D1807134

FOREIGN PARTS
GERMAN AND AUSTRIAN ACTORS ON THE BRITISH STAGE 1933–1960

LEGENDA

LEGENDA is the Modern Humanities Research Association's book imprint for new research in the Humanities. Founded in 1995 by Malcolm Bowie and others within the University of Oxford, Legenda has always been a collaborative publishing enterprise, directly governed by scholars. The Modern Humanities Research Association (MHRA) joined this collaboration in 1998, became half-owner in 2004, in partnership with Maney Publishing and then Routledge, and has since 2016 been sole owner. Titles range from medieval texts to contemporary cinema and form a widely comparative view of the modern humanities, including works on Arabic, Catalan, English, French, German, Greek, Italian, Portuguese, Russian, Spanish, and Yiddish literature. Editorial boards and committees of more than 60 leading academic specialists work in collaboration with bodies such as the Society for French Studies, the British Comparative Literature Association and the Association of Hispanists of Great Britain & Ireland.

The MHRA encourages and promotes advanced study and research in the field of the modern humanities, especially modern European languages and literature, including English, and also cinema. It aims to break down the barriers between scholars working in different disciplines and to maintain the unity of humanistic scholarship. The Association fulfils this purpose through the publication of journals, bibliographies, monographs, critical editions, and the MHRA Style Guide, and by making grants in support of research. Membership is open to all who work in the Humanities, whether independent or in a University post, and the participation of younger colleagues entering the field is especially welcomed.

ALSO PUBLISHED BY THE ASSOCIATION

Critical Texts
Tudor and Stuart Translations • *New Translations* • *European Translations*
MHRA Library of Medieval Welsh Literature

MHRA Bibliographies
Publications of the Modern Humanities Research Association

The Annual Bibliography of English Language & Literature
Austrian Studies
Modern Language Review
Portuguese Studies
The Slavonic and East European Review
Working Papers in the Humanities
The Yearbook of English Studies

www.mhra.org.uk
www.legendabooks.com

GERMANIC LITERATURES

Editorial Committee
Chair: Professor Ritchie Robertson (University of Oxford)
Dr Barbara Burns (Glasgow University)
Professor Jane Fenoulhet (University College London)
Professor Anne Fuchs (University of Warwick)
Dr Jakob Stougaard-Nielsen (University College London)
Professor Annette Volfing (University of Oxford)
Professor Susanne Kord (University College London)
Professor John Zilcosky (University of Toronto)

Germanic Literatures includes monographs and essay collections on literature originally written not only in German, but also in Dutch and the Scandinavian languages. Within the German-speaking area, it seeks also to publish studies of other national literatures such as those of Austria and Switzerland. The chronological scope of the series extends from the early Middle Ages down to the present day.

Managing Editor
Dr Graham Nelson, 41 Wellington Square, Oxford OX1 2JF, UK
www.legendabooks.com

Foreign Parts

German and Austrian Actors on the British Stage 1933–1960

R ICHARD D OVE

LEGENDA

Germanic Literatures 15
Modern Humanities Research Association
2017

Published by Legenda
an imprint of the Modern Humanities Research Association
Salisbury House, Station Road, Cambridge CB1 2LA

ISBN 978-1-781884-73-7

First published 2017

All rights reserved. No part of this publication may be be reproduced or disseminated or transmitted in any form or by any means, electronic, mechanical, photocopying, recording or otherwise, or stored in any retrieval system, or otherwise used in any manner whatsoever without written permission of the copyright owner, except in accordance with the provisions of the Copyright, Designs and Patents Act 1988, or under the terms of a licence permitting restricted copying issued in the UK by the Copyright Licensing Agency Ltd, Saffron House, 6–10 Kirby Street, London EC1N 8TS, *England, or in the USA by the Copyright Clearance Center, 222 Rosewood Drive, Danvers MA 01923. Application for the written permission of the copyright owner to reproduce any part of this publication must be made by email to legenda@mhra.org.uk.*

Disclaimer: Statements of fact and opinion contained in this book are those of the author and not of the editors or the Modern Humanities Research Association. The publisher makes no representation, express or implied, in respect of the accuracy of the material in this book and cannot accept any legal responsibility or liability for any errors or omissions that may be made.

Trademark notice: Product or corporate names may be trademarks or registered trademarks, and are used only for identification and explanation without intent to infringe.

© Modern Humanities Research Association 2017

Copy-Editor: Charlotte Brown

CONTENTS

❖

ACKNOWLEDGEMENTS

Writing a book is often a lonely business, but no book is just the product of its author, it also relies crucially on the help and support of others. This book is based largely on primary sources, above all the personal archives of three of the five actors who are its subject. I am indebted to Daniel Miller for information about his father, but above all for donating the treasure-trove of his parents' archive to the University of London. I am also most grateful to Ernest Rodker for giving me access to his father's personal papers and for patiently answering my questions, as well as to Rachel Ormerod for similar access to the personal papers of her grandmother Lilly Kann and for her generous help in supplying images. It is no exaggeration to say that access to these personal archives was invaluable: without them the book would not have been written.

There are others who have assisted in the writing of this book. I wish to thank staff at the National Archives, Kew, for advice on archival material. The staff at the Victoria & Albert Museum, Theatre and Performance Archives, were always helpful, as were staff at Westminster Reference Library. I am grateful to Matthew Chipping, BBC Written Archives' Centre, Caversham, for help with Lucie Mannheim's wartime career at the BBC and to staff at the Akademie der Künste, Berlin, in particular Stephan Doerschel.

I am also grateful to the Martin Miller and Hannah Norbert-Miller Fund, Institute of Modern Languages Research, University of London for financial help with the licence fees payable to reproduce certain illustrations and to Clare George, Project Archivist of the Miller Archive for help in securing some of the images used. At a personal level, I remain greatly indebted to the late Joan Rodker for her lucid and evocative memories of touring theatre in Ukraine. I should also particularly like to thank Charmian Brinson for her informed interest and encouragement. As always, I thank Iris for her steady support and advice. Finally, any errors that remain, either factual or stylistic, are mine alone.

R.D., London, January 2017

ABBREVIATIONS

AdK	Akademie der Künste, Berlin
BBC WAC	BBC Written Archives' Centre, Caversham
MN-MA	Martin Miller and Hannah Norbert-Miller Archive, Institute of Modern Languages Research, University of London
TNA	The National Archives
V&A TPA	Victoria & Albert Museum, Theatre and Performance Archives, Blythe House, London

LIST OF ILLUSTRATIONS

Frederick Valk

Frederick Valk as Dr. Kurtz in *Thunder Rock*, London 1940 (from *Shylock for a Summer* by Diana Valk)★

Frederick Valk as Shylock in *The Merchant of Venice*, for the Old Vic, New Theatre, London 1943 (Bristol University Theatre Collection: John Vickers Archive)

Gerhard Hinze/Gerard Heinz

Gerhard Hinze as Matvei in *Distant Point*, Ukraine 1936 (courtesy Ernest Rodker)

Gerard Heinz in the 1950s (courtesy Ernest Rodker)

Martin Miller

Martin Miller, 'The Führer Speaks', London 1940 (Martin Miller and Hannah Norbert-Miller Archive, University of London)

Martin Miller as Jacob in *Awake and Sing*, Arts Theatre, London 1942 (Martin Miller and Hannah Norbert-Miller Archive, University of London)

Lilly Kann

Lilly Kann (second from left) as Grete Hinkemann in *Hinkemann*, Staatstheater, Dresden, 1924 (courtesy Rachel Ormerod)

Lilly Kann as Mother Superior in *The Cradle Song*, London 1944 (courtesy Rachel Ormerod)

Lucie Mannheim

Lucie Mannheim as Annabella Smith in the film *The 39 Steps* (GB1935)

Lucie Mannheim as Rebecca West with Marius Goring as Rosmer in *Rosmersholm*, London 1948 (Bristol University Theatre Collection, John Vickers Archive)

★ *Shylock for a Summer* (copyright Diana Valk) was published in 1958 by Cassell, now part of Orion Group, who were unable to identify the current copyright holder 'due to lack of sufficient information in our records'. All attempts to trace the copyright holder were unsuccessful.

PROLOGUE

CHAPTER 1

Setting the Scene

Theatre aspires to be an international art form, but theatre practitioners do not always travel well, particularly across the frontiers drawn by language. The dramatist may find that a play requires much more than translation, needing to be adapted to different cultural conditions; the stage director may have to vary his or her principles according to local conventions, but the problem is most acute for the actor who may be rendered literally speechless.

This book tells the story of five actors who were banned from the German theatre as Jews or communists when the Nazis came to power and, arriving in Britain before the Second World War, made the difficult transition to the British stage: the German actors Lucie Mannheim, Gerhard Hinze, Friedrich Valk, and Lilly Kann, and their Austrian counterpart Martin Miller. Their story represents a unique episode in British theatre history, yet it is one that has been sadly neglected. The only attempts to engage with it were in a volume edited by Günther Berghaus, *Theatre and Film in Exile*.[1] However, the book focuses, as its title suggests, primarily on German theatre in exile, that is, on the theatre groups set up by German and Austrian exiles to perform for their fellow-refugees in Britain.[2]

In an uncertain profession, refugee actors faced many new uncertainties, being unusually dependent on language and diction in practising their craft. In addition, they had to find their way in a new theatre culture. This book will outline the theatre culture they came from, and recount their achievements on the British stage, their reception by critics and audiences, their relations with English colleagues, and their possible influence on English theatre practice, in particular on acting styles.

Acting has always been an itinerant profession — the touring companies of Victorian and Edwardian Britain were part of a long tradition which went back to the travelling players of Shakespeare's day — but the extent of such movements has, with a few exceptions such as the *commedia dell'arte*, been defined by the borders established by language. Moreover, these five actors did not come as travelling

---

1 Günter Berghaus (ed.), *Theatre and Film in Exile: German Artists in Britain 1933–1945* (Oxford, New York, & Munich: Berg, 1989). See particularly Berghaus's own essay, 'Producing Art in Exile', pp. 15–45, and Alan Clarke's contribution, 'They Came to a Country: German Theatre Practitioners in Exile in Great Britain, 1938–45', pp. 99–120.

2 Only two essays in the volume actually broach the subject of German-speaking actors on the British stage, and even they make no detailed investigation. Moreover, in the twenty-seven years since the book appeared, these tentative beginnings have never been followed up.

players, but as refugees. They arrived in Britain at different times after 1933, fleeing Germany, and later Austria or Czechoslovakia, to escape racial or political persecution by the Nazi regime. Britain had not been their refuge of first choice. On leaving Germany in 1933, they had gone initially to countries which shared the German language — Austria, Switzerland, or the German-language stages of Czechoslovakia — in the hope of continuing their stage careers.

They all left Germany in mid-career and in recounting their experience on the British stage, the narrative contains frequent echoes of the German-speaking theatre they had left behind, making it necessary to outline their earlier careers in Germany. While this inevitably evokes some fundamental differences in practice between the German and British theatres, the book is not an attempt to compare the two. Some implicit comparisons may emerge in passing, but the aim of the book is to examine how well actors whose background and experience were in the German theatre were able to adjust to the very different conditions of the English stage.

The course of their careers was, as so often in the 1930s and 1940s, subject to political events. It was the Nazi government which forced them into exile in 1933 — and the political decisions of the British government in 1938–39 which brought many of them to Britain. There was also a strong historical and political dimension to their performances: Martin Miller launched his career in Britain with his satirical impersonation of his fellow-Austrian, Adolf Hitler, broadcast live to Germany in 1940 in what the BBC considered a propaganda coup. Gerhard Hinze was interned as an 'enemy alien', before exchanging the improvised stage of an internment camp for the boards of a West End theatre, appearing as a Polish pilot (itself an exemplary political role) in Terence Rattigan's *Flare Path*. When Frederick Valk played Shylock for the Old Vic in 1943, his performance was viewed as a powerful statement on behalf of Jews everywhere.

Lucie Mannheim came to Britain in 1934, one of the first refugee actors to arrive in London; the other four arrived in 1938–1939. During the last troubled months of Chamberlain's 'peace for our time', the previous trickle of refugees arriving in Britain became a flood. Following the steady advance of Nazism across Central Europe in 1938–1939 — the annexation of Austria, the occupation of the Sudetenland, the 'Reichskristallnacht' pogrom, and the German invasion of Bohemia and Moravia — Britain became the default destination for refugees from the Third Reich.

By the outbreak of war an estimated 78,000 German-speaking refugees were living in Britain.[3] Among them were some 400 artistic professionals of all kinds, including many actors.[4] Only a small number, probably fewer than thirty, assimilated

3   The total number of German-speaking refugees who came to Britain has been the subject of lively academic debate, but the best estimate (based on Home Office figures released in 1943) is that by the outbreak of war there were some seventy-eight thousand refugees living in Britain. See Louise London, *Whitehall and the Jews 1933–1948: British Immigration Policy and the Holocaust* (Cambridge: Cambridge University Press, 2000), pp. 11–12.

4   See James M. Ritchie, 'Exiltheater in Großbritannien', in *Handbuch des deutschsprachigen Exiltheaters 1933–1945*, ed. by Frithjof Trapp and others, 2 vols (Munich: K. G. Saur, 1999), I, 343:

well enough to make a career on the English stage. Those who came to Britain in 1938–1939 arrived unsung: unlike those who had preceded them to London in 1933–1935, few if any of them were star names. Although they had established solid and successful careers in the German-speaking theatre before 1933, they were unknown outside it. Few of them spoke English, none spoke it to the level required for professional performance: in 1939 they were a surplus commodity, ill-equipped to find work on the British stage. Initially they were forced to resort to self-help, turning to the theatre groups set up by the refugees themselves, the 'Little Theatre' of the Free German League of Culture and its Austrian counterpart, the Laterndl, as the only opportunity to practise their craft.

While fewer than thirty German-speaking actors were eventually able to make their way on the British stage, perhaps as many as fifty found work in British films, though there is an obvious overlap between theatre and cinema, emphasising the links between the two mediums at a time when many films were adapted from successful plays. This study deals with stage actors — those whose ambitions lay primarily in the theatre, rather than film. There is no place in it for such successful central European actors as Lilli Palmer, Herbert Lom, and Anton Walbrook, who made their name in British films and remained faithful to that medium, despite occasional appearances on stage. (If they play any part in this narrative, it is only as extras.) Nonetheless, all the actors on whom this study focuses began their acting careers in Britain with small parts in film, where it was easier to find work. It was usually two or three years before they transferred to the British stage and even then they continued to play regular, if minor, film roles in order to make a living. Their faces are still familiar from British films of the period: their names are not. While their film work is therefore a frequent point of reference in this study, it was not the primary focus of their acting careers — and is therefore not the primary focus of this book.

Piecing together the details of the theatrical past has never been a simple matter. Every stage performance is ephemeral. All that survives in retrospect is its reflection in theatre reviews and criticism, and its echoes in the memory of the audience, who can say of an exceptional performance: 'I was there'. Theatre archives may well boast such treasures as an original play script or the director's working version of it, but more commonly contain items like theatre programmes, which usually convey little beyond the cast and the place of the event, or theatre reviews which can summon up a production, but are not always a reliable guide, giving a subjective view of a play and its performance that sometimes says more about the reviewer than about the play itself.

Furthermore, while contemporary reviews are frequently cited in this book, they have a strong bias towards London, whereas the bulk of theatre performances, particularly during the war years, were in the provinces, where touring theatre, once the norm in late Victorian and Edwardian days, found a new lease of life. It would have been highly desirable to interview the actors themselves but the last

Alan Clarke suggests that some four hundred 'artists' of all kinds arrived, the theatre practitioners forming the largest proportion ('They Came to a Country', p. 102).

survivor among them, Lilly Kann, died in 1978. Fortunately, it has been possible to consult the personal archives of three actors, Martin Miller, Gerhard Hinze, and Lilly Kann, without which this book would probably not have been written.

This study is not intended merely as a tribute to a few tenacious and gifted foreign actors; it seeks also to record a small, but significant part of *British* theatre history. In the four decades or more since these actors took their final bow, their contribution to British theatre — or even their very presence — has been forgotten. They do not receive so much as a passing mention in any recent study of the British theatre. Their careers on the British stage have not, of course, been 'hidden from history', they have simply faded from view, being now considered of interest only to a few academic specialists — and ignored by most of *them*. It is time to restore these actors to their rightful place in British theatre history. This is their story.

ACT I

A Tale of Two Cities:
London and Berlin

CHAPTER 2

'Dressed Up and in Good Company': The London Theatre in the 1930s

Monday, 30 January 1933, when Adolf Hitler was appointed Reich Chancellor, was a fateful day in German, and indeed, world history. At the time, however, it caused hardly a ripple on the calm surface of British life — least of all in the theatre. In London's West End, it was very much business as usual. On 30 January, a new play by Ben Travers, *A Bit of a Test*, had its opening night at the Aldwych Theatre, the ninth and last of the 'Aldwych farces'. The theatre critic of the *Observer* called the second act 'essential, victorious Aldwych nonsense', adding in declamatory style: 'O rare Ben Travers!'[1] Elsewhere in the West End, at the Criterion theatre, *Fresh Fields*, a new comedy by the actor, writer, and composer Ivor Novello was beginning what would prove to be a year-long run. In fact, Novello had two shows running: his 'non-musical play' *Flies in the Sun* had also just opened at the Playhouse Theatre.

Elsewhere in the West End, one notable theatre had temporarily gone dark. At the Coliseum, *Casanova*, 'a musical play of adventure and love', with music by Johann Strauss and musical arrangements by Ralph Benatzky, had closed two days earlier on 28 January. The Austrian composer Benatzky, best-known as co-composer of *The White Horse Inn* (*Im Weißen Rößl*), was in January 1933 still enjoying the fruits of his musical success in Berlin. He was not a Jew, but his first wife had been Jewish, and in the light of Hitler's rise to power, he was already making plans to leave Germany for Vienna, the scene of his early success. Five years later, as Hitler returned in triumph to the same city which had once rejected him, Benatzky was forced to flee again — this time to the USA. German and Austrian actors who arrived in London after 1933 were surprised, even dismayed, by what they saw. The West End theatre of the period was conservative, class-bound, and insular, its repertoire consisting largely of drawing-room comedies, thrillers, and musical revues. It catered almost exclusively to a middle-class audience, intent on watching its own reflection on stage. It was an audience which came to be entertained, but not challenged.

The conservative nature of West End theatre stemmed directly from its production values. The choice of play was dictated by purely commercial criteria: whether it could be expected to run long enough to make a profit. Plays which

---

1 Ivor Brown, *Observer*, 5 February 1933; see also *The Times*, 31 January 1933.

were considered 'difficult', that is, which made emotional or intellectual demands on the audience or which were likely to prove controversial, were, in consequence, best avoided.

Dramatists writing for the West End stage responded in kind, producing plays which fitted this conservative template. The result was a theatre repertoire which, while not dull, was certainly bland and predictable, offering few, if any, plays that tackled subjects of social or political concern. Although there were regular performances of the English classics, largely at the Old Vic, it is notable that there were fewer performances of Shakespeare in London in the six years 1933 to 1939 than there were during the six years of the Second World War.

English theatre suffered from a lack of new creative writing. The West End stage was dominated during the 1930s by a few already well-known names. Noel Coward, who perhaps best embodied the escapist world of 1930s theatre, had begun the decade with his 'intimate comedy' *Private Lives* and ended it with the semi-autobiographical *Present Laughter*, adding to the reputation he had won in the previous decade. Ivor Novello, who had acted in Coward's play *Sirocco* in 1927, wrote a series of enormously successful musical revues for the Drury Lane Theatre, including *Glamorous Night* (1935) and *Careless Rapture* (1936). George Bernard Shaw who had once turned the Edwardian theatre into an arena for debating social and political issues, was still writing, but none of the plays he wrote in the 1930s was as successful — or radical — as his earlier work. If he remained a controversial figure in British society, it was largely for his political views: he was among a number of credulous British visitors to the USSR who saw largely what they wanted to see.

A more original voice on the London stage was that of J. B. Priestley, who had made his name with his first novel *The Good Companions* in 1929, consolidating it with his second, *Angel Pavement*, in 1930. He had soon become equally well-known as a dramatist, establishing himself with *Dangerous Corner* (1932), the first of several successful plays throughout the 1930s. Like his novels, Priestley's plays contained a message of social criticism which helped to earn him a more radical reputation then he perhaps deserved. His dramas were naturalistic, with as yet few signs of experimentation — the dramatic innovations of *They Came to a City* or *An Inspector Calls* were still undreamed of in his imagination.

Priestley's plays from this decade are now rarely performed and it is easy to forget his pre-war standing. The journal *Theatre World*, for example, declared unequivocally:

> In 1939, seven years after his first play *Dangerous Corner*, J. B. Priestley stands unchallenged as the leading English dramatist of the day [...] *Johnson over Jordan* is one of the few inspiring plays of our time. It is up to all intelligent playgoers to accord it warm and instant support.[2]

In fact they did not. Following hard on the heels of the social satire *When We Are Married*, *Johnson over Jordan* marked a new departure in Priestley's work which, with its blend of realism and mysticism, was not always readily understood

---

2 *Theatre World*, April 1939.

The play concerns an ordinary businessman who reviews his past life from the vantage point of a post-death limbo. In both dramatic premise and technique, the play was innovative but, significantly, it failed to appeal to audiences, and after a few weeks was transferred to a smaller theatre, while Ralph Richardson, who was playing the title role, had to agree to appear unpaid for a few weeks to allow performances to continue. *Johnson over Jordan* was filmed as a television play in 1965 but has rarely been revived in the theatre.[3]

Among the few notable newcomers to the West End stage in the 1930s was Terence Rattigan, whose first play, the comedy *French without Tears* (1936), was an overnight success, receiving ecstatic reviews and running for 1049 performances at the Criterion Theatre. Rattigan went on to become a leading playwright, a skilful exponent of the 'well-made play', but he too was not a stylistic or dramatic innovator.

During the 1930s there was also a move to restore poetic drama to the theatre repertoire, exemplified by T. S. Eliot's *Murder in the Cathedral* (1935) — though the play was not commissioned for the London stage, but written at the request of George Bell, the Bishop of Chichester, for the Canterbury Festival and produced in the cathedral's Chapter House. It was later shown at the Mercury Theatre, Notting Hill, where it ran for several months. The Mercury also staged the verse drama, *The Ascent of F6*, co-written by W. H. Auden and Christopher Isherwood, in 1937. Neither play, however, set a trend in the mainstream London theatre. Not until after the war was there a revival of poetic drama with Eliot's *The Cocktail Party* and Christopher Fry's *The Lady's Not for Burning*.

English theatre in the 1930s made few attempts to stage experimental plays or use innovative production techniques. Above all, it remained highly insular, showing little interest in European drama. Although Berlin had become the theatre capital of Europe in the 1920s, modern German drama was still virtually unknown — or at least unshown — in Britain. The parochialism of West End theatre management and audiences meant that the production of modern foreign plays was confined to the 'little theatre' clubs, such as the Gate Theatre, or the Sunday evening play societies like the Stage Society, which were run on club lines. It was the Stage Society which had introduced Gerhard Hauptmann's *The Weavers* to the British stage and which later staged Ernst Toller's *Masses and Man*, produced by Lewis Casson, with his wife Sybil Thorndike in the leading role. From 1926, the Gate Theatre produced several Toller plays but by the early 1930s it had begun to lose direction and prestige, until it was revived under the management of Norman Marshall.

There was also keen interest in radical experiment from left-wing theatre groups. The Rebel Players, for example, which was affiliated to the Workers Theatre Movement, performed regularly in trade union and Labour halls during the early 1930s, presenting short agitprop pieces which they also took to the streets in London's East End. Similarly, the Salford-based Theatre of Action, which included Ewan MacColl and Joan Littlewood, performed agitprop plays and sketches in

---

3 Its only major revival recently was by Jude Kelly at the West Yorkshire Playhouse, Leeds, in 2001. See Michael Billington, '*Johnson over Jordan*', *Guardian*, 14 September 2001.

Manchester and the north west, concentrating on street performance. In the course of 1934–1935, however, the group made a gradual return to indoor performance, its members eventually moving on to form the peripatetic Theatre Workshop in 1945.

The Rebel Players, meanwhile, were to be the nucleus of Unity Theatre, founded in February 1936 to provide theatre for working-class audiences, pioneering direct political commentary on stage. In April 1936, Unity produced Clifford Odets's *Waiting for Lefty* in an American double bill with Albert Malz's *Private Hicks*. It was also Unity which in 1938 performed Bertolt Brecht's short play *Senora Carrar's Rifles*, the first production of a Brecht play in Britain. However 'professional' in execution, these were amateur performances which the West End theatre could afford to ignore.

In the prevailing conditions, it is small wonder that theatre artists arriving from Germany and Austria were disconcerted by what they encountered in the mainstream London theatre. Among those who pronounced their verdict on it was Julius Berstl, playwright, producer, and man of the theatre. Berstl had arrived in London in 1936, at the age of fifty-three, after working for two decades in the turbulent theatre world of Berlin. Accustomed to the variety and vigour of stage production in Germany, he could barely conceal his impatience with much of what he saw on the West End stage, describing the action of the typical drawing-room comedy as:

> Act 1 — Tea is served.
> Act 2 — Cocktails are served.
> Act 3 — Whisky is served.[4]

Berstl's concept of theatre, like that of many of his fellow-exiles, reflected Schiller's famous maxim that the theatre was a moral institution — claiming that theatre should aim to educate and instruct, as well as appeal to man's sense of the aesthetic.[5] Outlining the main differences between theatre audiences in England and Germany, Berstl contended that in Germany audiences were prepared for a didactic, as well as an aesthetic experience, whereas theatre in England was a social institution: audiences 'did not go to learn anything or to witness a literary experiment or to be involved in solving problems but simply to relax after a day's work and that, if possible, dressed up and in good company'.[6]

Other emigré observers shared Berstl's dyspeptic view of English theatre. The artist (and sometime playwright) Oskar Kokoschka felt crushed by the universal mediocrity of theatre in London, writing to the theatre director Heinz Wolfgang Litten that 'the journey in the Tube, past the advertisements for the theatrical offerings of this most unintellectual of cities is in itself alarming — sheer murder'.[7]

4   Julius Berstl, *Odyssee eines Theatermannes* (Berlin: Sarani, 1963), p. 178. All English translations are the author's own unless otherwise stated.

5   Schiller's lecture, 'Die Schaubühne als moralische Anstalt betrachtet' [The Stage as a Moral Institution], given in 1784, had continued to be a point of reference in German theatre 150 years later.

6   Berstl, p. 187.

7   Letter from Oskar Kokoschka to Heinz Wolfgang Litten, published in June 1944 in *Freie*

Bertolt Brecht, who made a brief visit to London in 1934, did not bother to conceal his contempt, dismissing the London stage as 'antediluvian' ('vorsintflutlich').

Berstl was certainly in a better position to judge the English stage than Brecht, who at that time spoke little English and had come armed with his own theatrical agenda. Berstl, on the other hand, had studied English as a young man and as late as 1927 had translated two comedies by Frederick Lonsdale, *The Last of Mrs Cheyney* and *On Approval*, for the Berlin stage. (It must remain an open question how far Berstl's close acquaintance with Lonsdale's work influenced his views on English theatre.) Berstl also remarked on the English style of acting:

> Like the English in general, the English actor avoids any strong outbursts of temperament and shows his strength through understatement. He is completely in his element when he can play himself [...] This private approach to acting is nowhere better demonstrated than in the English drawing-room comedy, whereas, on the other hand, as soon as he puts on a historical costume, the English actor becomes restricted, even stiff.[8]

According to Berstl, the typical English style of acting was low-key and under-stated, in which the actor sought to deliver lines with a minimum of emotion. The suppression of emotion and temperament contrasted strongly with the prevailing acting style in Germany which was more emotional, even visceral, attempting to portray the character from the inside.

Berstl was not alone in this perception. In his autobiography *Aller Tage Abend*, the Austrian actor Fritz Kortner noted that his own acting style was at odds with the expectations of London audiences, claiming that the English tradition of under-acting (he called it 'Ausdrucksanämie' [expressive anaemia])[9] had forced him, an actor who had always striven for expressiveness, to abandon his own highly emotive performance style — the very thing which had first singled him out for fame — and to adopt the 'charming virtuosity of expressive non-commitment' which British audiences expected.[10] Kortner had first become famous for his role in Ernst Toller's *Transformation* in the early days of the Weimar Republic in September 1919. Thereafter, his fortunes as an actor had closely matched the rise and fall of the Republic itself.

Deutsche Kultur, the monthly bulletin of the Free German League of Culture in London.

8   Berstl, p. 186.
9   Fritz Kortner, *Aller Tage Abend* (Munich: Kindler, 1959), p. 429.
10 Ibid., p. 428.

CHAPTER 3

Weimar — Before and After:
The German Stage in the 1920s and 1930s

It is almost impossible to begin any review of German theatre in the early twentieth century without introducing the name Edward Gordon Craig.[11] The English actor and stage designer had great influence in Germany before the First World War, helping the German theatre to abandon stage realism in favour of a more abstract, symbolic style. Craig believed in the primacy of the director, who should bring unity to any production, and his ideas were certainly taken up by leading directors like Max Reinhardt. While Craig's influence was strongest in design and direction, it also extended to acting and actors, helping to shape the performance styles of many German actors, including those in this study.

Craig's influence was greatest before 1914, but certainly extended into the early years of the Weimar Republic, founded in the wake of the Kaiser's abdication in 1919. The Weimar Republic has become, particularly in the English-speaking world, a byword for political failure, but it is also acknowledged as a seedbed of artistic modernism, not least in the theatre.[12] During the 1920s, Germany led the world in theatrical innovation and experiment. Among those who found fame in these years were dramatists like Ernst Toller, Georg Kaiser, Carl Zuckmayer, and Bertolt Brecht, whose work took a revolutionary view of stage production, and often of political development. Their plays were widely performed and often showcased by outstanding directors such as Reinhardt and Erwin Piscator. Men like Brecht and Piscator personified the combination of left-wing activism and theatrical experiment which dominated the Weimar stage, provoking violent opposition from nationalist groups such as the emerging National Socialist party. One highly effective Nazi tactic was that of audience disruption. Such 'events' were not so much spontaneous protests against left-wing political radicalism as well-orchestrated attempts to prevent a particular performance.

An early example was the production of Toller's *Hinkemann* [Brokenbrow] in Dresden in 1924.[13] Toller was a controversial figure in the Weimar Republic,

11   See Denis Bablet, *Edward Gordon Craig* (London: Heinemann, 1966).

12   See Peter Gay, *Weimar Culture: The Outsider as Insider* (London: Secker & Warburg, 1968); John Willett, *The Weimar Years: A Culture Cut Short* (London: Thames & Hudson, 1984).

13   See James Jordan, 'Audience Disruption in the Theatre of the Weimar Republic', *New Theatre Quarterly*, 1/3 (1985), 283–91.

dividing opinion like no other dramatist. *Hinkemann* was widely interpreted as an allegory of Germany, in which the soldier protagonist's emasculation stood for that of a defeated nation, provoking noisy disturbances by nationalist protesters which made much of the dialogue inaudible. Following death threats against the theatre director, *Hinkemann* was not performed again in Dresden, an early lesson in the baleful influence of nationalism on the theatre. Such interventions lapsed for some years, before growing more frequent in the months preceding Hitler's achievement of power.

The middle years of the Republic (1924–1929) saw a flourishing of the arts and sciences in which Jewish artists and intellectuals played a prominent role. In 1933, there were some half a million Jews living in Germany, representing less than one per cent of the population, but anti-Semitism had long been a central tenet of Nazi ideology and on assuming power they acted quickly to remove Jews from every area of public life, not least cultural life. Measures to undermine Jewish influence in the economy and society began on 1 April 1933 with a national boycott of Jewish businesses, enforced by storm-troopers who stood outside Jewish-owned stores to deter anyone from entering. Though lasting only one day, the boycott was an intimidating show of force — and a warning of worse to come.

On 7 April, less than a week later, the Nazi government passed the Law for the Restoration of the Professional Civil Service, excluding Jews from public employment, including national, regional, and local government. Anyone in government service had to prove their 'Aryan' ancestry; those unable to do so were dismissed. Curiously, this measure directly affected Jewish actors and other theatre practitioners: if they were contracted to the state theatres in Berlin or to one of the many municipal theatres, they were cursorily dismissed.

In the early months of Nazi rule, many theatre artists fleeing Germany had tried to continue their careers in countries with a common language and theatre culture, seeking work in Austria or in the German-speaking theatres of Czechoslovakia. Some German actors already knew these stages through seasonal contracts or guest performances. However, Austria did not prove a reliable place of refuge: the blight of anti-Semitism was already spreading there.[14] Nor did Czechoslovakia, where German-speaking areas began to fall under the spell of Nazism.

German-speaking actors who found their way to Britain had to contend with more than a new language and a different performance style; they also had to assimilate to a new theatre culture, in which the traditions and conventions differed, sometimes fundamentally, from those in Germany or Austria. The German theatre was more regionally orientated than the English, partly reflecting Germany's political history as a collection of minor kingdoms and dukedoms which were unified as a national state under the aegis of Prussia and Berlin only in 1870. In the 1920s and 1930s, most German towns of any size had a theatre, often municipally owned and subsidised, and usually a source of local pride. Partly for this reason, theatre and the theatrical professions enjoyed greater social status and prestige in Germany than in Britain.

---

14 Cf. Hilde Haider-Pregler, 'Exilland Österreich', in *Handbuch des deutschsprachigen Exiltheaters*, ed. by Trapp & others, I, 97–154.

Municipal theatres offered a programme of plays performed over a ten-month season. The theatre assembled a company, inviting actors to audition, though the decision as to which roles an actor was assigned generally lay with the director. The plays were performed in repertory, giving actors the chance to perform a wide range of roles, drawn from the European classics and contemporary German drama. It was a system that was largely duplicated in Austria, Switzerland, and the German-language theatres of Czechoslovakia.

The network of municipal theatres and the practice of yearly contracts gave actors — and other theatre artists — greater security than in Britain, where even a run-of-the play contract depended on short-term audience approval and might last only a couple of weeks. This security was underwritten by the German Stage Workers Cooperative (Genossenschaft deutscher Bühnenangehöriger: GDBA) which was founded as early as 1871 and quickly managed to negotiate standard salaries for various kinds of stage work. By comparison, the British actors' union Equity was not founded until 1930. German actors on the British stage tended to regard Equity as ineffective, though they were of course comparing it to something which no longer existed in Germany, the Nazi authorities having disbanded the GDBA after 1933.

In general, many of the conditions and practices in the German theatre remained unchanged throughout the Nazi era — but the careers of many actors did not. Some of the star names of the Weimar stage such as Elisabeth Bergner, Fritz Kortner, and Lucie Mannheim were Jewish. Others were communists — which in the political climate of 1933 was an even more dangerous connection. Actors who were neither Jews nor communists usually had little to fear. Among those who flourished in the Nazi era were Werner Krauss, perhaps Germany's greatest actor, Emil Jannings, who had become an international star after his appearance with Marlene Dietrich in *The Blue Angel*, and Gustaf Gründgens, whose admirers included Hermann Goering.

In September 1933 the Nazi government established the Reichskulturkammer [Reich Chamber of Culture] (RKK) under the auspices of the Propaganda Ministry. Purporting to be the professional organisation of all German creative artists, the RKK was in fact an instrument of *Gleichschaltung*, that is, of enforcing Nazi ideology across the arts. The Reichstheaterkammer [Reich Chamber of Theatre], as a subdivision of the RKK, began by summarily excluding from membership all Jewish artists (and other undesirables, such as communists) thus denying them the right to perform on the German stage. If they remained in Germany, they faced the choice of putting their career on hold or retreating into the cultural ghetto of 'Jewish Theatre'. The only other avenue of escape was emigration.

As well as actors, the Nazis were quick to ban the work of several leading dramatists, including Friedrich Wolf and Bertolt Brecht, because of their links to the German Communist Party, and Ernst Toller because of his past as an active revolutionary. Carl Zuckmayer, though neither a communist nor a revolutionary, was particularly hated by the Nazis, because of his success in lampooning traditional Prussian military virtues in the comedy *Der Hauptmann von Köpenick* [The Captain of Köpenick]. The Nazis also banned anti-Nazi writers like Erich Kästner, author of the children's classic *Emil and the Detectives*, whose works had frequently been adapted for film or stage. Kästner managed to remain in Germany, and even continued to write for films, though he was always credited under a pseudonym.

The abrupt change from the modernist innovations of the Weimar theatre to the 'traditionalism' of the Nazi stage was not simply a descent into cultural darkness. Some parts of the theatre repertoire remained little changed, notably the classics, which were simply appropriated to the new political agenda. The playwright most frequently produced during the Nazi period was Schiller, followed by Shakespeare, Goethe, and Lessing.

The importance of Shakespeare in the German theatre has long been acknowledged. In 1864 Germany celebrated the 300th anniversary of the dramatist's birth with the founding of the German Shakespeare Society (Deutsche Shakespeare-Gesellschaft) which, significantly, was founded in Weimar, the home of German classicism. Shakespeare, the Society's founders declared, was 'not a foreign poet, but one whom England must share with us, due to his inborn Germanic nature'. His popularity in Germany has continued uninterrupted ever since.

During the late Weimar period, the most popular Shakespeare play on the German stage was *A Midsummer Night's Dream,* which received more than forty separate productions in the years 1929 to 1932, performances being usually accompanied by the music of Felix Mendelssohn. Surprisingly, Mendelssohn's music continued to be played with productions of the play after 1933, with the tacit approval of the 'Reichsdramaturg' Rainer Schlösser: a triumph of tradition over ideology.[15]

The Nazis were quick to appropriate Shakespeare's plays to their own agenda, as can be illustrated, for example, by reference to *The Merchant of Venice*. Shakespeare's most controversial play provided an obvious focus for Nazi anti-Semitism, enjoying increased currency on the German stage after 1933.[16] Inevitably, there were some cuts in the text: the marriage of Jessica and Lorenzo was for example omitted, since it contravened Nazi racial laws.

Not all Shakespeare's plays were performed in Nazi Germany; some of the history plays, for example, were considered unsuitable, while *Othello* was ultimately suppressed on racial grounds. Even so, Shakespeare remained an indispensable part of the German theatre repertoire after 1933, so much so that in 1939 he became the only 'enemy dramatist' not to be banned in Germany. The experience of playing Shakespearean roles was certainly part of the theatre heritage which exiled German actors brought with them to Britain.

During the early years of emigration, only a handful of German-speaking actors came to London. Those who did were mainly star names, such as Elisabeth Bergner, Conrad Veidt, Oskar Homolka, Fritz Kortner, and Lucie Mannheim, who

15 Stefan Hüpping, *Rainer Schlösser (1899–1945): Der 'Reichsdramaturg'* (Bielefeld: Aisthesis, 2012), p. 162.

16 See, for example, Andrew G. Bonnell, 'Shylock and Othello Under the Nazis', *German Life and Letters*, 63/2 (April 2010), 166–78. See also Anselm Heinrich, 'It is Germany Where He Truly Lives: Nazi Claims on Shakespearean Drama', *New Theatre Quarterly*, 28/3 (2012), 230–42, and John Gross, *Shylock: A Legend and its Legacy* (New York: Simon & Schuster), 1993.

could hope to command lucrative contracts in British theatre, and above all film. Some, like Bergner and Veidt were already internationally known through their film performances; others, like Homolka, were to become so.

During the 1930s Elisabeth Bergner briefly became almost as famous in Britain as she had been in pre-Nazi Germany. She had made a working visit to London in late 1932 with her future husband, the film director Paul Czinner, to negotiate a film contract with Alexander Korda. Once Hitler came to power she did not return to Germany, transferring her career to the British stage. Just a year after her arrival in London, she made her English stage debut, through the mediation of the theatre impresario C. B. Cochran, in *Escape Me Never*, which the author Margaret Kennedy adapted from her own novel, writing the stage version especially for Bergner. The production ran for 232 performances, establishing Bergner as a star of the British stage. In 1934, she appeared in her first 'English' film, *The Rise of Catherine the Great*, an early production of Alexander Korda's London Films, directed by Paul Czinner, whom she had married in 1933. But Bergner was ultimately only in transit, leaving for the USA at the start of the war, and eventually resuming her career in post-war Germany.

Hard on her heels came the German actor Conrad Veidt, who arrived in April 1933. Beginning as a stage actor in Berlin, Veidt had subsequently made his name in silent films. His role as the murderous sleep-walker in *The Cabinet of Dr. Caligari* (1919) had made him an international star, whose face was familiar to cinema-goers across much of the world. In 1926 he was invited to Hollywood to work alongside John Barrymore, but the advent of sound films and his poor command of English put his career into reverse. He left Hollywood to return to Germany in 1929, busily re-building his film career against the background of Hitler's rise to power. Although he was not Jewish, he left Berlin for London in April 1933, together with his Jewish wife Lilly Prager, whom he had married only shortly before. His contacts with the British film industry quickly enabled him to establish himself. In 1934 he played the title role in *Jew Süss*, Lothar Mendes's philosemitic version of Feuchtwanger's famous novel. Such an anti-Nazi role cut off any possibility of a return to Germany. Veidt continued making films in Britain and in 1938 even became a British citizen. He was well established, financially secure, and much in demand. However, in 1940 he left Britain for Hollywood, where he was to play perhaps his most famous film role as Major Strasser in *Casablanca*.

The Austrian actor Fritz Kortner, who had made his career principally in Germany, had — like Elisabeth Bergner — withdrawn abroad in 1932, moving to Ascona in Switzerland. He too did not return after the Nazis assumed power. He made two brief stage appearances in Vienna before finally arriving in England in February 1934, planning to pursue his career in the British film industry.

He was initially able to secure a foothold in film with a cameo role in Berthold Viertel's *Little Friend*. By 1935, he seemed to have established himself in Britain, playing the title role in the film *Abdul the Damned*. Produced by the Hungarian-born Max Schach, directed by the Austrian Karl Grune, and based on a story by another Austrian, Robert Neumann, *Abdul the Damned* was hardly a British film at all, though, being made for the British market, it naturally had an English script. Kortner, still struggling to master the rudiments of the language, had learned his lines sentence by sentence:

> And then the assistant director would put his head round the dressing-room door and say: 'Mr. Kortner, we've changed these three sentences and taken that line out and added these few words here, so it's no longer that, it's this' — and he was gone, leaving Kortner in despair: 'How do I learn this at the last minute and how do you pronounce it anyway?'[17]

Kortner's despair was all too real, driving him to leave Britain for the USA in 1937.

Oskar Homolka, another Austrian-born actor who had made a career in Germany, came to Britain in January 1935. Homolka's path to fame is typical of many of his Austrian contemporaries. He had first gone to Germany in the mid-1920s, appearing frequently on the Munich stage, not least as Mortimer in the premiere of Brecht's *Edward the Second of England*, and then moved on to Berlin, where he appeared in some thirty silent films, before acting in the first 'talkie' made in Germany.

As an Austrian and a Jew, Homolka left Berlin rapidly in 1933, returning to his native Vienna. He left for London in 1935, where he was cast by Berthold Viertel in *Rhodes of Africa*, before appearing in other films like Alfred Hitchcock's *Sabotage*. Britain was not, however, his ultimate destination: like many of his contemporaries, he aspired to the lush pastures of Hollywood and in 1937 he finally received the American visa which allowed him to fulfil this ambition.

For most of these star performers, London was only a stepping stone on the way to Hollywood. Kortner and Homolka both moved on to the USA in 1937; Bergner and Veidt followed shortly after the outbreak of war, so that by 1940 some of the most famous names of German stage and screen had arrived in London and already departed. The only one of these 'early arrivals' who chose to stay was the film and stage actress Lucie Mannheim who, having first arrived in London in 1934, was to acquire British nationality in 1941 through her marriage to the English actor Marius Goring.

17 Robert Neumann, *Ein leichtes Leben* (Munich: Desch, 1963). See also Kortner, pp. 427-37.

ACT II

Getting Out 1933–1939

CHAPTER 4

Playing the Diva:
Lucie Mannheim in London

When the German stage and film actress Lucie Mannheim left Germany in 1933, her flight marked a complete break in her professional and personal life, ending not only her career on the German stage, but her long-term relationship with the theatre director Jürgen Fehling. Mannheim's stage career in Weimar Germany had developed very much in parallel to that of Fehling. As early as 1919, she joined the Volksbühne, Berlin, playing a leading part in Gogol's *Die Heirat* [Marriage], which Fehling directed. Mannheim was then just twenty years old, making the first of many stage appearances under Fehling's direction.

Known as a radical and innovative director, Fehling had first made his name with his productions of plays by radical young dramatists like Ernst Toller, Ernst Barlach, and Bertolt Brecht. In 1922, Leopold Jessner invited both Mannheim and Fehling to join the Berlin State Theatre (Preußisches Staatstheater). Mannheim became the company's principal actress, appearing, often under Fehling's direction, in such leading roles as Marie in Büchner's *Woyzeck*, Juliet in *Romeo and Juliet*, and Nora in Ibsen's *A Doll's House*. She played opposite most of the leading actors on the German stage, including Fritz Kortner, Werner Krauss, Albert Bassermann, and Oskar Homolka. Though all except Krauss were to follow her into exile, none of them ever appeared on stage with her again. Her most influential theatrical experience of the 1920s was the visit to Berlin in 1922 of Konstantin Stanislavsky's Moscow Art Theatre. Their performance of *The Cherry Orchard* was a revelation to her, helping to form the memorable acting technique she brought to London

During the 1920s Mannheim had also made her mark in the cinema, her screen credits including silent films by G. W. Pabst and F. W. Murnau. She then moved seamlessly into sound film, appearing in E. A. Dupont's *Atlantik* (1929), the first film on the *Titanic* disaster, and other early 'talkies' in Germany. In 1932, as the Weimar Republic drifted into extra-parliamentary rule, she starred in the remake of a popular silent film, *Madame wünscht keine Kinder* [Madame Wants No Children], which was shot in 1932, but released only in 1933 — after Mannheim had already left Germany.

At the height of her fame, when still only thirty-three years old, Mannheim found her career threatened by Hitler's sudden appointment as Reich Chancellor, forcing a fundamental re-appraisal of her life. As a Jew, she felt she could no longer stay in Germany, but emigration was a momentous decision, disrupting both her professional and personal life. Jürgen Fehling, as a non-Jew, felt no such compulsion to leave. Having devoted his life to the German theatre, he chose to stay, continuing his career with several landmark productions up to 1944, when the closure of German theatres forced him into inactivity. His career in post-war Germany never really recovered.

In 1933, Mannheim left Germany in some haste after her contract with the Berlin State Theatre was abruptly cancelled. Hermann Goering reputedly made efforts to have her treated as a special case, despite what the Nazis called her 'racial failing'.[1] Goering's readiness to intervene on her behalf is all too likely. Mannheim was an enormously popular star. And Goering's Nazi convictions could sometimes be quite flexible, as famously illustrated by his cynical rejoinder: 'I decide who's a Jew'.[2] Goering also had a taste for theatre which was matched only by his penchant for certain leading ladies. His second wife Emmy Sonnemann, whom he married in April 1935, was a talented provincial actress, whom he had first seen on stage in Weimar in the title role of *Minna von Barnhelm*. Despite Goering's involvement, Mannheim was determined to turn her back on Berlin, travelling first to Czechoslovakia, before making a brief stage appearance in Zurich, and finally arriving in London in 1934.

While the transition could not have been easy, she managed to achieve considerable early success on both stage and screen. She made her London theatre debut in September 1935, playing the title role in Bruno Frank's *Nina* at the Criterion Theatre. When first written and produced in Germany in 1931, *Nina* had been very much a text for its time. Like Frank's other work it mixed witty dialogue with social criticism. The play is a study of the construction of a public persona. Nina is a popular film star who wishes to retire from films in order to spend more time with her husband. She proposes to her producer that she should be replaced by her film double Trude Melitz, who looks and sounds so much like Nina that she could easily be the studio's new star. The producer agrees and the former stand-in rises from obscurity to become a star. She goes to Hollywood, where she learns vital lessons in the manipulation of the media. In the final act she returns to Berlin as a full-blown diva, with an impregnable aura of glamour.

The play was an ingenious star vehicle for its leading lady, cleverly written so that the same actress could play both parts. Frank had in fact written this bravura stage role for his mother-in-law, Fritzi Massary, the famous diva of operetta and cabaret in the Berlin of the 'Roaring Twenties'; she had played the role for over two thousand performances. While the play is a witty and entertaining comedy, it is also a political satire, offering obvious parallels with the rise on the political stage of Adolf Hitler, whose ability to manipulate the new media of film and radio had already helped to construct his self-image as the saviour of Germany. The analogy between theatrical and political reality was fully appreciated by any theatre

---

1   For Mannheim's own account of her meeting with Göring, see Rolf Lehnhardt, *Die Lucie-Mannheim-Story* (Rommerskirchen: Remagen-Rolandseck, 1973), pp. 36–37.

2   The words were originally attributed to Karl Lueger, who was mayor of Vienna before the First World War.

audience in the final years of the Weimar Republic. Well aware of what he had written, Frank prudently left Germany on the day after the Reichstag Fire; the play itself was banned shortly afterwards. Frank stayed briefly in Switzerland, before moving on to London, where he remained during 1933–1934, subsequently living in Salzburg in 1935–1937, before the deteriorating political situation in Austria finally precipitated his move to Hollywood.

Nina was in many ways an ideal play to showcase Mannheim's acting talents in front of a London audience: an opportunity to enact the creation of stardom, even though the political overtones were largely 'lost in translation'. The production was — perhaps predictably — a popular success, running for 185 performances. It was also a critical success, marking a distinct stage in public discourse on refugees in the theatre. A critic writing in the *News Chronicle* under the headline 'Hitler's new gift for Britain', praised 'the genius of Lucy Mannheim', calling her 'an actress of supreme talent and uncommon personality'.[3] The review in *The Bystander* struck the same note. Writing under the title 'A Gain from Germany', the reviewer asserted, with some insensitivity, that:

> English audiences should feel grateful to Herr Hitler [...] Thanks to his policy, they have the opportunity of seeing on the London stage some first-rate continental artists who have mastered the English tongue sufficiently to play their parts in that language: no mean feat in itself, but needs must when the devil drives.[4]

The *New Statesman* concurred, even contriving to grasp the political nettle of anti-Semitism directly, under the title 'More non-Aryan Brilliance'. The review concluded: 'At all events, she has vitality, humour, intelligence, spontaneity and resilience of mood beyond any comparison which this country can offer.[5] Other critics lauded her 'enchanting versatility' or asserted that 'last night she took London by storm'.[6]

Mannheim's double part was very physically demanding, placing her constantly on stage and requiring a series of rapid costume changes, switching from one part to another in as little as seventy seconds. However, so skilful was Mannheim's portrayal of the two characters that most of the audience did not realise, even after the final curtain had fallen, that both parts were played by the same actress.

The dual role was highly challenging for any actor: while the two characters looked alike, they had contrasting personalities. Perhaps the most perceptive appreciation of this double role was by the *Daily Telegraph*'s W. A. Darlington, who called Mannheim's performance:

> A remarkable feat of characterisation since the physical likeness between the two had to be emphasised [...] the actress was deprived of all the reliance on the

3   E. H. Baughan, 'Hitler's New Gift to Britain: Genius of Lucie Mannheim', *News Chronicle*, 18 September 1935.
4   'A Gain from Germany', *The Bystander*, 2 October 1935.
5   'More Non-Aryan Brilliance', *New Statesman*, [n.d.].
6   Ivor Brown, *Observer*, 22 September 1935; 'The Art of Lucie Mannheim', *Evening Standard*, 18 September 1935.

FIG. 1. Lucie Mannheim as Annabella Smith in the film
The 39 Steps (GB, 1935)

make-up box usual in such feats of doubling. The contrast between the two had to be made by acting and acting only. It was made with superlative skill.[7]

Amid the plaudits for Mannheim's impressive performance, the only real dissenting voice was that of the leading London theatre critic James Agate, who in a piece headed 'Note on Foreign Acting' demanded rhetorically whether an actress now had to have a foreign accent in order to appear on the West End stage:

> This pleasant boring little play [...] started one or two thoughtful hares... First, the engagement of one more foreign actress among whose assets is a rich inability to speak the English tongue, set one wondering whether the report is true that at agents' offices, the notice is now displayed: 'No English need apply'.[8]

Agate's xenophobic outburst does him little credit, even though it undoubtedly voiced a feeling that was more widely held; in the circumstances of this particular 'foreign invasion', it also had undertones of nationalism and anti–Semitism, which were occasionally echoed by others, such as Graham Greene in his film criticism. Significantly, Agate's piece was never reprinted in any of the volumes of his collected criticism which were published later.

Mannheim was moved by the warmth of her first night reception, calling it 'extraordinarily thrilling to me. I am more grateful than I can say for finding a country where I can work again'.[9] *Nina* was of course a stage contrivance, a virtuoso role for any actress, but more reflective critics wondered presciently how she might tackle a more 'normal' role.

Earlier in 1935, Mannheim had made her British screen debut in Alfred Hitchcock's *The Thirty-nine Steps*, a rollicking version of John Buchan's novel. Hitchcock had served a cinematic apprenticeship in the 1920s in Babelsberg with the famous director F. W. Murnau and would have been well aware of Mannheim's name and reputation. He offered her a part in the film without so much as an audition, creating for her the role of the mysterious spy 'Annabella Smith', a character who is not present in Buchan's original novel. The part was brief, but also significant: while she is killed off in an early scene, her death precipitates the subsequent action of the plot. Mannheim was originally engaged for three days' filming, but — largely due to Hitchcock's perfectionism and attention to detail — this eventually became thirteen days, bringing Mannheim a financial windfall of some £300. *The Thirty-nine Steps* was released in June 1935, becoming one of Hitchcock's first international successes.

The success of *The Thirty-nine Steps* gave Mannheim a modest financial independence, enabling her to move into a 'tiny' house with a garden in the middle-class suburb of St. John's Wood.[10] It also gave her a useful platform for two roles in the British cinema, both of which were variations on a colonial theme. In 1936 she

7   W. A. Darlington, 'German Star's Triumph', *Daily Telegraph*, 18 September 1935.
8   James Agate, 'Note on Foreign Acting', *Sunday Times*, 22 September 1935.
9   'Lucie Mannheim and her Biography. By a Correspondent', unattributed cutting in the production file, V & A Theatre and Performance Collection, London.
10   Ibid.

appeared in *East Meets West*, a vehicle for the veteran British actor George Arliss, newly returned from Hollywood, who donned a turban and monocle to portray a Middle Eastern sultan in one of the British cinema's frequent excursions into costume melodrama. Although the producer had assembled a talented cast, the film itself was undistinguished. There was a mixed reaction from the critics, though none was as scathing as Graham Greene, who warned his readers to 'avoid [it] like the plague'.[11] Mannheim won few plaudits for her role as the wife of an alcohol smuggler, though it served to keep her in the public eye.

In 1938, she appeared in *The High Command*, the first and only film made by Fanfare Films, in which she acted alongside James Mason, then a rising star of British cinema. Based on a contemporary novel, the plot centred on a British general, an officer of the old school serving in Africa, who has to confront his own past: the murder of a fellow-officer fifteen years earlier during the confusion of the First World War.[12] The general is juxtaposed with the factory-owner Martin Cloam, whom he despises as 'a common trader'. If the general is a symbol of military tradition, Cloam stands for the power of trade and commerce throughout the Empire. Significantly, both Cloam and his wife become foreigners in the film version (though they were not in the original novel): Cloam was played by the Hungarian actor, Steven Geray, his wife by Lucie Mannheim, both speaking English with a foreign accent and both representing part of the potential threat to British imperial interests in Africa. The film, with its focus on colonial mores, has not stood the test of time, but it also failed to please contemporary reviewers, the critic of the *Sunday Times* commenting: 'As for *The High Command*, this is a picture made by Fanfare, a new British company. Its avoidance of reality and its slowness make it a first-class soporific in this sultry weather'.[13] *The High Command* did little to enhance Lucie Mannheim's reputation. It was her last film role before the outbreak of war.

While Mannheim had made a triumphal debut on the West End stage, wiser heads waited to see how she would tackle a more 'normal' part. In fact, her opportunities were strictly limited, circumscribed by her age and foreign accent. Although her English had certainly improved, she retained a marked German accent which effectively prevented her from playing any of the classical female roles in the English stage repertoire, even those she had played in Berlin. Her subsequent stage career in England was frequently undermined by poor judgement in the choice of material, aggravated by differences of cultural context and taste.

Nina ran for some six months, but it was a further six months before Mannheim returned to the West End stage in Ferenc Molnár's comedy *Girl Unknown* in September 1936 at the New Theatre. She played the leading role of Anna, an ailing 'entertainer' who is rescued from a sailor's bar in Trieste by a benevolent

11   Graham Greene, *The Spectator*, 18 September 1936 (repr. in Graham Greene, *The Pleasure Dome: Collected Film Criticism 1935–40*, ed. by John Russell Taylor (Oxford: Oxford University Press, 1980), p. 101).

12   Lewis Robinson, *The General Goes Too Far* (New York: Puttnam, 1936).

13   Cited by Graham Greene in *Night and Day*, 29 July 1937, reprinted in *The Pleasure Dome*, pp. 156–57.

count who sends her to recuperate at a mountain sanatorium. There, she poses as a respectable woman, falling in love with an Italian fellow-patient (played by Ballard Berkeley) and then with a young post-office clerk who in turn obliges her by delaying messages from the count curtailing her stay in the sanatorium — a part played by the young actor Marius Goring. This was her first acquaintance with Goring, whom she herself chose for the part after finding his photo in the casting compendium *Spotlight*. In accordance with the role, which called for a younger actor, Goring was thirteen years her junior: the couple would marry in 1940.

Girl Unknown was a trivial affair, lacking in pace: 'its dilatory motion defeats even Miss Lucie Mannheim's performance as Anna', remarked the critic Ivor Brown who criticised the episodic structure, commenting drily that 'the screen rights should be valuable'.[14] The production was a major flop, closing after a mere twelve performances.

In September 1937 Mannheim played the role of Sonja Duveen in *The Last Straw* at the Comedy Theatre, the first London performance of a thriller by Edward Percy (i.e. Edward Percy-Smith), a popular playwright who later became a Conservative MP. Mannheim also produced the play, her first venture into direction in London. She had little experience of production and it is difficult to see why she chose this play for her directing debut. It was, after all, routine West End fare: a melodrama featuring a neurotic and homicidal undergraduate, played by Marius Goring.

The *Sunday Times* pronounced the verdict, 'Gripping is the word for this play'; the *Daily Mail* called it an 'excellent melodrama, an entertainment which should be very popular'.[15] W. A. Darlington paid tribute to some 'tense acting', citing the big scene between Goring and Mannheim:

> The contrast between Mr Goring's exhibition of jangled nerves and Miss Mannheim's taut, fierce grip on her panic makes a grand contrast. Their big scene together is beautifully timed and played and deserves all the applause it evoked last night.[16]

Following this initial praise, he concluded laconically: 'This is not much of a play'. Ivor Brown was less restrained: 'I fail to see how dramatic critics can be expected to prophesy the reactions of other people to these essays in bodeful nonsense'. While the play ran for a respectable fifty-two performances, it did little to establish Mannheim's reputation as a producer. Ivor Brown, for example, while careful to compliment her acting, was critical of her production: 'Miss Lucie Mannheim does considerably better work in the part of a benevolently intervening lady than as a producer of this play, whose lighting is crude and whose emotional atmosphere could easily be screwed up'.[17]

During her career in Weimar Germany, Mannheim had also appeared frequently in cabaret and musical theatre. In April 1938, she briefly played the leading role in the Viennese operetta *Mariza* [Countess Mariza], at the Theatre Royal, Birmingham.

14 Ivor Brown, *Observer*, 20 September 1936.
15 *Sunday Times*, 29 September 1937; *Daily Mail*, 30 September 1937.
16 W. A. Darlington, 'Tense Acting in a Thriller', *Daily Telegraph*, 30 September 1937.
17 Ivor Brown, *Observer*, 29 September 1937.

For whatever reason, she did not, however, play the role when *Mariza* opened three months later in London at the Palace Theatre. It is not known whether, despite her long experience of musical theatre, she was unhappy in the role, or whether she was simply unavailable.

At the end of 1938, the Duke of York's Theatre engaged Mannheim and Marius Goring to stage a season of plays which they would jointly produce. Goring, who later became famous for his roles in such films as *The Red Shoes*, had in fact first made his name as a young actor on the London stage. But, like Mannheim, he had little experience of directing.

Their association began promisingly but then petered out. The programme opened in February 1939 with Ibsen's *A Doll's House*, produced under the title *Nora*, with Mannheim playing the title role. The production was clearly an attempt, perhaps signalled by the change of title, to repeat one of her great successes in Berlin. Ibsen's reputation as a European dramatist had always been buttressed by his success in Germany, where he had been more widely performed than anywhere else. The first performance of *Hedda Gabler*, for example, had been given in Munich in the presence of the playwright. Neither Ibsen nor *A Doll's House* had ever enjoyed the same level of popularity in London, where his plays were still only grudgingly accepted as part of the modern theatre canon, as they were in Berlin. In particular, *A Doll's House*, a play challenging the traditional roles of wife and mother, had never been embraced by London audiences: this production by Mannheim and Goring was indeed the first staging of the play in London for fourteen years. At the first night, there were rows of empty seats, particularly the cheaper ones.

The critics had warm words for Mannheim and in some cases for the production. The *Daily Telegraph*'s W. A. Darlington commented that 'a good play can be just as good under a new title and certainly this is in some ways the most enlightening production of this masterpiece I have seen', continuing:

> Lucie Mannheim's Nora is a brilliant piece of work, attractive and intelligent in the highest degree. This is a very fine actress. She has a certain number of tricks — mostly tones and gestures which are exaggerated and make her momentarily inexpressive — but they really do not matter, since never for a moment do they make her lose her grip on her audience.[18]

The *Observer* judged the production 'in many ways excellently done', calling Mannheim's performance 'a very able rendering, a highly professional composition'.[19] *The Times* concurred, calling the play 'a masterpiece of story-telling' and commenting that 'Miss Mannheim is never dull' and 'we are bound to admit that [she] makes her extremely intelligent reading of the character clear'.[20] However, despite many good reviews, the production managed to run for only forty-three performances.

At the end of March, Mannheim and Goring appeared together in *Lady Fanny*, a new adaptation of Jerome K. Jerome's play *Fanny and the Servant Problem*, originally

18   W. A. Darlington, 'An Attractive Nora', *Daily Telegraph*, 4 February 1939.
19   Ivor Brown, 'Nora by Henrik Ibsen', *Observer*, 5 February 1939
20   *The Times*, 4 February 1939

written in 1908, but receiving its first-ever London performance. The production proved an expensive flop, being taken off after only six performances. Faced with the possibility of a dark theatre, the Duke of York's management put its faith in a revival of *Nina*, in a production by Mannheim and Goring, in which she played her accustomed dual role, while Goring took the part of the film director Schimmelmann. From the start, the production had an air of hasty improvisation. In an interview, Mannheim stated that 'we had only six days for rehearsal. We saw the scenery for the first time on Saturday'. There were no reviews, since the theatre management was not sure of being able to open as planned and so thought it 'inadvisable' to send out press tickets in case they had to cancel the arrangements.[21] The production opened on 10 April 1939 for 'a limited season', but lasted only two weeks and seventeen performances. It was their last production at the Duke of York's. Mannheim was learning the hard way about the professional and commercial risks of the West End theatre.

It is pertinent at this stage to ask why Lucie Mannheim failed to capitalise on her spectacular initial success in London. *Nina* was above all a vehicle for a star actress, Mannheim playing a part in which she excelled, but which she could not easily repeat. In fact, her very success made subsequent stage roles far more difficult to find, and, as previously mentioned, her German accent excluded her from certain roles. The major reason, however, that her career in London stalled seems to have been a poor choice of material, caused partly by her unfamiliarity with the English theatre context and perhaps too great a reliance on advice received from Marius Goring, with whom her professional and personal life were now closely entwined.

---

21 *Evening Standard*, 12 April 1939.

CHAPTER 5

Exit Stage Left:
Gerhard Hinze in the Soviet Union

Lucie Mannheim was a famous star, driven from the German stage because of her Jewish background. Gerhard Hinze, although well-known in the theatre, was not famous, nor was he Jewish. He had managed to escape from Germany after being arrested and imprisoned as a communist. Born in Hamburg in 1904, and raised in that city, Hinze had become an actor in 1921. His early career had been steady, but unremarkable. Like many of his contemporaries, he had served a long apprenticeship at provincial theatres throughout Germany and Austria including seasons in Stuttgart, Duisburg-Bochum, and finally in his native city Hamburg. Theatre in the Weimar Republic was very much a political sounding-board and the careers of many theatre artists were shaped by political events and their own response to them. The first turning-point in Hinze's career came in 1930, when he became a member of the German Communist Party (KPD): for the next decade and a half he subordinated professional ambition to political commitment. In the same year, Hinze became a leading actor at the Deutsches Schauspielhaus in Hamburg, thereby achieving — after less than a decade in the theatre — an important personal ambition. In 1932, as the political situation became increasingly polarised, he was dismissed by the theatre on account of his political views. In the same year, he formed his own company, the Hamburg Actors' Collective (Kollektiv Hamburger Schauspieler), to perform anti-Nazi plays and cabaret. In the light of political developments, the venture was short-lived. The company bravely continued to perform, even after Hitler came to power, but in March 1933 one of their performances was invaded by Nazi storm-troopers, leading to a pitched battle in the theatre, after which the Collective was closed down by the authorities.

After this traumatic incident, Hinze left Hamburg, where he was all too well known, for the anonymity of Berlin. He became part of a group around the communist actor Hans Otto, writing and distributing anti-Nazi pamphlets and leaflets. This activity too was short-lived: he was arrested on 15 November 1933, together with Hans Otto and others. After arrest, they were tortured and brutally beaten in various Nazi prisons, and finally taken to the notorious SA barracks in Voss-Straße, where they were tortured again. Hinze found himself crying out at the pain of these ferocious attacks. Many years later, Hinze told his son that, if he ever found himself in a similar situation, he should shout as loudly as possible, since it seemed to deter his captors from continuing. Hans Otto, on the other hand, suffered this brutal treatment in silence; his 'interrogators' continued their attacks, eventually beating him to death, before throwing his body into the street from a third-floor window to simulate suicide. Although Hinze managed to survive this ill-treatment, he was not released. Instead he was committed to Oranienburg concentration camp, where he spent four months (17 March to 14 July 1934) followed by a few weeks in another camp, Lichtenberg.[22] His sojourn in hell finally came to an end when he was released in October 1934, benefiting from an amnesty to mark the death of President Hindenburg. Hinze spent some months recovering from the effects of his maltreatment by the Nazis. During this time he managed, somewhat surprisingly, to acquire a passport (issued at Berlin-Wilmersdorf on 24 April 1935), and, when threatened by the Gestapo with re-arrest, fled to Prague in May 1935.

After some weeks in Prague, Hinze was engaged by the Schauspielhaus in Zurich — like Prague, one of the few remaining independent centres of German theatre — to play a summer touring season in Friedrich Wolf's anti-Nazi play *Professor Mamlock*. Interestingly, Hinze did not play the title role (a distinguished academic persecuted by the Nazis) but was cast as his Nazi antagonist. As he later explained: 'No, I was the Nazi, always I played the Nazi. You see, I know the Nazi mentality very well. I had been in a concentration camp and I was interested as an actor and as an anti-Nazi'.[23]

In October 1935 Hinze travelled to the Soviet Union, where he spent two years and three months, largely in Ukraine. However, he went first to Moscow, where he had been offered a part in *The Fighter*, an anti-Nazi film dealing with the Reichstag Fire. Shortly after, he was sent to join the German Kolkhoz Theatre (Collective Farm Theatre) in Dnepropetrovsk, an industrial city in eastern Ukraine. The theatre collective had been formed in May 1935 at the instigation of Erwin Piscator, who had appointed Maxim Vallentin as artistic director.[24] Before 1933 Vallentin had been the most notable Agitprop theatre director in Germany. He had established an Agitprop theatre collective in Berlin as early as 1925, a year before he joined the KPD. The group adopted the name Red Megaphone (*Das rote Sprachrohr*), performing widely at KPD propaganda meetings and even touring the USSR in 1929. When the Nazis came to power, Vallentin was forced to go underground, before escaping to Prague and from there to the Soviet Union in 1935.

The Kolkhoz Theatre in Dnepropetrovsk, which Hinze joined in 1935, was a *Wandertheater*, a touring theatre group travelling to German-speaking villages in Ukraine. The troupe included former members of the German agitprop group,

---

22 Dates and other details are taken from a subsequent statement by Hinze, describing his experience at the hands of the Nazis ('taken down on 10.3.55'), Gerard Heinz Papers.

23 See the transcript of Hinze's interview with the Interned Enemy Aliens Tribunal, 1 January 1942, TNA, KV2/2364, no. 33b.

24 Cf. John Willett, *The Theatre of Erwin Piscator: Half a Century of Politics in the Theatre* (London: Eyre Methuen, 1978), pp. 134–36. The fullest account of the Kolkhoz Theatre and other German theatre groups in the USSR is contained in: Peter Dietzel, *Exiltheater in der Sowjetunion 1932–1937* (Berlin: Henschelverlag, 1978).

FIG. 2. Gerhard Hinze as Matvei in *Distant Point*, Ukraine 1936
(courtesy Ernest Rodker)

Kolonne Links, including, among others, the actor Curt Trepte. A couple of years earlier, Hinze had brought Trepte into the Communist Party, now it was Trepte's turn to invite Hinze to join the new theatre group. Another member of the theatre was the young Englishwoman Joan Rodker, who was to become Hinze's companion over the next few years. She was the daughter of the poet and publisher John Rodker, who in the 1930s was also acting as agent for Preslit, the Soviet overseas literature organ. Joan had come to Moscow armed with little but a letter of introduction from her father and after a brief spell as a translator — brief but disastrous, as she herself commented — had been invited to join the new theatre group.[25]

The Kolkhoz Theatre was very much a propaganda theatre: Hinze played in various anti-Nazi plays, directed by Maxim Vallentin, including a dialectical adaptation of Kleist's *Der zerbrochene Krug* [The Broken Jug], a play drawn from the German classical repertoire which satirises the failings of the judicial system. Hinze played Gerichtsrat von Walter, a legal official charged with inspecting Adam, the village judge, and the way he runs his court. He also performed the leading role of Commander Malko in Alexander Afinogenov's contemporary Soviet play *Distant Point*, written in 1935 in the style of socialist realism. *Distant Point* is set partly in a railway carriage in which Malko, a Red Army general who we learn is dying of cancer, is delayed at a railway siding in a remote Siberian village. His presence provides the catalyst for a philosophical debate about life and death, social values, and the value of comradeship and dedication in the revolutionary cause. *Distant Point* was then completely unknown outside the Soviet Union, but it did not remain so. Unity Theatre later staged the play in London during the Battle of Britain, a strong marker of changing values in theatre production in the early war years.

Hinze's other parts included the role of General Galofa in Ramon Sender's one-act *The Secret (Das Geheimnis)*, a rather melodramatic piece concerning attempts by a brutal interrogator, a part played by Hinze, to extract information about strike plans from his prisoner, who succeeds in tricking him, choosing death rather than betraying his comrades. In a play with strong echoes of his own experience, Hinze played the role, not of the prisoner, but of the fascist interrogator, confirming his claim, as an actor, to know the 'enemy' and his twisted mentality.

At this point, it is important to note the obvious disparity between the official Soviet history of touring theatre and the more prosaic reality. Soviet accounts always painted a rosy picture of such propaganda tours, in which theatre groups were welcomed by enthusiastic villagers. Post-war accounts appearing in the GDR, written some thirty years after the event, continued to tell much the same story.[26] The reality was rather different. The inhabitants of the German-speaking villages visited by the theatre group were largely Lutheran Mennonite Christians, whose ancestors had first come to Ukraine over a century before. The village communities had lost their original autonomy under the impact of famine in the early 1920s, and the subsequent Soviet collectivisation of agriculture, which had turned each village

---

25 Author's interview with Joan Rodker, 5 August 2009.
26 Cf. Dietzel, *Exiltheater in der Sowjetunion.*

into a collective farm. The villagers were obliged to receive the travelling theatre troupe, even though they belonged to a religious community whose tradition shunned theatrical performance. The company performed in the open air or, if the weather dictated, in a central meeting hall, sometimes in what had once been the village church. Joan Rodker, then an ardent communist, remembered that the actors were all billed with local families, very often sharing their beds which she remembered they occupied immediately after the villagers had got up to go to work. Her abiding memory, however, was of the fleas which infested the bedding and which it was afterwards almost impossible to get rid of.[27]

Hinze continued to act with the Kolkhoz Theatre until it was disbanded in the autumn of 1936. In November he moved to Odessa to become artistic director of the German Theatre Collective (Deutsches Kollektivistentheater) run by Ilse Berend-Groa. This was a German-language touring company, comprising mainly young non-professional actors, which took theatre out into the countryside. According to Hinze's own recollection, he staged anti-Nazi plays, such as Friedrich Wolf's *The Trojan Horse (Das Trojanische Pferd)* as well as a performance of Shakespeare's *Othello.*[28] His recollections also suggest the considerable demands of working with actors who knew little about the theatre, let alone the European classics:

> We used to travel in the German districts and play before peasants. [...] It was hard work because the actors were actually peasant boys and were ordinary workers [...] and it was very difficult for them to read and to act, but it was very interesting — they were quite young boys.[29]

Hinze was a talented actor, with a strong stage presence. Joan Rodker remembered: 'He was a very good-looking man, very charming'.[30] Their relationship had flourished and their son Ernest was born in Odessa in May 1937. Ernest was born at the height of the Stalinist purges which had spread throughout the Soviet Union, their effects soon impinging on Hinze. Under the impact of the first big show trials in August 1936, Russian attitudes to foreigners (even foreign communists) changed abruptly. In the prevailing atmosphere of political mistrust, all Germans became suspect as potential spies. Some were arrested; most were 'merely' expelled. In Hinze's case, his contract was terminated and he was given twenty days to get out of the Soviet Union, leaving in January 1938.

At this point, Hinze and Joan Rodker were forced to separate temporarily. Unable to re-enter Germany, he returned to Prague, while she, together with their infant son, went back to London, where he planned to re-join her. Four months passed before Hinze was finally able to leave Prague for Britain, travelling first to Holland by air to avoid passing through Nazi Germany; in May 1938 he was at first refused entry to Britain.

When he arrived at the port of Harwich on 17 May 1938, he was initially

27   Author's interview with Joan Rodker.
28   Hinze to Under-Secretary of State, Aliens Department, 8 September 1941, Gerard Heinz Papers.
29   Interview with the Interned Enemy Aliens Tribunal. See note 2.
30   Author's interview with Joan Rodker.

refused leave to land. His wish to enter Britain was treated with some suspicion, undoubtedly because immigration officials found visas in his passport confirming that he had spent the previous two years in the Soviet Union, and therefore assumed (correctly) that he was a communist. Equally, 'although in possession of only £12, he expressed his intention of staying permanently in Britain'.[31] Such frankness was plainly unwise. In addition, Hinze spoke little or no English, but he declared, no doubt sincerely, that one reason he wanted to enter Britain was that he wished to learn English. He was finally given a visa for one month, 'on condition that he does no work, paid or unpaid'.[32]

Hinze was met at Harwich by Joan Rodker and her father John, whose presence Special Branch recorded, noting that their passports showed 'they had been resident in Russia for some time'.[33] Having been refused entry, Hinze was sent back on board the ferry to be returned to Holland, a country from which he might well have been repatriated to Germany. He was finally permitted to enter Britain only after the late intercession of the Labour MP Ellen Wilkinson who, without knowing Hinze, agreed to stand as his guarantor.[34] Her action possibly saved his life and certainly changed its course, enabling him to enter Britain and eventually to make a career on the London stage.

31 Special Branch report, Harwich, 18 May 1938, TNA, KV2/2364, no. 1A.
32 Ibid.
33 Ibid.
34 Author's interview with Joan Rodker. Cf. also Hinze to under-secretary of state, Aliens Department, 8 September 1941, Gerard Heinz Papers.

CHAPTER 6

'Restlessly Waiting Close to the Frontier': Friedrich Valk in Prague

The German actor Friedrich Valk had, like Gerhard Hinze, been brought up in Hamburg and had even made his first stage appearance there. On leaving Germany, he had, like Hinze, first taken refuge in Prague, where their paths certainly crossed from time to time. There the parallels end. Hinze had escaped from the Third Reich after being arrested and imprisoned as an active communist; Valk became a victim of the Nazis simply because he was Jewish.

Valk was born in 1895 in Elberfeld in the Ruhr but grew up in Hamburg, which was not only Germany's largest port, but also a theatre city of some standing. Originally destined for a career in business, Valk had turned instead to the theatre, making his earliest stage appearances at the Schauspielhaus Hamburg in 1915. The following year, he was conscripted into the Kaiser's army, serving in Northern France, but he was an unwilling soldier, admitting that the happiest day of his army service was when he finally discarded his uniform. On the very day he finally arrived back in Hamburg, he walked on in a production of *The Merchant of Venice* — a play with which his name became closely associated and which was to provide one of his outstanding roles on the British stage.[35]

After performing supporting roles in Hamburg, Valk moved on to play major roles in Lübeck, thirty five miles from Hamburg, where he made an instant impression in heroic (or villainous) parts, including Shakespeare's *Richard III*, a performance which strengthened his love of Shakespeare and earned him the local nickname of 'The King of Lübeck'. From Lübeck, Valk moved on to the Landestheater Darmstadt in 1924, where he made his second appearance in *The Merchant of Venice*, this time as Shylock.

In the same year Valk joined the Staatstheater Berlin, under the direction of Leopold Jessner, where he spent four years, appearing in various plays from the German classical repertoire, such as Hebbel's *Herodes und Mariamne* [Herod and Mariamne], Hauptmann's *Die Weber* [The Weavers], and Schiller's *Die Räuber* [The Robbers]. He also appeared in Shakespearean plays: *Hamlet* (as the ghost of Hamlet's father) in 1926 and *The Merchant of Venice* (as Tubal) in 1927.

35 Diana Valk, *Shylock for a Summer* (London: Cassell, 1958), pp. 32–33.

By then Valk had become a sought-after actor and in 1929 he joined the ensemble of the Schauspielhaus Düsseldorf which, under the artistic management of Louise Dumont and Gustav Lindemann, had become one of the most famous and successful theatres in Europe. Valk spent three seasons there (1929 to 1932) appearing as Mephistopheles in a historic production of *Faust Part II*, staged in April 1932 to mark the centenary of Goethe's death. It was Valk's most acclaimed role hitherto — and was to be the last he ever played on the German stage.

Confronted by the increasingly threatening political situation in Germany, Valk felt it wise to leave the country temporarily to watch developments from a safe distance. In November 1932 he accepted an engagement at the Neue Deutsche Theater (NDT) in Prague — and after Hitler's appointment as Chancellor did not return to Germany.

The NDT was the largest German-language theatre in Czechoslovakia, and could look back on a long and illustrious history, during which it had often acted as a geographical and cultural link between Austria and Germany. When Prague became the capital of the newly-founded Czechoslovakia in 1919, the NDT was reduced to the status of a minority theatre, but remained a cultural focal point for the substantial German-speaking population of Prague. During the 1920s it had produced predominantly plays from the modern Austrian and German repertoire. It had also remained a popular venue for touring companies and for guest appearances by well-known actors. Many of the actors forced to leave Germany after February 1933 had already appeared at the NDT; most others knew of its reputation, making Prague the first-choice destination for many refugees. Although there is no official figure of the number of theatre artists fleeing Hitler's Germany for the (temporary) safety of Czechoslovakia, the best estimate appears to be about 250, a figure including a substantial number of Czech nationals who had been pursuing their careers in Germany before being forced to return home.[36]

After 1933, Czechoslovakia was the only remaining democratic state in Central and Eastern Europe. Moreover, it adopted a liberal and generous policy towards refugees, as emphasised by the Foreign Minister Edvard Beneš, speaking in 1933:

> It will be a future source of pride for us, as it has been for centuries to England, America, France and Switzerland, that we have given asylum to political refugees. This is not just a self-evident truth for a state, which was born in the circumstances ours was, in which our émigrés played such a major part. It is also a consequence of the entire legal and political structure of our state.[37]

Beneš spoke from personal experience, having been a political exile himself, but in practice things were not so simple. Certain aspects of the government's policy towards refugees were flouted or forgotten as a consequence of disagreements between parties in the government coalition. Meanwhile, the Third Reich was making increasingly aggressive demands that the Czech government should rein in the activities of German refugees.

---

36 See Hansjörg Schneider, 'Exiltheater in der Tschechoslowakei', in *Handbuch des deutschsprachigen Exiltheaters*, ed. by Trapp and others, I, 157–92 (p. 157).

37 *Prager Tageblatt*, 9 November 1933, cited by Schneider, 'Exiltheater in der Tschechoslowakei', p. 160.

Czechoslovakia had a long border with Germany to the North, and a German-speaking minority, largely in the Sudeten border areas, which would become the focus of an international crisis in 1938. The ethnic German minority comprised some 23 per cent of the total population, although within the Sudetenland and in other linguistic enclaves, German speakers constituted a comfortable majority.[38] After 1933, large parts of the German-speaking minority moved to the right, supporting the Fascist party of Konrad Henlein, which in the election of May 1935 became the strongest party in parliament and increasingly took its cue from Nazi Germany, culminating in the inflammatory demand that the Sudetenland and its German majority should become part of the German Reich.

The tensions and troubles of the political situation after 1933 impacted heavily on the cultural scene in Prague, not least on the theatre. The NDT's artistic programme was affected throughout the inter-war period by the international situation and the growing threat to Czechoslovakia. After 1933, the NDT became, willy-nilly, a political focal point, its activities influenced by the vagaries of the political situation, and particularly by the noises off stage emanating from the country's northern neighbour.

Valk had been invited to join the NDT by its director, Paul Eger, a Swiss Jew of liberal persuasion and great experience in the theatre. Eger was anxious to steer the theatre along an unpolitical path, avoiding controversy and political backlash, though this proved difficult from the start. Valk's first part at the NDT was the title role in Sophocles's *König Ödipus* [Oedipus the King] which opened on 1 March 1933, the evening after the Reichstag Fire in Berlin.

The theatre also had to contend with the problems of domestic censorship which refused to sanction the production of controversial plays like Friedrich Wolf's *Cyankali* [Cyanide], which addressed the issue of abortion, or Ferdinand Bruckner's *Krankheit der Jugend* [Sickness of Youth] — both of which had been banned in Germany. The difficulties facing the NDT were indeed those of any German-language theatre operating outside the jurisdiction of the Third Reich — but not outside its sphere of influence.

Much of the theatre's repertoire, however, was less contentious, being drawn from the classical and modern European repertoire including works by Shakespeare and Shaw, Schiller, Lessing, Hauptmann, Büchner, Ibsen, Strindberg, Tolstoy, and Gorky. The breadth and scope of this repertoire offered Valk, as the company's leading actor, the chance to play an almost unprecedented range of classical roles, including those he would repeat on the London stage, such as Othello and John Gabriel Borkman.

It was also at the NDT that Valk first encountered the Czech-born director Julius Gellner, whom Eger had recruited following his dismissal — as a Jew — by the Münchner Kammerspiele. Several of Valk's stage appearances in Prague were made under Gellner's direction, most notably in two Schiller plays: as Verrina, the doughty Republican, in *Fiesco* and as President von Walter in *Kabale und Liebe* [Intrigue and Love], both in 1937. Gellner was to renew his collaboration with Valk

38   According to the Czechoslovak national census of 1930.

in London, directing one of his outstanding performances on the English stage.

After 1933, the NDT suffered growing financial problems, partly due to a decline in public subsidy, which made the theatre increasingly reliant on box-office returns. However, it also suffered from the small size of its target audience, which in the 1930s amounted to some forty thousand, although this number had been swollen by an influx of refugees from Germany.[39] This relatively small potential audience, allied to the lack of subsidy, made it necessary to change the theatre programme every week, so that each production ran, typically, for only five or six performances. Such short runs made great demands on all the theatre workers, but especially on the actors who had to learn different roles at frequent intervals. As the linchpin of the acting ensemble, Fritz Valk played many of the leading roles, meaning that he had to learn long parts and feel his way into a new role at short notice. In order to conserve his energies, he did not appear in many of the plays which filled out the programme, such as light comedies by Bruno Frank and Ferenc Molnár, though he did appear in 1933 as Professor Higgins in Shaw's *Pygmalion*. It might be thought that comedy was not Valk's forte, but one of his later admirers regretted that 'his superlative sense of comedy [was] never fully exploited in the theatre'.[40]

Czechoslovakia, and above all Prague, had by 1935 become the main centre of anti-Nazi resistance outside Germany. Valk played an important part in anti-Nazi activities in Prague, which inevitably impinged on the NDT. In 1935, anti-Nazi members of the theatre ensemble joined their Czech counterparts in organising a German-Czech Theatre Club (Deutsch-Tschechicher Bühnenklub), with the declared aim of preventing any further advance of fascism on the cultural front; Paul Eger tolerated this incursion into the political neutrality of the theatre, well aware that the future of the NDT itself depended on the political survival of the Czechoslovak Republic. In the prevailing circumstances, Valk, as the company's leading actor, needed little persuasion to become the joint president of the theatre club, together with his counterpart at the Czech National Theatre, Vaclav Vydra.

In August 1936, Radio Prague had begun foreign language broadcasting in several different languages, including German, which served as part of propaganda broadcasts to Germany. It should be emphasised that Radio Prague's broadcasts to Germany preceded, by at least two years, the BBC German Service, which was inaugurated only in 1938 in response to the Munich crisis. A number of refugees worked with the German section of Radio Prague, including Fritz Valk, who acted as an announcer, while also undertaking drama and poetry readings, roles he reprised in propaganda broadcasts for the BBC during the war. Radio Prague continued these broadcasts, even after the signing of the Munich Treaty, which surrendered the Sudeten territories to Germany — and ceased only after the Germans invaded what remained of Czechoslovakia in March 1939.

Valk's fine stage voice was well-known in Germany and these broadcasts alone would have placed him on the Gestapo's 'black list' when the Nazis marched into

39 In the same census of 1930 some forty-two thousand inhabitants of Prague claimed to speak German as their first language.
40 Donald Davis, 'A Tribute', in Valk, p. xix.

Prague in March 1939. Valk, it should be noted, had become a Czechoslovak citizen in 1937, a decision prompted by the urgent need for travel documents, his German passport having been withdrawn. His Czech passport would later prove to be a valuable asset.

The Neue Deutsche Theater suspended all performances at the end of September 1938 and, with the signing of the Munich Treaty, which dismembered Czechoslovakia, it finally closed its doors altogether. It never opened again as a German-language theatre.

German tanks rolled into Prague on 15 March 1939. Fritz Valk had left the city less than three weeks earlier, bound for Britain. He travelled from Prague to London by train, running a calculated risk by taking the most direct route straight across Germany, anticipating that, since he had not lived in Germany for several years, his true identity would be protected by his Czech passport. Luck was on his side and he passed through Germany without incident, arriving in London on a rainy evening at the end of February 1939.

CHAPTER 7

'The Great Tragedienne':
Lilly Kann

In February 1933, the German actress Lilly Kann was in the middle of her second season at the Neues Schauspielhaus, Königsberg, the capital of Germany's easternmost province, East Prussia. When Hitler came to power, things changed abruptly. She found that she and other Jewish colleagues were suddenly barred from entering the theatre. Her contract was arbitrarily cancelled, her employment terminated, leaving her career — after twenty-five years on the German stage — at a sudden crossroads.[41]

Kann was born in 1893 into an assimilated Jewish family in Peitz, Brandenburg, though she spent her early years in Kempen in Posen, a small town close to what was then the German border with Poland.[42] The family belonged to the cream of local society, her father being a lawyer at the district court. It was also an artistic family; her mother had trained as an opera singer before abandoning her career in favour of marriage. In very early childhood Lilly Kann lost the sight of her left eye; for the rest of her life she wore an artificial eye, a physical disability of which she was constantly aware, but which did not deflect her from pursuing her ambition to go on the stage.

The family moved to Berlin when she was seven, her mother dying shortly after. Lilly attended the Charlotten-Lyzeum (girls' high school) in Berlin and later trained at the theatre school of the Prussian State Theatre. She began her acting career when she was just fifteen at the Goethe Festival in Düsseldorf, going on to play her first professional season in Bonn, performing small parts in German and foreign classics.

Looking back on her career in an informal memoir, written in the 1970s, Kann cites an aphorism coined by the famous theatre impresario Max Reinhardt: 'Theaterspielen lernt man durch Theaterspielen' [You learn how to act by acting]. It is a maxim she illustrates through the example of her own career.[43] Her first season in Bonn was followed by seasons at other small-town theatres like Landsberg an der

---

41 Lilly Kann, *Der Ritt über'n Bodensee: Erinnerungen Einer Schauspielerin*, ed. by Charmian Brinson and Richard Dove (Bern: Peter Lang, 2017), p. 68. The manuscript of Kann's memoirs, contained in five notebooks, is part of the Lilly Kann Papers (privately held in London).

42 Kempen is now Kepno, the name being changed after Posen was ceded to Poland in 1919.

43 Kann, p. 84.

FIG. 3. Lilly Kann (second from left) as Grete Hinkemann in *Hinkemann*,
Dresden, 1924 (courtesy Rachel Ormerod)

Warte (now Gorzow Wielkopolski) and Nordhausen (Harz). Such small provincial theatres boasted an ambitious repertoire consisting mainly of ancient and modern classics. Moreover, because of the small local audience, the programme had to be changed regularly: Kann remembered 'learning and playing a big role every 10–14 days'.[44] She also played in Lübeck, a lively town where she stayed three years, playing leading roles by Ibsen, Strindberg, and in Euripides's *Medea*. Her long apprenticeship in provincial theatres gave her the chance to play a wide range of parts and taught her the rudiments of her trade. In later years she maintained that it was hard work and experience that had made her the accomplished actress she became.[45]

In 1922 she joined the Staatstheater, Dresden — 'the first really top rank theatre of my career'.[46] She began by playing the title role in Grillparzer's *Medea*, the first of many tragic roles, such as Clytemnestra in the Oresteia trilogy, Lady Macbeth, and the title role in Friedrich Hebbel's *Judith*. She also acted in contemporary plays, most notably in the notorious production of Ernst Toller's *Hinkemann* in 1924, in which she played Grete Hinkemann, the protagonist's wife. She recalled that the actors had tried to continue the performance in the face of noisy disturbances by nationalist protesters which made much of the dialogue inaudible. The play was taken off after the first performance.

From 1925 to 1928 Kann was part of the company of the Düsseldorf Schauspielhaus, run by the celebrated partnership of Gustav Lindemann and Louise Dumont, where she became known as 'die große Tragödin' [the great tragedienne].[47] There was also another side to her talent. She became famous for her dramatic recitations of poems by Heine (Dusseldorf's most famous son) at Sunday matinée performances. She also had a fine singing voice, perhaps inherited from her mother, and gave regular recitals of traditional and popular songs, which later became a feature of her career in London. After Düsseldorf, she continued her career in Frankfurt and Berlin, where she understudied the role of Mrs Peachum in the original production of Brecht's *Dreigroschenoper* [Threepenny Opera]. In 1930 she gave birth to a daughter, Karla, after a love affair with an Italian, Giulio Farina, of whom little is known but his name.

With Hitler's rise to power, Kann found herself, after twenty-four years on the German stage, effectively banned from it. She was an actress with a strong sense of vocation, for whom life without the theatre was no life at all. She decided to seek work abroad, travelling to Vienna to audition at various theatres, but without success: Austria was in the grip of economic recession and burgeoning anti-Semitism. She was still in Vienna when she received a letter from the dramatist and critic Julius Bab offering her a contract with the theatre of the newly-formed Jewish Kulturbund in Berlin. Her initial reaction was one of disbelief: she was all too aware of the striking anomaly of a Jewish theatre in a Nazi state. After verifying that the offer was genuine, however, she accepted it, returning to Berlin in time to join rehearsals for the theatre's opening production, Lessing's *Nathan the Wise*, staged —

44 Ibid.
45 'Hard Work Made Lilly Kann a Fine Actress', *Weekly Sporting Review*, 22 December 1949.
46 Lilly Kann, autobiographical outline, dated 13 January 1957, Lilly Kann Papers.
47 *Rheinische Post*, 10 February 1973.

in an echo of former theatrical glories — at the Berliner Theater in Berlin's West End. Kann played the role of Daja, a devout Christian and the female companion to Nathan's daughter Recha, an essential figure in the dramatic narrative.

The theatre of the Jewish Kulturbund was perhaps the most remarkable theatrical enterprise during the Nazi era. The Kulturbund (or KuBu, as it became known) staged plays, operas, and concerts in various cities, becoming effectively the only professional stage outlet for Jewish artists in Germany, and the only theatre Jews were permitted to attend.[48] All Jewish artists were required to join it: they therefore faced the choice between performing in the cultural ghetto of 'Jewish theatre' — or emigrating. From the outset, the KuBu theatre faced the steady loss of both its performers and its audience through emigration. It also faced constant financial problems. It was run as a subscription theatre, but since 'Aryan' Germans were not allowed to attend its performances, it had to rely entirely on the support of a suddenly impoverished Jewish community.

Kann spent the next six years with the KuBu, longer than she had spent with any other theatre. During this time she became a mainstay of the company, appearing in over thirty productions, often in leading roles. The theatre's repertoire was, of course, shaped by what the Nazi authorities would permit or rather what they considered suitable for performance in a 'Jewish theatre'. For example, they refused to sanction performances of the German classics — so familiar to both actors and audience — since a Jewish theatre was deemed unfit to perform them. Fortunately, this proscription did not apply to foreign classics, and Kann was able to perform in various classical productions, including Shakespeare's *Othello* (1933) and *The Winter's Tale* (1939), Ibsen's *The Wild Duck* (1934) and *Pillars of Society* (1937), and Pirandello's *Six Characters in Search of an Author* (1935).

Even her roles in such foreign classics illustrate the constant need to balance artistic considerations against the reality of Nazi censorship. Plays by Ibsen or Shaw, for example, often required significant cuts in dialogue. Ibsen, always a popular playwright in Germany, had been appropriated by the Nazis as a 'Nordic writer', but despite this, his plays often posed problems for Nazi censorship. In *Pillars of Society*, Ibsen's theme of political opportunism in a public figure is personified by his protagonist Bernick, a successful businessman and 'a pillar of society', whose façade of social concern is exposed as mere hypocrisy. Kann played the role of Lona Hessel, his former lover, whom Bernick had abandoned in order to marry for money. The play's final exchanges are between these two characters, ending with Hessel's line: 'The spirit of truth and the spirit of freedom — those are the pillars of society'. However, Kann did not speak these words, because the play's director had made cuts in dialogue, including these final exchanges, in order to make the play acceptable to the Nazi censors.[49]

---

48 For further details of the Jüdischer Kulturbund, see *Geschlossene Vorstellung: Der Jüdischer Kulturbund in Deutschland 1933–1941*, ed. by Akademie der Künste, Berlin (Berlin: Hentrich, 1992). An historical account is contained in a more recent monograph: Rebecca Rovit, *The Jewish Kulturbund Theatre Company in Nazi Germany* (Iowa City: University of Iowa Press, 2012).

49 Rovit, p. 127. Rovit even suggests that these cuts were so extensive that 'the core significance' of the play was lost.

In contrast to her earlier career, Kann also embraced comedy. Paradoxically, comedy represented an important part of the KuBu's repertoire — a surreal accompaniment to the tragedy unfolding off-stage. Prominent among comedies staged were those by Jewish authors writing in German, like Arthur Schnitzler, whose work had been banned from the German stage after 1933, except for performance by the KuBu. Kann also appeared in contemporary English comedies, like Shaw's *You Never Can Tell* and Merton Hodges's *The Wind and the Rain*, widening her knowledge of English theatre even before her arrival in England.

At the insistence of the Nazi authorities, a further strand of the theatre's repertoire consisted of Jewish plays (largely translated into German from Yiddish or Hebrew) which portrayed Jewish life in the East European *shtetl*, a world totally foreign to the KuBu's highly assimilated German-Jewish audience, most of whom had never even heard Yiddish spoken. Although Kann acted in several such plays, she was equally unfamiliar with this world; it was only much later that she encountered Yiddish theatre in London, when performing with the Yiddish actor Meyer Tzelniker. Kann's six-year spell with the Kulturbund could well be considered a paradigm of the theatre's repertoire.

In her informal memoir, written nearly forty years later, Lilly Kann is surprisingly brief in her references to the KuBu, having little to say about the exceptional circumstances of a theatre where the actors regularly performed under the watchful eye of the Gestapo. Her recollections include only fleeting impressions of life in Nazi Berlin, such as the notices outside public playgrounds stating 'Forbidden for Jewish Children' which, she records, upset her own daughter. But in general her account of life in the Kulturbund theatre is rather superficial, suggesting that both actors and audience adapted quickly to the abnormal situation, learning to tolerate the intolerable:

> What was life like in the Jewish Kulturbund theatre? Just like in any other theatre. Rivalry over roles, romantic attachments, both heterosexual and homosexual. The actor at the Jewish theatre in the Hitler years was not very different to the actor anywhere else. What interested him? Politics? No, his next role. Personal risk? Not so much as his next role.[50]

Her recollections do help to explain why she remained so long in Nazi Berlin, almost failing to escape Germany altogether: 'But, in any case, it was an existence, even if only a modestly paid one and as long as you had an existence, you put off the decision to leave and face the uncertainty of life in a foreign land'.[51]

While others, both actors and audience, gradually began to leave Germany, Lilly Kann stayed on. In the 1936–37 season alone she appeared in no fewer than six productions, including a cabaret evening in which she performed songs by Jean Cocteau. In November 1938 she played Mrs Macfie in Merton Hodge's light comedy *The Wind and the Rain*, which had run for over a thousand performances in London.[52] Opening on 2 November 1938, the play was directed by Fritz Wisten,

---

50 Kann, p. 72.
51 Ibid., p. 76.
52 The title alluded to Feste's song in *Twelfth Night*.

who, in parallel, was rehearsing the next production, *Benjamin, wohin?* [Where to, Benjamin?], in which Kann was to appear with the Austrian actor Martin Miller.

During 1939, Lilly Kann continued to appear at the KuBu, firstly in Shakespeare's *The Winter's Tale,* in which her daughter Karla, then aged six, also played a small role, then in another English play, J. B. Priestley's *People at Sea*, and finally in Ladislas Fodor's comedy *Märchen der Gerechtigkeit* (Fairy Tale of Justice) — a title so sharply at odds with the prevailing circumstances in Germany that one wonders how the Nazi authorities allowed it to be performed. Before her final departure, Kann gave a farewell performance with an evening of songs from theatre and cabaret, including the Brecht/Weill song 'Surabaya Jonny', a poignant showpiece which could not have been performed publicly anywhere else in Germany in 1939.[53]

Having sent her daughter to Britain on a *Kindertransport* in June 1939, Kann found her own departure delayed by the difficulties of obtaining the necessary visas. As she herself recounted, while entry to Britain required a visa (which was difficult to obtain) it was also necessary to obtain an exit visa, which was issued by the Nazi authorities only subject to time-consuming and often arbitrary requirements:

> There was an enormous room, the centre empty, tables all around the walls — and we had to proceed from one table to the next, showing a list on which was written every single item we wanted to take with us; every cotton reel, every needle had to be mentioned. I still have a copy of the list to this day.[54]

She finally managed to escape Germany at almost the last moment, leaving on 18 August 1939. Even then, she displayed little sense of urgency, breaking her journey in Brussels to stay two nights with her aunt, before travelling on to London, finally arriving just twelve days before war broke out.

---

53   Cf. the report of this 'Abschiedsabend' in *Jüdisches Nachrichtenblatt*, 11 August 1939, press cutting in Lilly Kann papers.

54   See Lilly Kann, 'Getting Out', undated typescript, Lilly Kann Papers.

CHAPTER 8

Changing Countries:
The Austrian Actor Martin Miller

While Lilly Kann spent six years at the Kulturbund, Martin Miller stayed barely six months. Miller was born Rudolf Müller in 1899 in Kremsier, Moravia, now in the Czech Republic, but then still part of the Austro-Hungarian Empire. The family later moved to Vienna, then the most celebrated theatre city in Europe with the possible exception of Paris. It was Vienna that nurtured Müller's theatrical ambitions — and there that he began his career, playing minor roles at the Raimund-Theater in 1921 under the stage name Martin Miller.

Miller soon sought to widen his experience, leaving Vienna to perform in some of the border outposts of German-language theatre. Over the next fifteen years, he worked in cities as far apart as Lodz, in Poland, where he spent two seasons in 1923–1925, and Strasbourg, where he acted in 1936, but he made his name and mastered his craft in the German-language theatres of the Czech Sudetenland. From 1926 he spent almost a decade as actor, and later director, in the German theatres of Reichenberg, Aussig, and Mährisch-Ostrau, playing a wide range of dramatic and comic roles, always to critical acclaim. He became indeed a major star in this minor firmament, beginning at the Stadttheater Reichenberg (now Liberec, Czech Republic) which, in common with other German theatres in the Sudetenland, played an ambitious repertoire of European classics that included Shakespeare, Strindberg, Gogol, Schiller, and Lessing, as well as modern plays by Carl Zuckmayer and Ferenc Molnár.

One of his greatest triumphs in Reichenberg was in *The Adventures of the Good Soldier Schwejk,* a stage adaptation by Max Brod and Max Reimann of Jaroslav Hašek's satirical novel about a Czech soldier in the Imperial army in the First World War. By that time, Schwejk had already become one of the traditional figures of Viennese cabaret: the archetypal little man, entangled in red tape, harassed by police, doctors, and clergy, but always coming out on top. Miller's performance as a comically subversive Schwejk had earned unqualified praise: 'The complete victory of the good soldier Schwejk belongs, however, to Martin Miller, who transformed the part into a star role. It is hard to imagine a better performance'.[55] Miller was to play Schwejk again in very different circumstances in London in 1940, but on that occasion there were no reviews at all.

55 'Die Abenteuer des braven Soldaten Schweyk', undated press cutting, MN-MA.

From 1933 to 1935, Miller worked as artistic director (and actor) at the newly-founded German Theatre in Mährisch-Ostrau (now Ostrava, Czech Republic), directing Grillparzer's *Der Traum ein Leben* [The Dream a Life] as the inaugural production. In 1935, in the mounting political crisis that was soon to engulf the Sudetenland, German-language theatres increasingly took their cue from Nazi Germany and Miller found his contract in Mährisch-Ostrau was not renewed, forcing him to turn elsewhere.

Finally arriving back in Vienna in 1935, at a time of political crisis and rising antisemitism, Miller had honed his skills in the newly-established *Kleinkunstbühnen*, or cabaret theatres performing satirical revue. Playing to a small audience, with little publicity, they were almost the last places in Austria where social and political criticism were still tolerated. In 1936 Miller appeared regularly at the 'Literatur am Naschmarkt', where his dazzling impressions of such famous actors as Max Pallenberg and Albert Bassermann were greeted by 'real gales of laughter'.[56] Miller's gift for comic impersonation did not translate readily into a second language, but his pitch-perfect impression of Adolf Hitler was nonetheless to launch his later stage career in London. He also performed at the ABC, the most politically radical of Vienna's cabaret theatres, where the resident writer was the young poet and dramatist Jura Soyfer, later to die in a Nazi concentration camp.

Cabaret theatres like the ABC vanished overnight in March 1938, finding themselves among the earliest casualties of Hitler's *Anschluss*. As a Jewish actor, Miller could no longer find employment, leaving him with little choice but to emigrate, if he was to continue his career. Miller was already a much-travelled actor, willing and able to change countries, but while prepared to act abroad, he had always confined himself to performing in the German language. He had no knowledge of English and no contacts with the English or American theatre. In the circumstances, it is perhaps not surprising that he chose to stay in Germany, at least temporarily, signing a six-month contract with the theatre of the Jewish Kulturbund in Berlin. It was the first time he had acted there. As he later explained in an interview: 'In Berlin I felt I was keeping something alive in the very jaws of death; in Vienna one felt almost frivolous playing in the theatre, while the European world collapsed'.[57] His contract, signed and dated September 1938, ran from 1 November 1938 to 31 March 1939, during which time he appeared in just three productions. The first of these was *Benjamin, wohin?* adapted for the stage by Hermann Sinsheimer from a story by the Yiddish-language author Mendele Moicher Sforim.

As early as 1935, the Gestapo had banned the use of stage names for artists performing at the Kulturbund theatre. Miller was therefore obliged to perform under his birth name, Rudolf Müller. Unwittingly, he had come to Berlin at perhaps the most turbulent and dangerous period of the Kulturbund's existence. On 9 November, a week after his arrival, the Nazis instigated the 'Kristallnacht' pogrom,

---

56 *Neues Wiener Abendblatt*, 8 August 1936, as cited in Ingeborg Reisner, *Kabarett als Werkstatt des Theaters* (Vienna: Theodor Kramer, 2004), p. 154.

57 'Jewishness and the Theatre', *The Jewish Telegraph*, undated cutting (*c.* 1967), MN-MA.

during which synagogues, as well as Jewish homes and businesses, were wantonly attacked. The theatre director Fritz Wisten, who was busily rehearsing *Benjamin, wohin?*, was arrested and sent to a concentration camp. Surprisingly, he was quickly released with the order to go back and continue with the production of the play — a sinister variation on the theatre adage, 'the show must go on'. And it did go on. Performances of *The Wind and the Rain*, suspended by order of the Nazi authorities on 8 November, were resumed on 22 November, by order of the same authorities, but the actors played to an almost empty house.

The production's director Fritz Wisten was at the same time rehearsing *Benjamin, wohin?*, in which Miller was to make his Berlin debut. In Wisten's absence, the premiere of *Benjamin, wohin?* had of course been delayed, finally taking place on 15 December 1938. The play was a picaresque tale of two itinerant pedlars, wandering through the landscape of the East European *shtetl*. Benjamin, played by Alfred Berliner, was a figure in the mould of Don Quixote, whose Sancho Panza, the wise and witty rogue Senderl, was played by Miller, who provided a wonderful comic foil to Berliner. The role of Selda, Senderl's wife, was taken by Lilly Kann: it was the first time she and Miller had appeared together.[58] The play itself was something of an anomaly, but gave the audience welcome comic relief from the gathering darkness outside the theatre. Miller made an instant impression, one critic paying tribute to his 'skill and maturity, as well as his heart and personality'.[59]

Even within the cultural ghetto of the Jewish Kulturbund, actors and other artists were subjected to humiliating and often nonsensical regulations, which had to be followed in order to gain the approval of the Nazi authorities. In January 1939 it was decreed that every Jewish male had to indicate his racial origin by adding the second name 'Israel'; women were correspondingly required to use the middle name 'Sara'. Miller accordingly appeared in the following production as 'Rudolf Israel Müller', Lilly Kann as 'Lilly Sara Kann'.

The Kulturbund opened its programme for 1939 with Ferenc Molnár's *Die Fee* [The Good Fairy]: staging yet another comedy while tragedy waited in the wings. The Hungarian dramatist Molnár had achieved great success in Germany in the 1920s, but he was a Jew and his work had vanished from the German theatre once the Nazis took power. *The Good Fairy* is a modern fairy tale, in which a poor cinema usherette uses a rich man's money to support a struggling lawyer, who she claims is her husband. As with any Molnár comedy, the sparkling dialogue drew frequent applause, even, as the reviewer noted, in the middle of a scene. Miller's portrayal of the struggling lawyer was described as 'a splendid and unforgettable performance, truly worthy of the spontaneous applause that broke out time and again, in tribute to Müller's performance and the whole, so completely successful production'.[60]

The third and final role of Miller's six-month season at the Kulturbund allowed

58 'Premiere im Kulturbund: Aufführung der Komödie *Benjamin, wohin?*', *Jüdisches Nachrichtenblatt* 8, 20 December 1938.

59 Julius Bab, 'Jüdische Schauspieler: Rudolf Israel Müller', *Jüdisches Nachrichtenblatt* 14, 17 February 1939.

60 Leo Hirsch, 'Premiere des Molnar-Lustspiels im Kulturbund', *Jüdisches Nachrichtenblatt* 9, 13 January 1939.

him to display another side of his talent in Shakespeare's *The Winter's Tale*, directed by Fritz Wisten and opening on 7 February 1939. Notably, the play was performed — as were all other Shakespeare productions at the Kulturbund theatre — in the classic translation by Dorothea Tieck, long familiar to German theatre-goers. Shakespeare's 'comedy' is in fact a tale of jealousy and remorse. Miller played Leontes, King of Sicily, a man so driven by ungovernable passion that he becomes unjust and tyrannical, until he is changed by the influence of female moderation. Lilly Kann played the leading role of Paulina, her daughter Karla, then aged six, also appearing in a minor part.

Once again it was Miller (or Müller) who stole the show. Reviewing the production, Leo Hirsch, the theatre's dramaturge, reported, using the hateful terminology that the Nazis imposed:

> Rudolf Israel Müller performs Leontes with resounding power and fury, with dawning delusion and such rapid heightening that its final rise and fall only manage to be softly whimpering, and thereby all the more touching, sounds from the heart.[61]

It was Miller's farewell performance. On 5 March 1939 he left Berlin for London, shaking off the involuntary persona of Rudolf Israel Müller and becoming once again Martin Miller — a name that would soon resound on the London stage.

---

61   Leo Hirsch, 'Die Premiere der Kulturbundbühne: *Das Wintermärchen*, *Jüdisches Nachrichtenblatt*, 12, 10 February 1939.

ACT III

'Enemy Aliens' on the British Stage
1939–1945

CHAPTER 9

Theatre in Britain
During the Second World War

The arrival of German-speaking actors on the British stage during the war years
is closely linked to the progress of the war itself, and the wartime fortunes of the
British theatre, including the important contribution of successful American plays.
The history of the British theatre during the war has been surprisingly neglected
by academic critics: even standard works of reference like *The Cambridge History of
British Theatre* have comparatively little to say on the subject. And yet the war years
were more than a history of survival; they were a time of significant change which
profoundly influenced post-war developments.[1]

Theatre, like other forms of public entertainment, suffered considerable restrictions
in wartime. In the interests of public safety, places of public entertainment were
immediately closed on the outbreak of war — and were only allowed to reopen
once the anticipated enemy air raids failed to happen. The short closure had had its
effect: 'the grave dislocation of the theatre industry throughout the country, with
its attendant distress and unemployment was not unforeseen', according to *Theatre
World* in October 1939.[2] By then, some West End theatres, as well as most suburban
and provincial theatres, had already been able to reopen. It had also become clear
that the continuation of most forms of public entertainment had official support,
since they were considered essential in maintaining civilian morale.

Even when allowed to re-open, theatres faced great difficulties in running
at all, not least because many actors and other theatre practitioners, including
directors and designers, not to mention those working back stage or front of the
house, were increasingly engaged in war work. Many younger actors joined the
armed forces, others joining up to entertain the troops with ENSA (standing for
Entertainment National Service Association, but popularly known, in the words

1 Baz Kershaw (ed.), *The Cambridge History of British Theatre*, 3 vols (Cambridge: Cambridge
University Press, 2004), III. In his own contribution, 'British Theatre 1940–2002', Kershaw mentions
such significant changes as CEMA and the wartime tours by the Old Vic only in passing. Equally,
Simon Trussler, in *The Cambridge Illustrated History of British Theatre* (Cambridge: Cambridge
University Press, 2000), offers only a brief summary of wartime theatre, see pp. 301–03. A welcome
exception (alas too short!) is the perceptive article by Anselm Heinrich, 'Theatre in Britain during
the Second World War', *New Theatre Quarterly*, 26/1 (February 2010), 61–70.
2 'Over the Footlights', *Theatre World*, October 1939.

of Tommy Trinder, as Every Night Something Awful). ENSA was set up in 1939 to provide entertainment to members of the British armed forces. Among those who performed with it were such popular entertainers as Gracie Fields, Vera Lynn, Joyce Grenfell, and George Formby, as well as actors like Paul Schofield and, later in the war, Laurence Olivier and Ralph Richardson. In 1940 ENSA requisitioned the Theatre Royal, Drury Lane — London's oldest theatre — to be used for forces' entertainment throughout the war. Similarly, the Covent Garden Opera House was taken over for use as a dance hall.

Wartime conditions made every aspect of theatre life more difficult. Theatre audiences declined, not least because the number of performances was greatly reduced. The blackout deterred many people from travelling in the evening, so that many theatres switched to afternoon or early evening performances. Even when performances did take place, they were sometimes disrupted by enemy air raids. Theatre programmes included instructions on what to do in the event of an air raid. Audiences were warned when an air raid was imminent (that is, when an air raid warning had sounded) and were told they could leave for a shelter if they wished, 'but the performance will continue'. In practice, most people stayed, preferring to sit back and enjoy the play.

In fact, many West End theatres closed altogether during the Blitz; others switched to matinee performances or sent shows out on tour, leaving *Theatre World* to complain in October 1940 that for the second time in a year, theatre activity had been transferred to the provinces until conditions improved: 'The choice of the Londoner is now restricted to the delights of the Revudeville at the Windmill and the lunch-time ballet hour at the Arts Theatre Club, to which must be added the brave venture of Shakespeare at the Vaudeville, matinées only'.[3] Matters improved after the Blitz, but there was no return to 'normal'. Indeed, as late as 1944 the new flying bombs, posing an unknown threat, once more caused widespread theatre closures. Significantly, the vast bulk of theatre performances in the war years took place outside London.

A few theatres remained closed throughout the war, and many others, both in London and the provinces, were destroyed or damaged in enemy air raids. Well-known London theatres like the Shaftesbury, Queens, and Little Theatres were completely destroyed by bombing; others, including the Duke of York's, the Embassy, and the Old Vic, were badly damaged. Indeed, the Old Vic was not rebuilt until 1950, when it reopened as the first home of a national theatre.

The Old Vic had had a long and varied history, since its foundation as the Royal Coburg Theatre in 1818. After 1914 under the management of Lillian Bayliss, it had quickly earned a reputation as the representative English theatre, performing a classical, largely Shakespearean repertoire. In the continued absence of a national theatre, an idea frequently proposed but never realised, the Old Vic became virtually a national theatre in waiting. With the destruction of the Old Vic theatre building in 1941, the depleted company left London and spent the next three years as a touring company, based at the Victoria Theatre, Burnley, from where they

3 'Over the Footlights', *Theatre World*, October 1940.

toured to a succession of venues in Wales, Northern England, and Scotland, visiting industrial towns, mining villages, and army camps, as well as larger provincial centres, playing to local audiences rather than the self-selected elite of the West End. Among actors who joined the Old Vic company was Fritz Valk, or Frederick Valk, as he had now become.

In its first two years as a touring company, the Old Vic conducted no fewer than fifteen separate tours 'carrying productions of ancient and modern classics all over England, Scotland and Wales', claiming that, despite the serious difficulties of touring in wartime, 'the scope of its work has been greatly enlarged'.[4] In 1942, an Old Vic company was also established at the Liverpool Playhouse, where the resident company had been disbanded because of the blitz. During this time, the Old Vic had also played two short seasons in London, finding a temporary home at the New Theatre, to which it finally returned on a more permanent basis in 1944.

While this brief summary might suggest that theatre in Britain during the war years could be described as a matter of dogged survival or even stylised as a contribution to the war effort, there is another, more significant side to the story. This was also the period which initiated an agenda of radical change that would transform the cultural landscape of Britain after the war. Signs of the post-war revolution in British theatre were already apparent in the wartime theatre repertoire.

Even more evident was the revolution in the funding of the arts, announced with the introduction of the Council for the Encouragement of Music and the Arts (CEMA), the forerunner of the Arts Council, which financed many arts undertakings including theatres and theatre companies. CEMA had been established in January 1940 with well-delineated responsibilities. Whereas ENSA was to offer entertainment to the armed forces, CEMA was concerned with the home front. CEMA's initial objective was to offer financial aid to drama and music societies which found it difficult to continue their activities; the broader aim which emerged was to use artistic performance to boost public morale. By 1942 the government had assumed full responsibility for CEMA, so that for the first time in British history, the state had effectively become a patron of the performing arts. Part of the rationale for this policy shift (which would have been unthinkable in the 1930s) was to compensate for the closure of many existing entertainment facilities, as well as for the long working hours and privations of war. In fact, the government became willing to subsidise the performing arts on an unprecedented scale, emphasising in its own propaganda the contribution of art and artists to the war effort. The best-known example of this public subsidy was the various tours undertaken by the Old Vic company for several consecutive seasons, which were extensively documented and widely publicised by the Ministry of Information. Through CEMA the government was pursuing the aim of arts provision for all, a concept which pointed beyond the end of the war.

In the course of the war, theatre was increasingly conscripted to a patriotic

---

4 Theatre programme for *Othello*, New Theatre, July 1942, copy in V&A TPA. The New Theatre is now renamed the Noel Coward Theatre.

narrative. Theatre performances were regarded as a contribution to the war effort: an important source of recreation and therefore of maintaining public morale. In addition, they were to become a means of instruction, even contributing to the process of nation-building. These functions are best illustrated by the example of Shakespeare who, as the 'national playwright', was regarded as part of the cultural heritage the war was being waged to defend. Shakespeare's plays were increasingly performed in the war years — in marked contrast to the 1930s, when the number of performances had dwindled.

In 1940 there were few, if any stage parts available for the many foreign actors stranded in London by the tides of war. In most cases this was because they had not sufficiently mastered the English language, but their prospects of finding work on the English stage were further diminished by the presence of the 'reserve army' of English actors, waiting in the wings. Austrian and German actors also had to contend with the prevailing negative perception of them as 'enemy aliens'. In the crisis months of May and June 1940, the British government hastily introduced a policy of mass internment of 'enemy aliens', detaining them in makeshift camps and in some cases deporting them to Canada or Australia.

In May 1940 British public opinion, fanned by alarmist headlines in newspapers such as the *Daily Mail*, had broadly backed the government's policy of mass internment. Public disquiet at the deportation of refugees was strengthened when the *Arandora Star*, a cruise liner requisitioned to take internees to Canada, was sunk by a German submarine with the loss of over six hundred lives. Gerhard Hinze was among those deported on the very next vessel bound for Canada, spending some eighteen months there in difficult conditions. By the time of his return early in 1942, public opinion had shifted back in support of the refugees.

During 1941 there were various overlapping developments which impacted on the London theatre. One was the growing 'manpower problem': the absence of many British actors, serving in the armed forces, made it increasingly difficult to cast certain parts. Another factor was the growing social acceptance of refugees, aided by their progressive integration into the British 'war effort', typically into the armaments industry, but also helping to ease the transition of some émigré actors to British stage and screen. A third development was the emergence of a new cultural agenda, shaped partly by the requirements of the Ministry of Information, which brought changes to the West End theatre repertoire. While some London theatres remained closed, those that were open began to present plays that explored topical themes — even the war itself — offering unexpected opportunities to refugee actors and thrusting a few of them into the spotlight of the West End stage.

This trend becomes clear with reference to a handful of topical new plays produced in London, which included *Thunder Rock* (1940), *Watch on the Rhine, Awake and Sing*, and *Arsenic and Old Lace* (all 1942), All but one of these plays were written by American dramatists, emphasising the dearth of new dramatic writing in Britain, a situation finally relieved by the staging of Terence Rattigan's *Flare Path*.

Thunder Rock was a highly topical play by the successful dramatist Robert Ardrey. The plot concerns a campaigning journalist who withdraws from the world, disillusioned by its craven response to fascism. In search of solitude, he becomes a lone lighthouse keeper on Lake Michigan at Thunder Rock, the scene of a tragic shipwreck ninety years earlier, when a ship carrying a group of migrants to the USA had sunk with the loss of life of everyone on board. Gradually, the journalist enters into a dialogue with these long-dead souls, and is finally convinced by their moving stories that he cannot isolate himself and must return to the world, and his previous political commitment.

The story was a thinly-disguised appeal for America to abandon its policy of isolationism, an unpopular message when the play was premiered in New York shortly after the outbreak of war in Europe. *Thunder Rock* had been first performed by the Group Theatre on Broadway in a production directed by Elia Kazan, the cast including Lee J. Cobb and Frances Farmer. It opened on 14 November 1939 but closed after only three weeks. By contrast, the play had far greater success in London a year later, when it seemed to catch the prevailing mood of wartime defiance. *Thunder Rock* became indeed something of a focal point in the depleted landscape of London's theatre, thrusting Frederick Valk into the theatrical limelight. Supported by the Ministry of Information, it also became an early example of state sponsorship, something that the British theatre had hitherto always shunned.

Thunder Rock was the precursor of four other notable plays, all staged within a few months of each other in 1942, the first of which was another American play, *Watch on the Rhine* by Lillian Hellman, which opened at the Aldwych Theatre in April. The play's title derives from a patriotic German song which was popular during the First World War: a title that Hellman subverted through the play's call for an international alliance against Nazism. First performed on Broadway on 1 April 1941, *Watch on the Rhine* ran for 378 performances, winning the New York Drama Critics award as the best American play of the year. It is hardly surprising that it should be staged in wartime London, where there was a lack of new plays and new writers. At a time when the London theatre repertoire was still depleted, *Watch on the Rhine* enjoyed considerable success in a production by Emlyn Williams, running for eighteen months and 673 performances.[5] The protagonist Kurt Müller, a fervent anti-Nazi, was played by the émigré actor Anton Walbrook, returning to the London stage after his success in the film *Dangerous Moonlight*. When Walbrook eventually left the cast because of another film commitment, the part was taken by his fellow-émigré, Frederick Valk.

Precisely because of its strong contemporary resonance, *Watch on the Rhine* has only rarely been revived, unlike *Awake and Sing*, the third play in our wartime anthology. Like its two predecessors, *Awake and Sing* was an American play, written in 1935 by Clifford Odets, and briefly establishing him as America's finest young dramatist. While Odets had been highly regarded in the USA, the pre-war British theatre had kept its distance, finding his work too radical. On the other hand, the left-wing Unity Theatre, after considering *Awake and Sing* for production, had rejected it as 'too sentimental'.[6] Suspicions of Odets as a playwright of class

5   The play ran from 22 April 1942 to 4 December 1943.
6   Colin Chambers, *The Story of Unity Theatre* (London: Lawrence & Wishart, 1989), p. 78.

revolution, a reputation earned through the success of his early agitprop piece *Waiting for Lefty*, had melted away during 1941 following the Nazi invasion of the Soviet Union, and that country's mutation into a war ally.

In May 1942, *Awake and Sing* was produced by Alec Clunes at the Arts Theatre club. Despite Odets's radical reputation, *Awake and Sing* is essentially a family drama, charting the struggles of an impoverished Jewish immigrant family in the Bronx district of New York. Searching for authentic performances to convey the texture of this Jewish immigrant milieu, Clunes took a calculated gamble by casting two Jewish refugee actors — Martin Miller and Lilly Kann — in the leading roles. They rewarded him with two of the richest performances on the London stage during 1942.

Like its American counterparts, Terence Rattigan's *Flare Path*, written in 1941 and staged in August 1942, was very much a play of its time, depicting the war itself and its effect on the lives of those involved. The action is set in a hotel adjacent to an RAF Bomber Command airbase, covering forty-eight hours in the lives and loves of a group of air crew and their wives, a scenario which drew on Rattigan's own wartime experience as an RAF tail gunner. Indeed, at the time he wrote the play, he was still on active service. The prominent producer Bronson Albery had shied away from staging the play, believing that theatre audiences did not want to see plays about the war, but it was finally taken up by 'Binkie' Beaumont of H. M. Tennent, who staged it at the Apollo Theatre.[7] The script had to be approved by an air adviser to the Ministry of Information. Directed by Anthony Asquith (better known for his work in film) *Flare Path* proved an outstanding box-office success, running for eighteen months. Among those who came to see it was the prime minister Winston Churchill, who reputedly called it 'a masterpiece of understatement'.[8] The production also gave Gerhard Hinze his first role on the West End stage.

7   See Dan Rebellato, 'Introduction', in Terence Rattigan, *Flare Path*, intro. by Dan Rebellato (London: Nick Hern Books, 2011), p. xxv.
8   *Daily Sketch*, 12 January 1943.

CHAPTER 10

'A Particularly Honourable and Decent Character': Gerhard Hinze

When Gerhard Hinze first came to Britain in 1938 he was thirty-four years old; he was to spend the remaining thirty-four years of his life there, establishing a successful career in British theatre and film. This apparent symmetry suggests a continuity to his life in the theatre which the facts deny. The most striking aspect of his long theatrical career is the dichotomy between its two halves which differ not only in language and theatre culture, but also in aspiration and motivation.

Arriving at Harwich in May 1938, Hinze was formally admitted to Britain, 'on condition that he does no work, paid or unpaid', for a period of one month.[9] In fact, he was to remain in the country for the rest of his life (except for the eighteen months he spent in a British internment camp in Canada) taking British nationality, and eventually establishing a successful acting career in London.

Early in 1939, as Chamberlain's 'peace for our time' began to unravel, Hinze felt impelled to help colleagues who were still stranded in Prague. He contacted the Actors Refugee Committee (ARC), one of several such committees which sprang up to support those who had fled from Czechoslovakia, and those still there.[10] The ARC comprised many of the great and the good of English theatre: Sybil Thorndike and Lewis Casson, Dame May Whitty, Walter Hudd, Franklin Dyall, and Llewellyn Rees, who was shortly to become the secretary of the British actors' union Equity The ARC's purpose was to raise money to support refugee actors already in Britain, but above all to finance a plan to rescue those trapped in the logistic bottleneck of Prague. Hinze played a vital role in providing the names and contact addresses of actors in Prague, most of whom were fellow-communists with whom he had acted in Ukraine: Emmi Frank and Fritz Richter, Erich and Nina Freund (and their young son), Leo Bieber, Paul Demel, and Erwin Geschonnek. The courier sent to contact them and give them money, together with instructions for their escape, was Rolf Brandt, brother of the photographer Bill Brandt. His already dangerous mission became more dangerous — and more urgent — when on 15 March the German army invaded what remained of Czechoslovakia. Brandt carried out his mission, enabling most of the group to escape in adventurous

---

9 Special Branch report, Harwich, 18 May 1938, TNA, KV2/2364, no. 1a.

10 The best-known of these was the Artists' Refugee Committee, which was set up to rescue members of the Oskar-Kokoschka-Bund, based in Prague.

circumstances across the border into Poland. The escape group, including Richter, Bieber, and Demel succeeded in crossing the frontier. The only exception was Geschonnek who had the misfortune to be caught and handed over to the Gestapo, spending six years in Nazi concentration camps. From Poland, the others managed to reach Britain. Joan Rodker remembered them 'spending their first night on the floor of our one-room flat in Boundary Road'.[11]

Although Hinze was a versatile actor of wide experience, whose life story was more dramatic than any of his stage roles, his prospects of finding work on the British stage seemed slim: he spoke little English and knew little about the British theatre system. He did of course have some good contacts, through whom he was able to appear at Covent Garden, walking on in a production of Smetana's *The Bartered Bride*, allowing him a modest cultural reunion with Czechoslovakia.

During these months, however, the British stage was no more than a distant aspiration for Hinze, who was more concerned with plans to establish a German refugee theatre in London. He played an influential role in founding the Free German League of Culture (FGLC), which was to become the main cultural, social, and political organisation representing German refugees in war-time London. The FGLC staged a regular programme of cultural events, ranging from concerts and theatre productions to publications and art exhibitions. In view of the restrictions on political activity imposed on refugees by the British authorities, this cultural programme also served very much as a surrogate for political activity: the continuation of politics by other means.[12] A Special Branch report to MI5 early in 1940 noted Hinze's membership of the FGLC, which it described as 'an organisation under strong communist influence if not control'.[13] MI5 concurred, considering the FGLC to be little more than a 'communist front'.

Hinze was an active member of the FGLC from its inception in December 1938, later claiming that it was really his brainchild, and that he had first proposed the idea to the artist Fred Uhlman, a claim which can no longer be verified.[14] He was certainly a member of the League's Executive Committee and was elected chairman of its Actors' Section, confirming the respect he enjoyed amongst his theatre colleagues.

One of the central features of the FGLC was its 'Little Theatre', which aimed to offer refugee audiences the cultural solace of German-speaking theatre in London, but would also enable the many refugee actors — driven first from Germany and then from Czechoslovakia — to practice their craft in exile. For a few actors, their performance became an audition for the London stage: among the audience for the theatre's early performances were English actors and directors who came in search of a European performance style, but who sometimes also acted as talent-spotters.

---

11 Details of the Actors' Refugee Committee were supplied by Joan Rodker in a letter of January 2010.

12 See Charmian Brinson and Richard Dove, *Politics by Other Means: The Free German League of Culture in London 1939–1945* (London & Portland, OR: Vallentine Mitchell, 2010).

13 Report from Special Branch to MI5, 5 January 1940, TNA, KV2/2364, no. 6a.

14 See the transcript of his interview with the Interned Enemy Aliens Tribunal on 1 January 1942, TNA, KV2/2364/ 33b.

Hinze did not appear in these early productions, but he remained an influential figure behind the scenes.

On the outbreak of war in September 1939, Hinze was one of the signatories to a press statement by the FGLC, thanking the British people for their help and hospitality 'in this grave hour' and declaring their readiness 'to play their part loyally in the defence of freedom, culture and democracy'.[15] Shortly after, he and other members of the League handed a memorandum to the Ministry of Information offering their services to the British war effort. MI5 was sceptical, if not suspicious, of these offers of help, suggesting they 'should be treated with reservation'.[16]

On 1 January 1940, Hinze was elected secretary of the FGLC. MI5 continued to keep him under surveillance, reporting that he was living 'with a woman who is alleged to be one half Russian and who is not married to him. [...] It seems that Hinze lives on his "wife"'s' earnings and on what he can get from Bloomsbury House'.[17] Questions of propriety soon gave way to those of national security.

Even before the war, the British government had considered a policy of general internment of 'enemy aliens', but had decided against it. Instead, aliens were required to appear before special tribunals, charged with assessing the degree of risk they represented and placing them accordingly into one of three categories: 'A' (to be interned), 'B' (exempt from internment, but subject to restrictions), or 'C' (exempt from internment and restrictions). Although the vast majority of refugees were placed in category 'C', Hinze was not. When he appeared before a tribunal on 22 January 1940, he was placed in Class 'B', presumably because of his stay in the Soviet Union. However, he was not detained at this point.

The position of 'enemy aliens' took a turn for the worse as the war situation suddenly deteriorated. In an atmosphere of near panic as the German army overran Holland and Belgium, the British government, now led by Winston Churchill, reversed its previous policy, beginning the large-scale internment of 'enemy aliens'. On 15 May, it ordered the arrest of all 'B' category male refugees. Among them was Gerhard Hinze, who was arrested on 16 May 1940.[18] Joan Rodker remembered police swooping on their home in 31 Boundary Road, St John's Wood.

Anti-German sentiment was widespread, and was further inflamed by newspapers such as the *Daily Mail*, which published wild rumours that the refugees constituted a 'fifth column' which was preparing to sabotage British defences and smooth the path for a military invasion of Britain.[19] Worse was to come, following the evacuation of the British Expeditionary Force from Dunkirk and the fall of France: the French surrendered on 22 June. As fears of invasion grew, the government reversed its previous policy, ordering the mass internment of German and Austrian refugees, including 'C' category refugees officially listed as 'victims of Nazi persecution'.

15 *The Times*, 5 September 1939.
16 MI5 memorandum, 18 September 1939, TNA, KV2/2364, no. 4a.
17 Internal Report M 11 to B5b, signed 'WAY' (=William Younger), 25 February 1940, TNA, KV2/2364, no. 7a.
18 The dates relating to Hinze's internment are contained in his Aliens Registration Book, a copy of which remains in his security file: TNA, KV2/2364.
19 See, for example, G. Ward Price in the *Daily Mail*, 24 May 1940.

Hinze was sent to the Isle of Man, being held in Central Promenade Camp, Douglas, but on 3 July, he was one of a large group of internees who were deported to Canada. The men sent to Canada encountered some of the harshest conditions of all internees. The arbitrary nature of internment was reinforced by the capricious manner of deportation: as the men lined up for trans-shipment, they did not actually know where they were bound for. They were shipped out on the troopship *SS Ettrick*, which left Liverpool on 3 July: the first such ship to make the voyage to Canada since the sinking of the *Arandora Star* with great loss of life.[20] Like others from the *Ettrick*, he was initially interned in Camp L, outside Quebec City, on the Plains of Abraham.

This is not the place to describe life in the camps in Canada (a story which has, in any case, already been well told), except to say that despite daunting material difficulties there was a remarkable number of cultural events, including musical and theatrical performances, which helped to sustain morale in the camps.[21] One fellow-inmate in Camp L recalled that Hinze gave recitals of poetry and scenes from plays:

> His Bühnendeutsch [stage German] diction was flawless. For a group of men speaking every known dialect of German (and Austrian), listening to Hinze was more than a pleasure, it was an education. His exquisitely manicured pronunciation was the height of verbal elegance.[22]

These performances were, of course, given from memory, as during these early days of internment there were few, if any, books or play-texts available.

Hinze did not remain in Camp L long enough to start a drama group. In October, the internees there were dispersed to different camps, Hinze being moved to Camp A, at Farnham, in Quebec province. Drama groups were eventually set up in most of the internment camps in Canada, but the most active group seems to have been the one formed by Hinze in Camp A. He organised a reading of Goethe's *Faust*, and directed a performance of R. C. Sherriff's *Journey's End*, followed by Chekov's one-act play *The Proposal*, in which the leading role was taken by the young Anton Diffring, and a performance of the first scene of *The Importance of being Earnest*. Shortly before his release, Hinze also gave a performance of songs from Brecht's *Dreigroschenoper*.[23]

In Camp A, Hinze was reportedly on friendly terms with the politician Wilhelm Koenen, formerly a communist member of the Reichstag. Together with Koenen and five others, Hinze presented a letter to the camp Commandant protesting against the provocative behaviour of Nazi Germans in the same camp. As a result all seven men were forcibly transferred to Camp S, a detention centre reserved for Italian fascists, and released only after representations in the House of Commons

20 Re. the sinking of the *Arandora Star*, see Peter and Leni Gillman, *Collar the Lot!* (London: Quartet, 1980), pp. 190–201.

21 See Eric Koch, *Deemed Suspect: A Wartime Blunder* (Toronto: Methuen, 1980).

22 George W. Brandt, 'Thespis Behind the Wire', in *Theatre and Film in Exile*, ed. by Berghaus, p. 226. Brandt was later Professor of Radio and Television at Bristol University.

23 Alan Clarke, 'German Refugee Theatre in Internment', in *Theatre and Film in Exile*, ed. by Berghaus, p. 213.

by Labour MPs D. N. Pritt and Ellen Wilkinson — who had initially stood as his guarantor to allow him to enter Britain.[24] Hinze was finally released from Camp S on 5 November 1941, and shipped back to Britain, landing at Liverpool on 25 November 1941. His internment ended suddenly, almost farcically, in Liverpool. Fifty internees from this shipment, including Hinze, who were due to be re-interned on the Isle of Man while their cases were reviewed, were actually released by mistake.[25]

Hinze's personal life had been totally disrupted by internment. In October 1940 Joan Rodker had travelled to the USA with their young son in the hope of being reunited with Hinze. There had been strong rumours that the US government would permit those released from internment in Canada to enter the USA; the rumours were in fact unfounded, as no such plans existed. Hinze was eventually shipped back to Britain, while Joan Rodker was left stranded in New York. They did not see each other again until 1947 and by then the break in their relationship had become permanent.

Despite his absence from Britain, Hinze's MI5 file had continued to grow. Among the more singular documents it contains is an internal memorandum citing a report by an agent code-named 'Kaspar'.[26] While informants tend to supply incriminating information, Kaspar's report is little short of a character reference for Hinze, describing him as 'a very talented actor' and continuing:

> Hinze is a member of the Communist Party and according to all reports is a particularly honourable and decent character. It is said that if he gave his word to do nothing against the interests of this country, he could be depended on to keep it to the letter but since he is an orthodox and sincere communist it is considered unlikely that he would make such a declaration.[27]

The proceedings leading to Hinze's final release from internment certainly confirm that he commanded the respect of his fellow-exiles. The Free German League of Culture had made a formal application for his release under Category 20 of the relevant White Paper, 'which comprises persons of eminent distinction who have made outstanding contributions to art, science, learning or letters'.[28] The letter referred to 'his profound knowledge of German classics and progressive literature', knowledge acquired during his lengthy apprenticeship in German provincial theatre. In fact, Hinze was officially released under Category 19 of the White Paper, which embraced those who had 'consistently, over a period of years, taken a public and prominent part in opposition to the Nazi system'. Appearing before the

---

24 See *Der Stacheldraht*, newspaper produced in Farnham internment camp, November 1941.

25 MI5 internal memorandum, E5(5), TNA, KV2/2364, no. 28a.

26 'Kaspar' was a code name for the bogus Austrian aristocrat Josef Otto von Laemmel, see Charmian Brinson and Richard Dove, *A Matter of Intelligence: MI5 and the Surveillance of Anti-Nazi Refugees 1933–50* (Manchester: Manchester University Press, 2014).

27 MI5 internal memorandum, dated 8 March 1941, TNA, KV2/2364/19a. The memorandum is signed by William Robson-Scott, later well-known as a Germanist. The travelling scholarship he endowed at the Institute of Germanic Studies still bears his name.

28 'Application for Release from Internment', submitted by the Free German League of Culture (Luise Dornemann), 17 December 1941, TNA, KV2/2364/15b.

Interned Enemy Aliens Tribunal on 1 January 1942, Hinze admitted that his views were left-wing, but insisted: 'I was never an organised communist [...] I am not a member of the Communist Party'.[29] The security services clearly took a different view. A Special Branch report over a year later continued to affirm that Hinze was a member of the German Communist Party in Great Britain, that he had joined the party in 1930 and noted his association with the composer Ernst Hermann Meyer 'and other prominent communists in Berlin'.[30]

Hinze's return to London began a development which eventually saw him exchange the makeshift stage of an internment camp for the boards of a prestigious West End theatre. It was however a slow transition. After the misfortunes and frustrations of internment, Hinze lost no time in resuming his role at the Free German League of Culture — and MI5 was equally quick to resume surveillance. One of Hinze's first actions as head of the Actors' Section was to call a meeting to discuss 'efforts to affiliate members to [the British actors' union] Equity'.[31] His main priorities at this time, however, were to help revive dramatic performances at the FGLC, which had declined with the loss of so many male actors through internment, and to revive his own stage career. After an enforced absence of eighteen months, he marked his return to the stage in a 'Gerhard Hinze evening' at the Free German League of Culture on 10 January. Among those present was the German writer Kurt Hiller, a diligent informant for MI5, who knew how to whet the appetite of his masters, reporting that:

> The German Party Communist and actor Gerhard Hintze [sic], who has just returned from Canada, gave a programme of songs and recitations. In the programme there were poems and flashbacks to life in the Internment Camps. [...] There were also poems by Rolf Anders (= Rudolf Thoel) and Erich Fried, of which some were decidedly revolutionary in tone and others sung the praises of the Red Army and the Soviet Union.[32]

The following month, Hinze turned to the Austrian Centre to pursue his work as a stage director in the revue *Here is the News*. He directed the dramatic sketch *Scorched Earth* by his fellow-communist Franz Hartl, in which he also acted. This short play which confronted its audience with the brutal consequences of total war proved highly controversial: the veteran theatre critic Monty Jacobs wrote a hostile review which provoked a wider debate as to the purpose of exile theatre.[33]

At this stage of his career, Hinze clearly wished to concentrate on directing. In June 1942, he was invited by the Ministry of Information to direct a cast of German refugee actors from the FGLC in a performance of *The Four Freedoms*, a play by the English writer Montagu Slater, at the New Theatre, Oxford. The performance took place under the auspices of the ministry as part of a large propaganda rally

29 See the transcript of his interview with the Interned Enemy Aliens Tribunal (see above note 6).

30 Special Branch report to MI5, 17 May 1943, TNA, KV2/2364, no. 53a.

31 MI5 internal report by W. A. Younger (M11) to ADF Mr. R. Hollis, 12 January 1942, TNA, KV2/2364/33a.

32 MI5 internal report by E7, source Hi, no. 214, 16 January 1942, TNA, KV2/2364/34a.

33 *Die Zeitung*, 6 February 1942; 'Was erwarten wir vom Theater?', *Zeitspiegel*, 7 March 1942.

in support of the war effort. The request to Hinze to arrange this performance certainly confirms an about turn in the attitude of the British authorities towards refugees, not least refugee actors. In fact, the performance was a triumphant success, as documented in a letter to Hinze from the ministry: 'We owe a great debt of thanks to you and your troupe which we can scarcely repay. Your production on Sunday was truly wonderful [...] I hope that I will have the great pleasure of working with you again in future events'.[34]

In fact, Hinze was unable to attend the actual performance, since he was appearing at the Oxford Playhouse in a matinee performance of Terence Rattigan's new play *Flare Path*, part of a pre-London run of the play, which went on to open at the Apollo Theatre on 13 August 1942. Drawing on the considerable popularity of the RAF in the aftermath of the Battle of Britain, the play concerns the lives and loves of a group of air crew. The main plot involves a love triangle between Teddy Graham, a bomber pilot, his actress wife Patricia, and Peter Kyle, a well-known Hollywood actor. After a love affair with Kyle in Hollywood, Patricia has returned to London and married Teddy after a 'whirlwind romance'. When Kyle suddenly appears at the hotel to ask her to marry him and return to Hollywood, Patricia plans to tell Teddy she is leaving him. However, she changes her mind, following, not her heart, but her sense of duty, an ending suitably in tune with the times.

The topicality of a play about Bomber Command was underlined by the customary short notice in the theatre programme which read:

> In the event of an Air Raid Warning an announcement will be made from the stage. Patrons are advised to remain in the Theatre, but those wishing to leave will be directed to the nearest official air-raid shelter, after which the performance will be continued for so long as is practicable.[35]

The production marked a turning-point for Rattigan, giving him his first success on the London stage for some five years. It was an even more significant change in the career of Gerhard Hinze, marking his first appearance in the English theatre. He never looked back, becoming a regular performer on the West End stage.

Hinze, credited as 'Gerard Hinze', played the role of Count Skriczevinsky, a Polish pilot officer with the RAF. The role is a highly political one, evoking the Polish contribution to the Battle of Britain. While only a supporting role, it placed Hinze centre stage at a crucial moment in the action. When the squadron flies a dangerous mission over Germany, the Polish pilot fails to return and is posted 'missing', presumed dead, only to reappear suddenly and miraculously in the final act: a highly theatrical moment which Hinze must have savoured. His unexpected reappearance is the cue for an impromptu celebration, curtailed only by the final curtain.

Count Skriczevinsky has a poor command of English, but, after the defeat of Poland, he has come to Britain to continue the war against Nazism, a character with whom Hinze could easily identify. The role required him to speak lines in broken English, stumbling over some words and mispronouncing others, the first of the 'foreign accent' roles in which Hinze would later specialise. As already indicated, it

34 Quoted in 'M.O.I. dankt Refugee-Schauspielern', *Zeitspiegel*, 4 July 1942.
35 Theatre programme for *Flare Path*, Apollo Theatre, August 1942, copy in V&A TPA.

is unclear when and how Hinze learned English. Nor is it known how he came to audition for the role in *Flare Path*. He was, however, part of a distinguished cast that included Phyllis Calvert and Kathleen Harrison, as well as a young George Cole.

Reviews of the play were overwhelmingly positive, welcoming Rattigan's return to the West End. There was, however, some criticism of the development of the plot. James Agate, for example, considered the reappearance of Count Skriczevinsky at the end of the play to be too sentimental — and even implausible, given that air-crew who 'ditched' in the sea rarely survived. Interestingly, when the play was adapted for the cinema in 1945, under the title *The Way to the Stars*, Rattigan radically rewrote the script, dispensing entirely with the character of Count Skriczevinsky.

Agate also questioned the resolution of the love triangle, in which Patricia returns to her pilot husband, although it is hard to imagine that the play could have been produced in wartime with any different outcome, which might have been considered prejudicial to the war effort and would scarcely have survived the scrutiny of the Ministry of Information. In general, however, Agate was impressed with the production, calling it 'extraordinarily lively. A laugh every minute, a roar every five minutes and a tear every ten', adding that 'notable acting by everybody makes the piece safe for a year'.[36] As so often, Agate was right: *Flare Path* was both a critical and a popular success, running from 13 August 1942 until 22 January 1944 and being seen by almost half a million people. The play proved a decisive turning-point for Hinze. He was ever-present throughout the long run, appearing in no fewer than 679 consecutive performances. Moreover, his presence in such a successful production gave him a firm foothold on the West End stage, offering the prospect of a post-war stage career in Britain. When the play's run finally ended in January 1944, he quickly found a new role in *Zero Hour*.

Zero Hour was a new play of great topical interest, set on the eve of the D-Day landings and first performed only weeks before they actually took place. Hinze took the part of Carl Baumer, a German parachutist, taken prisoner, who believes that a harsh peace will keep the fires of Nazism burning. Critics found the play itself too discursive, but the critic of *The Times* noted that 'Mr Gerard Hinze lights an impressive fire of fanaticism in the prisoner'.[37] Hinze was to repeat the role of the fanatical Nazi more than once in his subsequent career.

Despite his growing success on the London stage, Hinze remained committed to German exile theatre. While still acting in *Flare Path*, he also made a vital contribution to two highly successful refugee productions. He was co-producer, with Koka Motz, of the revue *Immortal Austria* which was staged at the Kingsway Hall on 13 March 1943 to mark the fifth anniversary of the *Anschluss*. Styled 'a British-Austrian Rally and Pageant', *Immortal Austria* was written by Eva Priester and the young Erich Fried; Hinze's involvement was a significant example of the cooperation between German and Austrian theatre exiles that flourished in London during the war years, a cooperation that was often lacking on the political stage.[38]

36 James Agate, 'A Moot Point', *Sunday Times,* 16 August 1942.
37 *The Times*, 15 June 1944.
38 Cf. letter from Free Austrian Movement to Hinze 26 March 1943, Gerard Heinz Papers.

Two months later Hinze played a vital part in the most ambitious event yet staged by the Free German League of Culture, which hired the Scala Theatre in central London for a performance to mark the tenth anniversary of the Nazi book-burnings in Germany. Under the evocative title *Fires in May* the programme included dramatic presentations of work by Heinrich Heine, Heinrich and Thomas Mann, Ernst Toller, Bertolt Brecht, and others. Among those performing were both German and Austrian artists, such as the actors Frederick Valk and Anton Walbrook and the violinist Max Rostal. British friends appearing included J. B. Priestley, who gave the opening address. However, the centre-piece of the evening was Hinze's production of J. R. Becher's *Schlacht um Moskau* [Battle for Moscow], which Becher had written two years earlier in the Soviet Union. The performance featured two stalwarts of the FGLC's Little Theatre, Josef Almas and Leo Bieber. Due to severe constraints of time, Hinze produced a much shortened version of Becher's epic play, linking the scenes through an English narrative spoken by the actress Beatrix Lehmann.[39] The performance of *Fires in May* attracted an audience of over a thousand refugees and British supporters, by far the largest audience for a single dramatic performance by German refugees in Britain during the war. Hinze's production of *Schlacht um Moskau* was the high point of the evening: it also proved to be his swan song as a stage director.

In parallel to his work on stage, Hinze also played several minor roles in British wartime films. Indeed a Special Branch report in May 1942 gave his occupation as 'film artist', listing his employment by Charter Film Productions, Piccadilly, in the film *Thunder Rock*.[40] Like other émigré actors, Hinze was able to find work in the British film industry even before making his debut on the London stage. He had only limited experience as a film actor — when he had first entered films in Berlin in 1928 the industry was still in the silent era. His only other experience of film acting had been in a German-language film produced in Moscow in 1935.

Despite his release from internment, Hinze remained under security surveillance until (and well beyond) the end of the war. Ironically, some of the only information available on his nascent film career is in the reports prepared by Special Branch for MI5. As noted, his first role was in *Thunder Rock* (1942), a cinematic version of the successful stage play. Directed by Roy Boulting, and starring Michael Redgrave and James Mason, the film also featured other German actors such as Frederick Valk and Lilli Palmer in leading roles. *Thunder Rock* was completed in March 1942 and shown later that year to enthusiastic reviews. The *Manchester Guardian* called it 'more interesting technically than anything since *Citizen Kane*'.[41] In fact, Hinze spent just three days (25–27 March 1942) working on *Thunder Rock*.[42] His minor role was uncredited, but it gave him a modest entrée into British films.

39 See 'Brände im Mai', *Zeitspiegel*, 29 May 1943.

40 Charter Film Productions was owned by John Boulting.

41 *Manchester Guardian*, cited in *Halliwell's Film and Video Guide*, ed. by John Walker (London: HarperCollins, 1999, p. 811) (hereafter referred to as *Halliwell*).

42 See Hinze's identity book, issued by Bow Street police station. Copy in Hinze's MI5 file, TNA, KV2/2364.

A further Special Branch report from May 1942 noted: 'Erich Freund is busy acting in films at Denham, as are Gerhard Hinze and Gerhard Kempinski, both of the Lantern Theatre. They are earning a lot of money there'.[43] A later report on Hinze stated that 'This man has since worked for other British film companies, the last being for Metro Goldwyn Mayer's British Studios, Denham in the film *Sabotage Agent*'. *Sabotage Agent* was an early title for the film *The Adventures of Tartu*, released in 1943, though there is no record that Hinze played any part in it.[44]

In fact, Hinze's next appearance was in *Went the Day Well?* (1942), on which he started working on 13 May 1942 at a rate of £7 a day.[45] The film was based on a story by Graham Greene, in which English villagers resist the invasion of their village by German paratroopers, despite the treachery of the village squire. It was directed by Alberto Cavalcanti, making his first feature film. It was well staged and acted, making effective wartime propaganda, its contemporary resonance audible in the enthusiastic reviews it received. Hinze's role was once again uncredited. Perhaps inevitably, he was cast as one of the invading Germans, a role he was destined to repeat in the post-war years.[46]

During the early months of 1944 Hinze was employed by Verity Films Ltd, a production company run by Sidney Box, making short documentary films for the War Office and the Ministry of Information. Hinze's work for Verity Films (hitherto unnoticed) was very much in the service of the British 'war effort'. A Special Branch report noted that he worked on the film *Our Story*, one of over two hundred wartime shorts produced by Verity Films.[47] Later that year, Hinze appeared in *English Without Tears*, a film scripted by Terence Rattigan and produced by Sidney Box, in which he played a minor role as a Polish officer: his first credited film role in Britain. While modest in themselves, Hinze's wartime film roles were the beginning of what became a long and prolific post-war career in British films.

For a time, Hinze seems to have been able to balance the different, and often conflicting, demands of the West End stage and the German émigré theatre. Even before the end of the war, however, he was faced by the decision confronting every refugee: whether to stay or to return. Many of the activists of the Free German League of Culture's Little Theatre were committed to returning to Germany to take part in the work of cultural and political reconstruction, as decreed by the Communist Party.

In March 1945 a meeting was held to address this very question, attended by some thirty 'political' refugees. The meeting took place in the house of Hans Flesch, a former Chairman of the FGLC, whose memoirs provide the only surviving account of the occasion.[48] According to Flesch, the tone of the meeting was set by the

43   Extract from Special Branch report, TNA, KV2/2364/42a.
44   There is no mention of Hinze in the cast list for *The Adventures of Tartu,* even in an uncredited role.
45   The original title of the film was *They Came in Khaki.*
46   Cf. Hinze's own remarks in the transcript of his interview with the Interned Enemy Aliens Tribunal (see above note 6).
47   Special Branch report to MI5, 23 March 1944, TNA, KV2/2364, no. 62a.
48   Hans Flesch-Brunningen, *Die verführte Zeit: Lebenserinnerungen* (Vienna: Brandstätter, 1988), pp. 116–19. According to Flesch, the meeting took place on the day after Allied troops crossed the

Communist Party ideologue Alfred Meusel, who gave a long address, extolling the victorious Red Army. Meusel ended by saying there was no question 'whether' communist refugees should return, merely 'how'. All of those present were then asked to state where they wished to return to. One after the other rose to say that they would return home 'as soon as possible', mostly 'to Berlin'. When Hinze's turn came, he announced that he could say nothing, since he would probably not return at all, at least for the present. His statement drew the wrath of Alfred Meusel, who harangued Hinze, reminding him that he was contravening a directive of the Party. If he did not conform, he must face the consequences. 'We are not some masonic lodge,' he declared, 'We are the Party'. 'Of course I know you're the Party', Hinze retorted, 'but I didn't know you were a slave-master'. In the ensuing uproar, Hinze walked out, pursued by Meusel's pronouncement that he was expelled from the Party with immediate effect.

Rhine at Remagen on 7 March 1945. Flesch's memoirs, written many years after the events (and after Hinze's death), may not be reliable in detail, but there seems little reason to doubt the general accuracy of his account. Hinze himself left no written record of the event.

CHAPTER 11

Shylock on Tour:
Frederick Valk

Fritz Valk's transition to the English stage was remarkably rapid. He arrived in London with strong acting credentials. He had played a remarkable range of roles which testified to the breadth and scope of the German theatre repertoire before Hitler, and which few English actors of his generation could have equalled, much less by the age of forty-five. The roles he had played in the German-speaking theatre underline his love of the German classics, particularly Schiller, but his career had also fostered his enthusiasm for Shakespeare. Among the leading Shakespearean roles he had already played were those which later made his name on the English stage: Othello and Shylock.

Valk had left Germany behind, but not his German roots. Within a month of arriving in arriving in London, he was plunged back into the concerns of the German émigrés and their fight against Hitler. On 28 March 1939, he appeared at the first public meeting held by the Free German League of Culture with the aim of gathering support amongst refugees and English well-wishers. The watchword of the evening was 'German Freedom', a theme addressed by several speakers. It was Valk who brought the evening to an emotional close by reciting the famous scene from Schiller's *Don Carlos* in which the Marquis of Posa implores the absolutist monarch, Philip II, to grant his people intellectual freedom: 'Sire, give them freedom of thought'. It was Valk's last chance to perform Schiller for some years.

Just over three months after his arrival, Valk played his first English role in London in Sidney Howard's *Alien Corn*. Howard had gained a considerable reputation as a playwright on Broadway, having won the Pulitzer Prize in 1925. In all he wrote no fewer than seventy plays and became one of the first Broadway playwrights to go to Hollywood. Indeed, he is probably better known for his screenplay for *Gone With the Wind* (1939) than for any of his plays.

The British production of *Alien Corn* opened at Wyndham's Theatre on 5 July 1939, six years after its success on Broadway. The play is a rather melodramatic study of thwarted ambition. Elsa Brandt is a young and talented concert pianist, originally from Vienna, who is obliged to work as a schoolteacher in order to support her crippled and widowed father, but who dreams only of realising her talent and returning to Vienna. The role of Elsa was played by the young actress Margaretta Scott, who had originally come to notice as one of the signatories to the document that established the British actors' union Equity in 1934. By 1939 she had become one of the country's leading young actresses. Valk played the role of her father, Ottokar Brandt, a once famous Viennese violinist, now unable to play because of infirmity. It was a substantial part for his London debut and Valk made the most of it. 'Fritz Valk, an actor from Berlin and Prague, is very happily cast as Elsa's father and makes the explosive old man a real figure', wrote the *Daily Telegraph*.[49] *Theatre World* concurred: 'Fritz Valk contributes a gutturally effective study of old Ottokar Brandt'.[50] James Agate declared that 'the play makes excellent entertainment and is grandly acted', before commenting with dry approval on Valk's stentorian stage voice.[51]

The *Daily Mail* agreed, writing that '*Alien Corn* is so splendidly acted and has such shrewdness, wit and character that it grips the attention all the way and deserves to be a roaring success'. Despite this endorsement, the production was not a success, running for only two months and sixty-one performances before being taken off.[52] It probably fell victim to the lapse of time and the changing political scene in Europe since its first performance in 1933. The Vienna to which Elsa Brandt so fervently wished to return no longer existed.[53] And in the real world, war was just a week away when the play was taken off.

Despite favourable reviews for his performance, Valk was not seen again on the London stage for several months. An actor who had never been out of work, he found that, with the closure of London's theatres, stage parts were impossible to find and, like other refugee actors, turned to the film industry. He had little experience of film acting, and probably few expectations. In fact, his career in British films began inauspiciously with a minor role in Carol Reed's *Night Train to Munich* (1940), starring Margaret Lockwood and Rex Harrison. The plot of the film is romantic and exciting, as well as occasionally implausible, thus providing something of a template for British war film production. The film opened as the Germans marched into Prague in 1939, forcing the last-minute escape of Dr Axel Bomasch, a scientific specialist in armour plating. While the narrow escape virtually matched Valk's own, he did not play the part of the escaping scientist, appearing instead — still credited as 'Fritz Valk' — in the role of a Gestapo officer at Munich Station, an irony he would certainly have appreciated. It was the first of several minor film parts which provided a vital financial lifeline.

Valk was absent from the London stage for some six months before returning in another play by Sidney Howard, *They Knew What They Wanted*, at the small Embassy Theatre in Swiss Cottage. The Embassy, which will feature again in our narrative, was a local theatre which changed its programme regularly to cater for a largely local audience, so that the play ran for only a week, opening on 18 March.

---

49 'Play Nobody Wanted: *Alien Corn* has a Success', *Daily Telegraph*, 6 July 1939.
50 'Alien Corn', *Theatre World*, August 1939.
51 'Mr. Fritz Valk, by speaking from the stage at Wyndham's in a voice which doubtless penetrates the auditorium at the [adjacent] New Theatre, gives English actors a much-needed German lesson', James Agate, *Sunday Times*, 9 July 1939.
52 The play ran at Wyndham's from 5 July to 26 August 1939.
53 'Alien Corn', *Theatre World*, August 1939.

They Knew What They Wanted was a comedy set in the American prohibition era. Tony, a sixty-year-old Italian immigrant who runs a vineyard, sends a photograph of himself to Amy, a waitress he met briefly in San Francisco, with a proposal of marriage: except that the photo is not of himself but of Joe, his hired hand — and a much younger man.

Reviewers from national papers rarely ventured as far north as Swiss Cottage, but a sympathetic review was published in *The Times*:

> The Embassy production is inclined to move too slowly [but] the individual parts are, in their detail, admirably played. Mr Frederick Valk gives Tony, the old man who sends Joe's photograph instead of his own, a child-like goodness and simplicity which explains why Amy should turn to him in the end.[54]

Three months later, Valk appeared in the role of Dr Stefan Kurtz in Robert Ardrey's *Thunder Rock*, which opened at a small theatre outside the West End. Written in 1939 in opposition to American isolationism, *Thunder Rock* espoused what was then an unpopular political position in the USA. The plot centres on a political journalist, David Charleston, who, after discovering that his reports have been censored by the editor of his newspaper so as not to offend the German government, decides to turn his back on the world. Seeking solitude, he takes the job of a lone lighthouse keeper on Lake Michigan at Thunder Rock, the scene of a tragic shipwreck ninety years earlier, in which a ship, carrying a group of migrants hoping to start a new life in the USA, had sunk with the loss of everyone on board. The supernatural plays a major role in the drama as Charleston begins to conjure up the ghosts of these victims who recount their stories. As Charleston gradually enters into a dialogue with the dead, their eloquent testimony forces him to realise that he cannot live in isolation and that he must return to the world of political commitment.

The plot, described by one reviewer as 'a tract for the times', was of course a thinly-disguised plea for America to abandon its policy of isolationism, a message which determined its contrasting reception in the USA and Britain. First staged in New York by the Group Theatre and directed by Elia Kazan, it famously flopped, being taken off after three weeks. A year later in wartime London it became a theatrical event. Seeming to catch the prevailing mood of wartime defiance, the play became a focal point in the depleted landscape of London's theatre.

The performance history of *Thunder Rock* in London echoes the turbulent time in which it was produced. It was first staged at the Neighbourhood Theatre, a small playhouse in South Kensington, on 18 June 1940, in a production by the director Herbert Marshall, who also ran the Neighbourhood Theatre.[55] Marshall had sent the play to the actor Michael Redgrave, who 'thought it one of the most exciting plays I had read'.[56] Redgrave agreed to play the role of Charleston, and it was his inspirational performance that ensured the play's transfer to the West End — and its place in London theatre history. In his dialogue with the spirits of the dead, Charleston is particularly drawn to the Kurtz family. Dr Stefan Kurtz, played by

---

54   *The Times*, 20 March 1940.
55   Herbert P. J. Marshall, a stage and film director, was a disciple of Stanislavsky.
56   Michael Redgrave, *In My Mind's Eye* (London: Weidenfeld & Nicholson, 1983), p. 160.

FIG. 4. Frederick Valk as Dr. Kurtz in *Thunder Rock*, London 1940

Frederick Valk (as he had now become), is a Jewish physician in Vienna, who has bravely and successfully pioneered the use of anaesthetics, but who becomes the victim of anti-Semitic persecution, forcing him and his family to leave Vienna for a new life across the Atlantic.

In the heightened political atmosphere of 1940, Valk had been able to escape internment, protected by his Czechoslovak passport, which gave him, in contrast to his German and Austrian counterparts, the status of 'a friendly alien'. The emblematic role of Dr Kurtz offered many parallels with Valk's own experience, enabling him to give a notable performance which drew the attention of influential theatre figures like Tyrone Guthrie

The production of *Thunder Rock* was staged just two weeks after the military defeat in France and the subsequent Dunkirk evacuation. German air raids had begun in earnest and all but two theatres in the West End were 'dark' in the week that *Thunder Rock* opened. The play was an instant success, catching the mood of audiences and critics alike. Michael Redgrave remembered that 'the critics heaped praise upon us: "A tonic to the mind and a bath to the spirit" said the *News Chronicle*'.[57] At such a crucial moment in the conduct of the war, the Ministry of Information (MOI) calculated that the play could make a contribution to boosting morale on the home front and therefore quickly arranged for £600 to be advanced to help with the cost of transferring the play to the West End. The production reopened at the Globe Theatre on 30 July 1940 with, once again, Redgrave in the leading role and Valk playing Dr Kurtz.

The significance of the play for the London theatre can be read in the reviews, which acknowledged, and approved, the play's politically didactic intention. The critic of the *Observer*, for example, called the play 'a tract for the times; propaganda in fancy dress'.[58] It enjoyed a successful — and highly eventful — run.

A number of performances were given at the height of the Blitz. Michael Redgrave later recalled that when the air-raid warnings sounded, the audience stayed in their seats. He would then stop the play, come to the front of the stage and offer to entertain the audience 'in a rather more basic manner' until the all-clear was sounded. During this 'interval' he gave rousing versions of music hall and wartime songs, such as 'Run, Rabbit, Run' and 'Hang Out the Washing on the Siegfried Line'.[59] These impromptu performances became the talk of the town and members of the audience from other theatres began to join the audience at the Globe whenever the air raid sirens sounded. 'For many it was a disappointment when the performance of *Thunder Rock* resumed'.[60] The production ran for forty-eight performances.

As the Blitz intensified, London theatres were, with few exceptions, forced to close. Some stayed open, but gave only matinee performances, while many companies were sent out on tour. This was the case with *Thunder Rock*, as *Theatre*

57 Ibid.
58 H. H., *Observer*, 4 August 1940.
59 Redgrave, pp. 160–61.
60 '*Thunder Rock*', in *The Methuen Drama Dictionary of the Theatre*, ed. by Jonathan Law (New York: Methuen, 1999).

World was quick to report: 'As Mr Redgrave is now engaged in filming, his part is being played on tour by that fine young actor Alec Guinness. The others of the original company remain'.[61]

There is no record of the company's, or Valk's, experience of the English provinces, though it must have been brief. In fact, *Thunder Rock* was born again in February 1941, reopening in a new production at the St. Martin's Theatre, where it ran for a further forty-six performances.[62] As Redgrave was still unavailable, a fresh cast was assembled for the new production, with Walter Hudd in the role of Charleston and Cyril Cusack as Streeter, but with the ever-present Valk still playing the part of Dr Kurtz. He was ultimately the only constant feature of these productions — apart from the background presence of the Ministry of Information, keeping a watchful eye on the government's investment. Thanks to the play's popular success, the £600 loan from the Treasury was finally repaid.

Michael Redgrave was conscious that *Thunder Rock* marked a turning-point in his career, recalling: '*Who is Who* wrote to me for the first time asking for an entry. *Picture Post* put me on their front page. I felt I had arrived'.[63] Frederick Valk too had arrived, the production playing a decisive part in establishing his presence on the London stage. His role as Dr Kurtz, with its strong undertones of prejudice and persecution, not only matched his own biography, but also touched on the experience of Shakespeare's Shylock, a role which he would shortly undertake in English and which always remained associated with his name.

In the summer of 1941, at a time when other refugee actors were still suffering the consequences of internment — Gerhard Hinze, for example, was still detained in Canada — Valk was able to take a significant step in his career on the British stage. Fresh from his long involvement with *Thunder Rock*, which had finally ended its run in April, he accepted an offer to join the Old Vic company on tour.

In the 1930s the Old Vic had become England's leading theatre, producing ancient and modern classics, above all Shakespeare, at its London stage in Waterloo Road. However, the company was abruptly forced to redefine its wartime role after the theatre building received a direct hit in a bombing raid on 10 May 1941, suffering severe damage, and forcing the company to re-evaluate its activities. Partly subsidised by the government through CEMA, the Old Vic became a touring company, bringing Shakespeare and other classics to the industrial heartlands of Britain. While it found a temporary home for performance in London at the New Theatre, the Old Vic company moved north, establishing its base at the Victoria Theatre, Burnley.

Valk was invited to join the Old Vic by its director Tyrone Guthrie who had seen — and vividly remembered — his performance in *Thunder Rock*: 'I first saw Frederick Valk act in a piece called *Thunder Rock*. He played a doctor, and gave the impression, which is one of the hallmarks of top-flight acting, not of being just a particular doctor, but of the Idea of Medicine; he was an archetype of doctor'.[64]

61   'Plays on Tour', *Theatre World*. October 1940.
62   The production ran at the St. Martin's Theatre from 25 February to 5 April 1941.
63   Redgrave, p. 161.
64   Valk, p. xi.

FIG. 5. Frederick Valk as Shylock in *The Merchant of Venice* for the Old Vic, London 1943 (Bristol University Theatre Collection, John Vickers Archive)

It was Guthrie who chose *Othello* and *The Merchant of Venice* for the touring repertoire and who cast Valk in the leading role in both plays, giving him his first Shakespearean roles on the English stage. Guthrie was well aware of the anomaly of a German actor, albeit one with a Czech passport, joining such a traditional English institution as the Old Vic. Even more startling was the idea that he should play two leading Shakespearean roles. Although Valk had already performed both Othello and Shylock on the German stage, and therefore knew the dramatic dimensions of both roles, it was a completely different matter to play them in English in England. The difficulty of learning lines was greatly magnified in a still unfamiliar foreign language.

Despite heroic efforts to learn English, Valk, a fine speaker of verse in his native German, never entirely mastered the cadences of English speech, nor the intricacies of English pronunciation. Moreover, he never lost his strong German accent, which restricted his career on the British stage to roles in which a foreign accent was permissible, thus excluding him from most of the great roles in the Shakespearean canon that he longed to play. Tyrone Guthrie observed: 'I shall always regret that no opportunity came for him to play *King Lear* in English'.[65]

Given these limitations, it was perhaps inevitable that Valk's initial triumphs on the British stage were in Shakespeare's two classic outsider roles, in which he could turn his foreign accent to advantage. While Othello is a noble general with a record of military success, he remains a foreigner, a black man in a white society; Shylock is despised by Venetian society as a money-lender, a profession which the same society has compelled him to follow. As a Jew, he too is a foreigner, whose cruelty in insisting on his bond is a product of the society which has spurned him. Valk could feel a natural empathy with both characters, without being blinded to their shortcomings.

In the autumn of 1941, the Old Vic had no fewer than three companies on tour, including a production of *The Merchant of Venice*, with Valk as Shylock, which took the play to mining communities in Scotland and County Durham, performing in a succession of miners' clubs, school halls, and community centres.[66] Tours usually consisted of two productions performed in turn and on this tour Valk alternated the role of Shylock with that of Nick, the barman in *The Time of Your Life* by the American playwright William Saroyan.

Shylock was a role for which Valk seemed to have been predestined. He brought to it much of his own personal and professional experience. As a Jew, he had been thrust by the Nazis into the role of social outcast, declared a foreigner in his own country. Professionally, he had acted in at least two productions of *The Merchant of Venice* during his career in Germany. He had first played Shylock in 1924 at the Landestheater, Darmstadt, a theatre originally built as a court theatre for the Dukes of Hesse: an inescapable contrast to the school halls and miners' clubs he was now to visit. After moving to Berlin he had appeared in a landmark production of *The*

65 Ibid., p. xiii.
66 George Rowell, *The Old Vic Theatre: A History* (Cambridge: Cambridge University Press, 2005), p. 132.

Merchant of Venice by Leopold Jessner in 1927; Shylock had been played by the more famous Fritz Kortner, while Valk had been cast as Tubal, 'a role he treasured as a super-Shylock'.[67]

The production values of the Old Vic touring company were — in keeping with the working conditions of the tour — notably austere. Many of the performances were for a single night only, some at workaday venues where the theatre space was occasionally improvised. In consequence, scenery had to be simple and adaptable (in one tour, the scenery consisted of screens which could be turned round for use in the second production); costume and design were unostentatious: Valk played Shylock in a long flowing black robe, a costume in apparent contrast to Shakespeare's description of the character as 'a rich Jew'. One popular name for these tours was 'Shakespeare at the Coalface', but they were seen and enjoyed by audiences who might never have been inside a 'proper' theatre.

In the summer of 1942, the Old Vic brought its new production of *Othello* to London, playing it in repertory with *The Merry Wives of Windsor* at the New Theatre, the company's temporary London stage. This short London season was financially supported by CEMA, whose assistance in staging the event was credited in the theatre programme — the first time its support had been so openly acknowledged. *Othello* was given forty-five performances from July to September 1942, Valk playing the title role to the Iago of Bernard Miles, who had appeared with him in the original production of *Thunder Rock*. The play was directed by Julius Gellner, with whom Valk had first worked in Prague.

The sense of anticipation preceding the Old Vic's short London season is captured by James Agate's review of the production, headlined 'The Moor at Last'. The review is a notable attempt to place Valk's performance in the long perspective of English theatre:

> *Othello* is the most formidable of Shakespeare's tragedies. Over and over again it has defeated the English actor. Free of the English handicap, the Czech actor Mr Frederick Valk struck at once the right note of immense dignity. [...] any playgoer with half an eye and half an ear must have been satisfied that here was an authentic tragedian [...] Mr Valk conveyed what should be conveyed in Titian-like gestures and with sufficient poetry. His exits had a sweeping grandeur more satisfying than most English actors' entrances.[68]

The overall impact of the production was exceptional, critics hastening to acclaim Valk's 'virile, masculine acting' in the title role.[69] Under the heading 'An Impressive Othello', W. A. Darlington wrote in the *Daily Telegraph*:

> Frederick Valk, the refugee actor, proved his quality in no uncertain manner as Othello at the New Theatre last night. In all respects but one he is the ideal choice for the part. He has stature, virility and dignity. He has a wide emotional and vocal range. On occasion he can make most effective use of monotony and stillness, at another moment he will get his effects by flinging himself about and running up and down the scale like a singer. He lacks one thing, the ability

---

67 Valk, p. 35.
68 James Agate, 'The Moor at Last', *Sunday Times*, 26 July 1942.
69 *Daily Worker*, 14 September 1942.

to speak Shakespeare's verse like an Englishman [...] Yet even with this great handicap, Mr Valk's must rank among the best Othellos I have seen.[70]

There was indeed a critical consensus that Valk's foreign accent was a handicap that he had overcome through the extraordinary range of his voice and his ability to convey overwhelming emotion through the sheer power of his physical acting.

Gellner's production was also widely praised, most perceptively in the *Spectator*:

> Julius Gellner's production [...] gives us the play not merely as Shakespeare wrote it, but also, surely, as he felt it. The dialogue throughout is taken at natural speed — that is, about twice as fast as the average Shakespearian delivers it — and is also spoken with every attention to its colloquial import. That all this is achieved without the loss of a single line of poetic value is a yardstick to the success of the production.[71]

Agate too praised the 'first-class production by Mr. Julius Gellner', while Darlington called it 'full of imaginative touches', adding that 'the Old Vic company may look upon it with pride'. In retrospect, it became one of the most memorable Shakespeare productions of the war years. Ironically, it was the *Daily Worker* that struck a note of unusual patriotism, complaining that 'It is a sad commentary on the state of our drama that [...] the best production of Shakespeare [has been] by a foreign director with a foreign lead'.[72]

Othello was unique in Valk's career, in that he played the role more frequently in English than in German. Altogether, he appeared in four productions of the play in the English-speaking theatre, as against a single, but formative performance in Prague.[73] For a few years he was to make the role very much his own, his interpretation a bench mark for others. In fact, this one short season as Othello proved enough to establish Valk's reputation in Britain as a *Shakespearean* actor.

Valk was a man of powerful physique and commanding stage presence, which seemed to predestine him for some of the great classical roles in the theatre. Photographs show a well-built man of above average height, with a massive head, set on broad shoulders — his head and chest were, according to Tyrone Guthrie, 'those of a giant' — with dark hair and a sallow complexion that gave him a slightly exotic air.

His voice matched his physique. His stage delivery was such, James Agate commented drily, that he could be heard in the next theatre.[74] In fact, his voice had a remarkable vocal range. Guthrie, a connoisseur of Shakespearean acting, remembered it as 'a warm and velvety baritone with an upper register of extraordinary brilliance and power [...] I do not think I have ever heard a man's voice which had the same ringing, uninhibited power at the top'.[75]

Valk's impact on stage was also due to his performance style. In an interview in 1946 — while he was appearing in a highly acclaimed production of *The Brothers*

---

70 W. A. Darlington, 'An Impressive Othello', *Daily Telegraph*, 23 July 1942.

71 *Spectator*, 30 July 1942.

72 *Daily Worker*, 14 September 1942.

73 Valk played Othello again in London in a production by Donald Wolfit, then later with the Citizens Theatre, Glasgow (17–29 April 1950), and finally in Toronto in 1955.

74 James Agate, *Sunday Times*, 9 July 1939.

75 Valk, p. xii.

Karamazov — Valk acknowledged that his style of acting was different from what British audiences normally saw, or expected: 'I fully recognise [...] that my way of dramatic expression is different from that which is most commonly appreciated in this country'.[76] In a theatre culture which placed the greatest importance on the spoken word, he was unable to match the perfect diction of English actors like Gielgud or Redgrave, choosing to rely almost entirely on the characteristic style of acting which had first won him fame in Germany. Like Fritz Kortner, his apprentice years had spanned the Expressionist decade of German theatre, in which heightened emotion was paramount, in contrast to what Valk (and other German actors) perceived as the suppression of emotion on the English stage

Perhaps what most distinguished Valk from other actors was the emotional impact of his performance. The words most commonly used to describe his acting were 'powerful' and 'passionate'. He had the physical ability to convey primeval passion which was normally contained — but which could, under stress, break out with terrible consequences. His acting style was at odds with the prevailing mode of cool detachment on the English stage which placed emphasis on perfect declamation of the verse, sometimes failing, in Valk's view, to reach the emotion which underlay it. In a rare statement of his own on the art of the actor, Valk emphasised the need to 'live the verse':

> Shakespeare's tragedies are born in hell and an actor who dares to play them must make a trip to hell. He can't return from there in a very orderly manner! [...] But most of the actors don't go down to hell. Either they don't know the way or they don't want to go at all. They prefer a temperate ante-room where one can sit and behave like a gentleman, delivering a declamation beautifully, with legs nicely crossed, in well-pressed trousers. Surely they will deliver the poetry — not a word will be lost — but it will be a dehydrated poetry and you will not hear the voices of Macbeth, Lear or Othello — baked in hell.[77]

Following the extraordinary success of its short London season, the Old Vic began a provincial tour of *Othello* which lasted, in all, nearly nine months, embracing the usual mixture of mining villages, small industrial towns, and larger provincial centres, such as Liverpool, where it performed *Othello* in November 1942, helping to bring life back to the Playhouse, which had been closed for two years.[78] The company had to contend with the usual problems of a touring theatre, heightened by the adverse circumstances of wartime. The handsome black and gold stage set, for example, shed its colour as wartime paint failed to withstand wartime transport conditions. Valk particularly remembered the special problems of removing dark grease-paint after playing Othello, due to the poor quality of wartime soap and the refusal to issue extra rations to anyone but chimney-sweeps.[79]

The year 1943 was a landmark for Valk, in which he consolidated his reputation on the London stage through his performance as Shylock, the part with which his

---

76 Edgar Ralph, 'Acting at Home and Abroad: Frederick Valk Talks on Two "Schools"', *The Stage*, 4 July 1946.
77 Frederick Valk, 'Acting and Poetry', *New Theatre*, July 1946, p. 10.
78 Theatre programme, *Othello*, New Theatre 28 July 1942, in V&A TPA.
79 Valk, pp. 76–77.

name was subsequently always linked. The Old Vic had already toured *The Merchant of Venice* for some months before finally bringing the production to London in February 1943, where it ran, once more at the New Theatre, for a total of forty-eight performances.[80] The play was one of the most popular in the Shakespearean canon in Britain in the 1930s and became the most frequently produced Shakespeare play during the war years in London — a total of seven productions, including the Old Vic production with Frederick Valk.

With London's theatre life still stripped to the bare bones, the Old Vic's return to the capital was eagerly awaited. Critical anticipation focused notably on Valk, whose performance as Othello six months earlier still resounded. When he returned in *The Merchant of Venice*, the popular magazine *Picture Post* ran a two-page photo spread, under the headline 'Valk Plays Shylock', calling him, with some hyperbole, 'the outstanding Shakespearean actor in Britain'.[81]

More soberly, the *Daily Mail* reported that:

> The Old Vic company returned to the New Theatre last night with the *Merchant of Venice*, and Mr Frederick Valk, the distinguished Czech actor as Shylock. This is beyond question a fine performance in a part in which a foreign accent is not a serious handicap.[82]

Ivor Brown in the *Observer* was far less reserved in his enthusiasm, calling Valk's Shylock 'an immense performance, full of muscular volubility, tremendously vehement in hate, but cleverest in the early raillery, when Shylock, having still his daughter and his ducats, has not sunk his judgement in his fury'.[83]

Valk's Shylock contrasts vividly with the notorious anti-Semitic portrayal by the great actor Werner Krauss, just two months later at Vienna's Burgtheater in May 1943. Krauss's performance, which was used to endorse the tenets of Nazi racial ideology, was to pursue him into the post-war years of de-Nazification. In contrast to Valk, Krauss never played the part again.

For one critic who saw Valk play Shylock, his performance lived on long after the actor had died. In his memoir of London's literary and theatrical world, the translator and biographer Michael Meyer included a chapter devoted to Valk, entitled simply 'My Greatest Actor', in which he described the elemental effect which Valk's Shylock had had on him:

> Valk could have been forgiven if he had, at this stage in the war, sentimentalised the Jew but nothing could have been further from the case. His Shylock was mean but he was so because of the attitude of everyone around him. It was an age of fine acting in Britain: Olivier, Richardson, Gielgud, Donat and Redgrave were all at, or approaching their peak. But now I found myself confronted by a power and — what can I call it? — savagery unlike anything I had experienced [...] I simply knew that I had been moved and shaken as never before in a theatre, or anywhere else.[84]

80 The play was performed from 16 February to 27 March 1943.
81 'Valk Plays Shylock', *Picture Post*, 9 March 1943.
82 'Czech Actor as Shylock', *Daily Mail*, 17 February 1943.
83 Ivor Brown, 'Theatre and Life', *Observer*, 21 February 1943.
84 Michael Meyer, *Not Prince Hamlet: Literary and Theatrical Memoirs* (London: Secker & Warburg,

Meyer was not alone in thinking Valk the best actor he had seen. Many years later, he was having lunch with Ralph Richardson who suddenly asked him to name the greatest actor he had ever seen. Meyer hesitated out of deference to the great actor sitting opposite. After a pause, Richardson asked: 'Valk?' And both men agreed.[85]

Despite the impact of Valk's performance in *The Merchant of Venice*, not everything he touched was so successful. In August, he took part in one of the most ambitious theatre productions of the war years, a stage version of Tolstoy's *War and Peace* at the Phoenix Theatre.[86] The production was almost a demonstration of central European stage techniques: the play was adapted by the Austrian Robert Lucas, directed by the Czech Julius Gellner, whose production for the Old Vic had framed Valk's Othello, and designed by the German Hein Heckroth. Despite the technical innovations of Gellner's production, Tolstoy's novel proved intractable material for the stage. There were thirty-two scenes, countless characters, and an actor-narrator to link the often isolated episodes.

The Times called the production 'an exciting experience', praising Gellner's innovative stage techniques, which owed much to the ideas of Edward Gordon Craig:

> All the mechanical resources of the stage are enrolled [...] Scenes [are] projected onto a permanent backcloth. A group of glittering chandeliers suggests the courtly elegance of Count Pierre's ballroom, a Byzantine roof the interior of the Razumovsky chapel and the same evocative discretion is shown in adumbrations of a battlefield or of burning Moscow.[87]

Valk appeared 'in all the growling splendour' of Kutuzov, the Commander of the Russian army, while Peter Illing played 'a somewhat Hitlerish Napoleon', a performance meant to emphasise the contemporary parallels in the play. The production had a resolutely topical focus: the defence of Moscow in 1941–1942 was already a symbol of Soviet resistance to invading German forces. This contemporary significance of the historical narrative was evoked through the dramatic device of framing the action with a modern artillery post outside Moscow.

The production began with a short provincial tour in Blackpool and Manchester before opening in London, but though a critical success, it quickly became a commercial failure. The producer Tom Arnold had originally been persuaded to back the play in response to 'the outcry against the prevalence of revivals and lack of anything new in the theatre', but the show closed after just twenty performances, as 'demand at the box office has grown steadily less and less'.[88]

After *War and Peace* Valk appeared in Lillian Hellman's *Watch on the Rhine*. Exceptionally for the West End stage, the play explored the hazards of political exile, the intricacy of patriotic loyalties, and the ever-present threat of espionage.

Hellman's German protagonist Kurt Müller, played in the original production by Anton Walbrook, is a fervent antifascist who arrives in the United States with his American wife to stay with her family after spending seventeen years in Europe. His

---

1989), p. 237.

85   Ibid., p. 247.

86   *War and Peace*, by Leo Tolstoy, adapted by Robert Lucas, Phoenix Theatre, 8–21 August 1943.

87   *The Times*, 7 August 1943.

88   *Evening Standard*, 20 August 1943.

role as an active antifascist disturbs the peace and plenty of a well-to-do American home. Another house-guest, a sinister Romanian count, finds a pistol in Müller's room as well as a sum of money intended for the resistance in Germany. He attempts to blackmail Müller by threatening to report him as an anti-Nazi to the German Embassy. Unwilling to compromise the resistance movement in Germany, Müller kills the Romanian and prepares to return to Germany to continue the political fight.

Reviews of the original production were predictably enthusiastic, endorsing the play's ideology and Walbrook's outstanding performance. The *Tatler and Bystander*, in a two-page photo feature, called it 'the best play since the war [began]'.[89] The *Observer's* Ivor Brown called it 'a play of its time', using its theme to refute Vansittart's claim that all Germans supported Hitler: 'But the essence of the drama is in the soul of Kurt Müller and most exquisitely does Mr. Anton Walbrook open the windows on that heroic heart. Lord Vansittart, both as playwright and as politician, should be interested in Müller'.[90]

Despite the attraction of a play on political exile and the chance to play the anti-Nazi Kurt Müller, the play was not as career-defining for Valk as *Thunder Rock*. In fact, he appeared only during the final months of the play's run, playing the role originally acted by Walbrook, who had left the cast because of film commitments.[91]

In October 1944, Valk returned briefly to the Old Vic company, playing the role of Stefan in Noel Coward's *Point Valaine* at the Liverpool Playhouse, 'a performance which Coward saw and admired'.[92] During 1944, Valk was also increasingly involved in broadcast propaganda. When the BBC German Service transmitted, in German translation, the text of the major speeches by Churchill, Roosevelt, and Stalin, each was spoken by Valk, making him probably the only actor to play all three world leaders in rapid succession.

Throughout the war years, Valk also played various supporting roles in British films. His strongly-accented English, ostensibly a drawback for a career in the English theatre, became something of a trademark in film. Combined with his imposing physical stature, it led ironically to his being cast frequently in British films as a Nazi figure of authority, variously credited under such titles as 'Gestapo officer', 'Kommandant', or 'Sturmführer'.

As already noted, Valk began his English film career with a minor role in Carol Reed's *Night Train to Munich* (1940), appearing as a Gestapo officer, the first of several such roles playing one of the very Nazi henchman who had driven him out of Germany. He was credited as Fritz Valk, a name he quickly chose to anglicise. In *Neutral Port* — one of the earliest war films actually shot in wartime Britain — he appeared as a U-Boot Commander, while in the 1941 film *Gasbags*, an adventure comedy in which the Crazy Gang 'invaded' Germany, he was cast as a 'Sturmführer'. In both these films he was credited as Frederick Valk, his new name

89   *Tatler & Bystander*, 27 May 1942.
90   Ivor Brown, 'At the Play', *Observer* 26 April 1942.
91   When Valk in turn left the cast, the part was played by Roger Livesey.
92   Meyer, p. 239.

marking a prudent shift of identity at a time when German names were regarded with suspicion.

During his early years in Britain, Valk was offered work in several notable film productions, but only in minor roles. In *Dangerous Moonlight* (1941), a star vehicle for Anton Walbrook, who was playing the role of a Polish pilot and piano virtuoso, Valk appeared as a Polish bomber commander. He also appeared in Carol Reed's *The Young Mr Pitt* (1942), a biographical film of William Pitt the younger, covering his long war with revolutionary France, a theme inviting obvious contemporary parallels. The film was a major production, starring Robert Donat as Pitt and featuring costumes by Cecil Beaton, but Valk played only a minor role, which was uncredited.

He fared much better in the successful film version of *Thunder Rock*, made in 1942 and released at the end of that year. The contemporary convergence of stage and screen — at a time when a successful play was often followed by a film version — was emphasised by the film's rather stagy production. Directed by Roy Boulting and produced by John Boulting for their production company Charter Films, the film starred Michael Redgrave, repeating his role as Charleston, and James Mason, but still had several substantial parts for émigré actors: Valk once again featured as Dr Kurtz, with Sybille Binder as his wife and the young German actress Lilli Palmer as their daughter.

Valk's was not the only career to prosper after *Thunder Rock*; the greatest success in the film was achieved by Lilli Palmer. She had already appeared in supporting roles in British films such as *The Secret Agent* (1935), *Sunset in Vienna* (1937), and *The Man With a Thousand Faces* (1938), but *Thunder Rock* was the film that became her 'film career-maker', after which she went on to become an international star.[93] The film also provided minor roles for other refugee actors, including Gerhard Hinze and the Czech actor Arnold Marlé, although both were uncredited. The cameraman was Mutz Greenbaum, a highly-respected cinematographer who had made his name in Britain by shooting a series of films in the 1930s under the auspices of Alexander Korda. He was usually credited as Max Greene.

The film *Thunder Rock* was both a popular and a critical success, helping to disarm any lingering objections to 'German' actors appearing in 'British' films. Unlike the original play, the film was well received on both sides of the Atlantic. When released in America in 1944, it ran to packed houses for three months in New York, where the original stage production had folded after three weeks.

With the exception of *Thunder Rock*, Valk's early film roles did little to advance his career or reputation, though they may have given him some financial assurance. In 1944, however, his growing reputation on stage, based largely on his success with the Old Vic, led to the offer of more substantial film roles. The first of these was in *Hotel Reserve*, released in June 1944. *Hotel Reserve* was a spy film, set in the South of France in 1938, starring James Mason as Peter Vadassy, an Austrian refugee who stumbles into a case of espionage. An innocent abroad, Peter is asked by the police to help identify a spy among his fellow hotel guests.

93 <IMDb.com//Lilli Palmer/nm0658339> [accessed October 2015].

The film co-starred Lucie Mannheim as the hotel proprietor, Madame Koch, while other refugee actors such as Martin Miller and Herbert Lom played supporting roles. Valk played Paul Heimberger, a member of the anti-Nazi resistance in Germany who has escaped to France. Produced by RKO Radio, the film was notable for having a trio of directors — Lance Comfort, Victor Hanbury, and Mutz Greenbaum (credited as usual as Max Greene) — who were also the film's producers. The ubiquitous Greenbaum was the director of photography too, though on this occasion his work as cameraman was uncredited. The film was based on Eric Ambler's novel *Epitaph for a Spy*, but despite the quality of its source and a distinguished cast, it received poor reviews — 'Slow, obvious and poorly made suspenser from a good novel' was one judgement — and it is mainly interesting today for the outstanding cameo roles it offered émigré actors.[94]

Having managed to escape typecasting as a Nazi henchman, Valk was finally able to create a different niche playing doctors, psychiatrists, or criminologists, where the German accent which had become his trademark was actually considered an asset. Two such roles came in *Dead of Night* and *Latin Quarter* (released in September and October 1945 respectively).

Dead of Night is something of an oddity, establishing a claim to fame as an early, and successful, British horror film. In a curious (and little-known) instance of wartime censorship, the British government had banned the production of horror films for the duration of the war: the success of *Dead of Night* therefore rested on its novelty as well as its notoriety. The film was made by Ealing Studios, escaping the studio's usual template and influencing subsequent British films in the genre. It was a portmanteau film, consisting of different dramatic episodes within a framing narrative. The different episodes had different directors, including Alberto Cavalcanti and Charles Crichton, better known for his direction of Ealing comedies. Michael Redgrave, his career once more interlocking with Valk's, appeared as the mad ventriloquist who believes that his amoral dummy really is alive. Valk played a major part as the psychiatrist Dr van Straaten, who appeared in two of the film's episodes. It is perhaps his best-known screen role.

Latin Quarter, released in London in October 1945, was a mystery thriller, set in 1890s Paris. The film was taken from a French play *L'Angoisse* by the writers Pierre Mills and Charles Vylars who also wrote the screenplay. Valk played the criminologist, Dr Ivan Krasner, appearing alongside fellow-émigrés Lilly Kann and Martin Miller. The story is told in a series of flashbacks, as related to Dr Krasner, giving Valk a central role, framing the episodes of the narrative. Valk thus played two of his best film roles in the same year.

94 'Hotel Reserve', in *Halliwell* (1999), p. 380.

CHAPTER 12

'The Führer Speaks':
Martin Miller

The most remarkable, indeed unexpected transition to the English stage amongst this small group of actors was that of the Austrian Martin Miller. When Miller arrived in London with the help of the Quakers in March 1939, he seemed to have little hope of continuing his acting career. He was thirty-nine years old, a provincial actor who spoke no English, had no English contacts, and knew nothing of the English stage. Yet by the end of the war, he had established himself in London as a character actor of great versatility. From the outset he proved remarkably resourceful; within days of arriving he had joined other Austrian émigré actors in founding the small cabaret theatre 'Das Laterndl' [The Lantern], of which he became the artistic director and star performer.

In the tolerant, but alien, environment of London, the Laterndl had set out to recreate the typically Viennese cabaret theatre. The theatre programme for the opening revue *Unterwegs* [On the Road] stated the tiny theatre's *raison d'être*: 'the LANTERN will preserve one of the characteristic forms of Austrian culture'.[95] The Laterndl was therefore founded as an explicitly *Austrian* theatre, a symbolic assertion of national identity at a time when Austria had been wiped off the political map.

This opening programme faithfully followed the format of the Viennese revue: a succession of short dramatic sketches and songs, alternating the serious and the comic. It was played largely in German, but English guests in the audience could orientate themselves via the *conférencier*, or master of ceremonies, whose commentary linking the different sketches was given in English. Among the original sketches written for the revue was 'Bow Street', portraying events in the waiting-room and interview-room of the Aliens Office where all refugees had to register, and 'Der blühende Garten' [The Garden in Bloom], a sketch mocking Hitler's declared intention of turning Vienna into a garden in bloom. Among the songs was Jura Soyfer's 'Lied des einfachen Menschen' [Song of the Simple Man], sung by Martin Miller.

The audience greeted this programme, parts of which enacted their own experience, with predictable enthusiasm. Less predictable was the enthusiastic reception of the British press from *The Times* to the *Manchester Guardian*, the *News Chronicle*

---

95 Copies of theatre programmes for most of the Laterndl productions are in MN-MA. The text of the programme is reprinted in Hilde Spiel, 'Keine Klage über England', *Ver Sacrum: Neue Hefte für Kunst und Literatur* (1972), 21–25.

FIG. 6. Martin Miller, 'The Führer Speaks', London 1940
(Martin Miller and Hannah Norbert-Miller Archive, University of London)

to the *Star*, and the *New Statesman* to the *Spectator*. *The Times* wrote that the revue 'made an extremely favourable impression',[96] but perhaps Goronwy Rees, writing in *The Spectator*, best caught the general sense of admiration with his comment, 'We should be grateful to Herr Hitler for the Lantern. Austria's loss has been our gain.'[97]

Martin Miller had a particular reason to be grateful to 'Herr Hitler'. His name first reached a wider audience in wartime Britain through his satirical impersonation of his fellow-Austrian in the sketch 'Der Führer spricht' [The Führer Speaks], which he wrote and performed as part of the Laterndl's second revue *Blinklichter* [Beacons] in late 1939. In Miller's disconcertingly accurate impression, the 'Führer' praised Columbus's discovery of America, 'based on the experiments of German scientists and supported by German apparatus and instruments', and went on to declare the USA a German protectorate:

> Since the year 1492, I have remained silent and have left these problems untouched in the interests of peace. But now my patience is at an end. Let Mr. Roosevelt take note that it is my unshakeable will finally to take the seat in the White House which Providence has destined for me and thereby transform it into the Brown House.[98]

Among the audience for the opening performance was Richard Crossman, then head of the German Section of the Political Warfare Executive, a clandestine government organisation responsible for broadcast propaganda to enemy countries. At Crossman's instigation, Miller was invited to perform the sketch for the German Service of the BBC, the programme being broadcast live to Germany on 1 April 1940.[99] So authentic was Miller's satirical impersonation that the American broadcaster CBS (which had not actually heard the programme) contacted the BBC in some consternation to ask where it had picked up the broadcast.

Miller remained the director of the Laterndl for the next three years, taking leading roles in all the first ten programmes. In March 1940 he produced *Der unsterbliche Schwejk* [The Immortal Schwejk], a montage of scenes from the life of its eponymous hero, with himself in the title role. Schwejk was one of the traditional figures of Viennese cabaret: the archetypal little man, constantly put upon by the authorities, but always emerged unscathed. As already noted, Miller had first played Schwejk a decade earlier in Reichenberg, where press reviews had made his performance a local sensation. In the London of 1940 there were, by contrast, no reviews at all, but the production did not pass unnoticed, receiving a double-page photo spread in the popular weekly *Picture Post*.[100]

---

96   *The Times*, 28 June 1939.

97   *Spectator*, 7 July 1939.

98   'Seit dem Jahre 1492 [...] habe ich geschwiegen und im Interesse des Friedens diese Probleme unberührt gelassen. Aber nun ist meine Geduld zu Ende. Herr Roosevelt möge zur Kenntnis nehmen, daß es mein unerschütterlicher Wille ist, endlich den mir von der Vorsehung bestimmten Stuhl im Weißen Haus einzunehmen und es damit zum Braunen Hause zu machen'. A typescript copy of the 'speech' is held in MN-MA.

99   The broadcast was reported in several newspapers, e.g. the *News Chronicle*, 2 April 1940, where it appeared on the front page.

100   *Picture Post*, 27 April 1940. *Picture Post* was a publication founded by the émigré Stefan Lorant.

By far the greatest difficulty to confront the Laterndl and other refugee theatres in 1940 was the problem of internment. Following *Schwejk*, Martin Miller staged Brecht and Weill's *Dreigroschenoper*. This ill-fated production opened on 26 May 1940, coinciding with the British government's introduction of mass internment of 'enemy aliens', a measure which quickly robbed the Laterndl of most of its actors and much of its audience. No fewer than three actors, for example, rehearsed in turn the central role of Mack the Knife, the first two being interned before the role was assigned to a third. It is not known how long the production actually ran, though performances were certainly curtailed by the steady disappearance of both cast and audience. Under the pressure of internment, both the 'Laterndl' and the 'Kleine Bühne' were eventually forced to close, remaining dark for over a year.

Miller himself was not interned, doubtless because he was considered indispensable to the BBC's war propaganda. The BBC was just beginning to use short satirical sketches (or 'features') as part of its propaganda war against the Third Reich. 'The Führer Speaks' was only the first of several 'Hitler' impersonations that Miller was asked to write and perform for the BBC German Service in 1940–1941, including 'Hitler Speaks in an Air-raid Shelter' (11 October 1940), 'The Führer Speaks to his Gauleiters' (May 1941), an address 'To German Women and Girls' (4 December 1941), and 'Hitler's New Year Message' (27 December 1941).[101] Among the rare archive material relating to Miller's wartime broadcasting career is a letter from the BBC to the newly-established German and Austrian Labour Exchange, listing the 'very many useful things' that Miller had done for them, 'When we wished to give an imitation of Hitler speaking, Mr. Miller has both written a script and performed. He is the only man in London we have been able to find to do this'. In addition, Miller had 'acted as an occasional speaker in the Austrian programme' and had also 'written short feature scripts that have been a great success'.[102]

Many years later, the writer and broadcaster Carl Brinitzer vividly recalled one of Miller's broadcasts:

> I shall never forget New Year's Eve 1940, when Miller-Hitler gave a speech which ended with the words: 'It is my unshakeable will that the year 1940 shall end today, and let the world, including Mr. Roosevelt, take note that I am determined to give the German people, this very night, the gift of a new year — the year 1941'.[103]

In the course of 1940 Miller had also made his British film debut. A brief snatch of Miller as Hitler, addressing a Nuremberg Rally, was included in the film *Let George Do It*, a comedy vehicle for the hugely popular star George Formby. Miller's brief appearance was uncredited, but it nonetheless launched a long career in British films.

101 Drafts of these and other Hitler parodies are held in MN-MA. For further details of Miller's wide-ranging career at the BBC, see Charmian Brinson, 'The Go-Between: Martin Miller's Career in Broadcasting', in *German-speaking Exiles in the Performing Arts in Britain after 1933*, Yearbook of the Research Centre for German and Austrian Exile Studies, vol. 14, ed. by Charmian Brinson and Richard Dove (Amsterdam & New York: Rodopi, 2013), pp. 2–14.
102 Letter dated 6 October 1942, in MN-MA.
103 Carl Brinitzer, *Hier spricht London: Von einem der dabei war* (Hamburg: Hoffmann & Campe, 1969), p. 112.

FIG. 7. Martin Miller as Jacob in *Awake and Sing*, London 1942
(Martin Miller and Hannah Norbert-Miller Archive, University of London)

Despite his work for the BBC, Miller had not deserted the Laterndl. When the little theatre finally reopened in September 1941, he produced a new revue, *Laterna Magica* [Magic Lantern] and played the title role in a production of Carl Zuckmayer's comedy *Der Hauptmann von Köpenick*. Miller's last major role at the Laterndl was in March 1942, in Stefan Zweig's adaptation of Ben Jonson's *Volpone*, a production to commemorate Zweig, who had committed suicide a few weeks earlier. The Austrian exile newspaper *Zeitspiegel* lavished praise on Miller's production and his performance in the title role, the reviewer concluding: 'I am sorry for anyone who doesn't see this *Volpone*'.[104] Miller had no time to savour this local triumph, for he had already moved onto a larger stage.

In early 1942 the English actor-director Alec Clunes took over the management of the Arts Theatre. Situated just off Leicester Square, the Arts was within the West End, but certainly not part of it. It operated as a club theatre, open only to members and their guests, thereby escaping the censorship of the Lord Chamberlain's office; club status also encouraged a more innovative programme of experimental and controversial work, including plays which had little prospect of being produced in the commercial theatre. The company was run on egalitarian lines, members being paid a flat fee of five pounds a week, a pittance for a leading West End actor, but a considerable sum for a refugee.

Clunes's first production for the Arts Theatre, opening on 20 May 1942, was Clifford Odets's *Awake and Sing*. First produced in New York by the Group Theatre in 1935, the play had established its author's reputation as a rising star of American theatre. Miller was invited to audition for the role of Jacob, the Jewish grandfather, and though he later admitted that he understood barely a word of the lines he was asked to read, he was offered the part, playing alongside Lilly Kann, who was cast as his daughter, and the nineteen-year-old English actor Richard Attenborough, later world-famous as the director of *Gandhi* and *Cry Freedom*, who played his grandson.

If Clunes's decision to produce *Awake and Sing* was courageous, his choice of Miller and Kann to play the two leading roles was little short of inspired. Neither had acted before on the English stage, but Clunes clearly chose them not only as Jewish actors but as refugees, capable of conveying the hopes and fears of the migrant translated to a strange land.

Miller was always keenly aware of his Jewish heritage, and of the great Jewish roles he had played in the theatre. In a newspaper interview in 1967 he declared that 'Jewishness and the theatre, these are my interests in life'.[105] Thirty years earlier in Vienna, swimming against the tide of the times, he had performed an evening of *Judenrollen* [Jewish roles], comprising recitations from scenes that featured some of the great Jewish characters he had portrayed: Shylock in *The Merchant of Venice*, the title role in Lessing's *Nathan der Weise*, a drama in praise of religious tolerance, and the Jewish physician Professor Bernhardi in Schnitzler's play of the same name.[106]

---

104 *Zeitspiegel*, 4 April 1942.
105 'Jewishness and the Theatre', *Jewish Telegraph*, undated cutting, in MN-MA.
106 See the card advertising this event at the Jüdisches Kulturtheater, dated 23 May [1937], in MN-MA.

The role of the Jewish grandfather in *Awake and Sing* was therefore one he could relish. Jacob is a larger-than-life figure, a defeated idealist who has never reconciled himself to the ways of the New World. He still holds firmly to the two great loves of his youth: the onward march of socialism and the great tenor Caruso, whose songs he has assembled in a treasured collection of gramophone records. He is a man who acknowledges that he has failed and now invests all his hopes in his grandson. It was a role in which even Miller's rather broken English could be turned to advantage.

Plays at the Arts Theatre normally ran for three weeks, but *Awake and Sing* proved so popular with audiences that it was brought back for a further three weeks, running for thirty-two performances in all, before transferring to the Cambridge Theatre in August.

The production of *Awake and Sing* proved a milestone in the careers of its three leading actors. Richard Attenborough, performing his first major role on the London stage as Miller's grandson, never looked back, going on to play the teenage gangster Pinky in Graham Greene's *Brighton Rock*, a role he repeated on screen. Attenborough's theatrical career intersected more than once with Miller's on the post-war London stage, not least in Agatha Christie's *The Mousetrap*.

Miller's powerful, yet poignant performance had also drawn the attention of West End theatre circles. He was offered a leading part in the American play *Arsenic and Old Lace*, which opened at the Strand Theatre on 23 December 1942. *Arsenic and Old Lace* is a macabre comedy in which two sweet old ladies cure the loneliness of their gentlemen callers by giving them poisoned elderberry wine to drink and burying them in the cellar. Upstairs lives their brother Teddy who — because he believes he is Teddy Roosevelt — is digging the Suez Canal in the cellar (which contains eleven bodies). The two old ladies were played by Lillian Braithwaite and Mary Jerrold, an actress who specialised in playing sweet old ladies. Miller was cast in the role of Dr Einstein, a drunken plastic surgeon with criminal tendencies and a German accent. It was a part that he played up to the hilt, consolidating his reputation as a character actor in West End theatre circles.

The critics admired both the play and the performances. *The Times* called it 'certainly the most amusing comedy on the London stage today [...] Every new corpse adds to the by no means ghoulish fun [...] The joke is sustained without seeming effort to the play's last line'. The *New Statesman* noted: 'If the fun occasionally flags, the general effect is riotous. Nor could the performance be better. Over-acting would wreck everything. [...] Mr. Martin Miller, as a criminal surgeon, carries entire conviction'. Even James Agate concurred, praising Miller's portrayal of Dr Einstein as 'a polite lunatic, owing something to *The Belle of New York* and something to Grand Guignol'.[107]

Arsenic and Old Lace quickly became an iconic production whose continued performance was credited with helping to stiffen wartime civilian morale. Among prominent visitors to the play were Churchill and his wife, the military hero Field

107 'Arsenic and Old Lace by Joseph Kesselring', *The Times*, 24 December 1942; *New Statesman*, 2 January 1943; James Agate, 'Arsenic and Old Lace', *Sunday Times*, 27 December 1942.

Marshal Montgomery, and King George with his wife and the two princesses, Elizabeth and Margaret. The visits were certainly part of war propaganda, serving to underline the message: 'Britain can take it'. The Strand was practically the only London theatre that continued to perform throughout the V2 rocket attacks in 1944. Perhaps for that reason, the play's black humour seemed to catch a certain mood of the moment, confirming the arbitrary nature of life and death. Like other members of the cast, Miller had been given a run-of-the-play contract — and the play ran for 1337 performances in London before it was finally taken off in March 1946. It was the first of many long-running productions in which Miller was involved.

Parallel to his success on the West End stage, Miller had also made his mark as a character actor in several British feature films, a success which was all the more remarkable as, before coming to Britain, he had had little experience of film acting. His English film debut in *Let George Do It* was followed by a substantial role in the film *Squadron Leader X*, an early product of the celebrated collaboration between Michael Powell and Emeric Pressburger. The film starred Eric Portman, an actor whose fame was then at its height. Portman was among several British actors who had seen the production of *Awake and Sing*. So impressed was he by Miller's performance that he recommended him for a supporting role in his next film *Squadron Leader X*, a spy thriller produced by RKO Radio and directed by Lance Comfort. The film was highly successful, a success which the critic C. A. Lejeune attributed to the merits of Pressburger's original story: 'Mr. Pressburger, as you may have noted if you are a smart reader of credit titles, wrote the story of *49th Parallel* and *One of Our Aircraft is Missing*. His speciality is escape'.[108] *Squadron Leader X* is indeed about the attempt by a Nazi airman (played by Portman) to escape from England. Miller played the role of an Austrian grocer who is blackmailed into being an unwilling collaborator: a performance which elicited a glowing review from the American magazine *Variety* on 27 January 1943:

> The outstanding characterisation is that of a Swiss [sic] cook who is blackmailed into assisting Nazi espionage in England. Temperamentally his technique is more that of an Italian, but he nevertheless gives an especially moving performance. His name, Martin Miller, is unknown, but report has it that he is an Austrian refugee.

Miller's performance was also acclaimed by James Agate:

> I gave it as my opinion recently that the best performance in *Arsenic and Old Lace* was by a Mr. Martin Miller. In the present film easily the best performance is that of the Austrian grocer, who [...] is a Mr. Martin Miller. As somebody of the same name ran away with *Awake and Sing*, I begin to think this Mr. Martin Miller must be just about the best actor in England.[109]

Unfortunately this view can no longer be verified, since no print of *Squadron Leader X* has survived. The BFI lists it as one of the '75 most wanted films', describing it as 'missing, believed lost'.

---

108 *Observer*, 3 January 1943.
109 James Agate, 'Myself at the Pictures', *Tatler and Bystander*, 13 January 1943.

However, British film-makers were quick to endorse Agate's judgement. Over the next three years, Miller played character roles in several British films, beginning with *The Adventures of Tartu*. Produced by MGM at the Gainsborough Studios and shot mainly during July and August 1942, the film was a spy thriller, featuring the popular star Robert Donat. While it was an important production for MGM, the studio's first British production in two years, the film itself was undistinguished. It was made very much as a propaganda vehicle, in which the resistance figures were heroic and self-sacrificing and the Nazis were venal and self-serving. Miller played Dr. Novotny, the local leader of the Czech resistance, a role to be relished by an actor who had been born in what later became Czechoslovakia. Released late in 1943, the film was a successful flag-waver.

While appearing nightly on the stage of the Strand theatre throughout 1944, Miller still found time to appear in two major film productions — *English Without Tears* and *Hotel Reserve*. *English Without Tears* can be summarised in a single sentence: the niece of a British aristocrat falls in love with her butler, a story-line captured in the American title *Her Man Gilbey*. This unmistakably English whimsy managed to find parts for a few foreign actors, including Miller as 'Schmidt', a character whose relevance to the plot is tenuous, and Gerhard Hinze (under the stage-name Gerard Heinz) as a Polish officer, a role in which he was beginning to feel at home.

A striking aspect of the films in which Miller appeared — and indeed of the British film industry in wartime — is that so many of the cast were fellow-émigrés. There was one notable difference between him and them. While Miller's own film career had resulted directly from his success on stage, many of his compatriots had taken the opposite route. Confronted by a new theatre culture and a new language, they had found it easier to establish a foothold in film than in the theatre.

Remarkably, while enjoying success on mainstream stage and screen, Miller still found time to remain active at the BBC, working for the German Service and later for the separate Austrian Service, set up in 1943. He acted in numerous one-off programmes as well as several of the satirical series, notably the 'Kartenstelle' series, listed in the BBC's wartime schedules under its English title 'Daily Worries'. The programme was broadcast at roughly fortnightly intervals from May 1943 until the end of the war, following, like most successful comedy programmes, a consistent and recognisable format. Set in Vienna's *Kartenstelle für Bedarfsgegstände* [Ration Card Office for Household Necessities], the farcical proceedings usually featured the harassed official (played by Miller) and the comical Herr Mayerhofer (played by Josef Almas), whose literal interpretation of Nazi proclamations reduced them to absurdity and Miller's hapless official to complete despair. A selection of the scripts still survives in the BBC Written Archives, as well as one recording which enables the listener to savour Miller's measured delivery of bureaucratic banalities and his perfect comic timing.[110]

---

110   See Richard Dove, 'It Tickles My Viennese Humour' in *'Stimme der Wahrheit: German-Language Broadcasting by the BBC'*, Yearbook of the Research Centre for German and Austrian Exile Studies, Vol. 5, ed. by Charmian Brinson and Richard Dove (Amsterdam/New York: Rodopi, 2003), pp. 57–74.

It is remarkable that these regular broadcasts were carried out almost at the margins of his burgeoning stage and film career. Miller's wife Hannah Norbert later recalled Miller's good fortune that his BBC broadcasts were made from Bush House, the Headquarters of BBC European broadcasting, which was located only a couple of hundred yards from the Strand Theatre, where he was appearing in the long-running *Arsenic and Old Lace*. Miller would often arrive at the theatre just in time for his initial appearance at the end of the first act, with the doorman waiting in some anxiety for him to appear.[111] By the time he reached the stage door, Miller, the man of many faces, had already slipped into role as the eccentric Dr Einstein.

111   Brinson, 'The Go-Between'.

CHAPTER 13

'An Actress of Distinction and Repute': Lilly Kann

Lilly Kann finally reached London in the nick of time. Arriving on 21 August 1939, twelve days before war was declared, she was met at Victoria Station by two 'kind and helpful gentlemen' from the Jewish Refugees Committee; they took her to her accommodation at a hostel near Regents Park, where, for the first time in her life, she had to share a room with a stranger — an early introduction to the minor indignities and discomforts of life as a refugee.

Like many other refugees, she was virtually penniless, after leaving Germany with just ten Marks (approximately £4), the maximum amount émigrés were permitted to take with them. Furthermore, she had lost almost all her possessions, which were being shipped over on a German vessel that was actually on its way to London when it was ordered to return to Hamburg, as war had broken out. The incident emphasised how narrowly she herself had escaped Nazi Germany.

Like other refugees she spent 'long hours' in Bloomsbury House, where the Jewish Refugees Committee was located, and where she went regularly to collect her 'one pound a week'.[112] Faced with the immediate problem of subsistence, she began, like many other refugees, in domestic service, working briefly in the kitchen of a hostel in High Wycombe, though she was evidently ill-suited to the job:

> Mrs Lilly Kann has been with us for a fortnight. She is leaving because she does not like doing the washing up [...] She says she is not very strong and of course she needs to be here as there are twenty-two people to cook for. Mrs Kann has taken lessons in German and Viennese cooking and would be all right, I should imagine where there is a kitchen maid.[113]

As an 'enemy alien', which she had automatically become with the outbreak of war, Kann was obliged to appear before an Aliens' Tribunal which was required to assess whether she represented a risk to British security. The secretary of the local refugee committee wrote in her support:

> Miss Lilly Kann is known to me personally, having been introduced by members of our committee, and having been for ten days a guest in our

112 Kann, p. 78.
113 Letter from A. S. Bolton, Woodside Hostel, High Wycombe, 25 September 1939, Lilly Kann Papers.

house. In Germany she is an actress of distinction and repute, and exercised her profession in the Jewish theatre in Berlin up to August last. I consider her a person of integrity and feel that any consideration accorded to her by the Tribunal would be in no way abused.[114]

The tribunal agreed, placing her in the 'C' category of refugees representing no risk.

Her life as a refugee in England was for several years unsettled and insecure. A list compiled by the Aliens Section of the Metropolitan Police confirms a restless pattern of life, giving nineteen different addresses for her (mostly in London, but extending to Shropshire and Derbyshire) between 1939 and 1944.

Her professional prospects seemed bleak. Up until then, she had spent her entire life in the theatre. Now the Nazis had stolen not only her theatrical career, but the rich theatre heritage which had nurtured it — and even the very language of her livelihood. Although the major problem she faced was the language barrier, this was exacerbated by her age. When she arrived in Britain she was forty-five years old, an age at which many actresses, even today, find that their careers begin to peter out. Yet only six months after her timely escape from Germany, she was able to make her first stage appearance in London, albeit not yet in English.

She appeared in the inaugural performance at the Little Theatre of the Free German League of Culture in Belsize Park on Sunday, 24 March 1940. The evening consisted of two one-act plays by J. M. Barrie: *Der Dreihundert-Schilling Blick* (*The Twelve Pound Look*) and *Mein lieber Sohn* (*The Old Lady Shows her Medals*), translated and adapted by Fritz Gottfurcht, formerly a scriptwriter at the Berlin cabaret 'Larifari', and with stage designs by John Heartfield. The choice of J. M. Barrie for this inaugural performance may seem strange, but following his death in 1937 Barrie's reputation in Britain still far transcended his name as the author of *Peter Pan*.

The performance was attended by Sybil Thorndike, one of the League's twenty-two British patrons and a staunch friend of the refugees, who spoke briefly from the stage:

> The greatest of English actresses came on stage at the end and congratulated the actors. She had sacrificed one of her rare free evenings, had spent two hours in a tiny hall listening to a performance in a strange language and now stood embracing Lilly Kann, shaking her colleagues' hands and speaking from the fullness of her heart to them and the audience below, constantly interrupted by loud applause.[115]

This was Lilly Kann's first and last appearance at the 'Little Theatre'; shortly after, she made her debut at its Austrian counterpart, the Laterndl. Her appearance there is, at first sight, surprising, since, despite her long career on the German stage, she had never acted in Austria. The invitation to perform at the Laterndl clearly came from Martin Miller, with whom she had acted at the Jüdischer Kulturbund.

Her first appearance at the Laterndl was in Miller's production of *The Immortal*

114 Letter from the secretary of Chesham, Amersham and District Refugee Council to Aliens Tribunal, Lilly Kann Papers.
115 *Freie Deutsche Kultur*, April 1940.

Schwejk in March 1940; there were no reviews, and though the production did receive a double-page photo spread in *Picture Post*, none of the images show her in role.[116] Indeed, it is uncertain which role she played, since no cast list has survived.[117]

Following *The Immortal Schwejk* Martin Miller staged Brecht and Weill's *Dreigroschenoper*. Lilly Kann played the part of Mrs Peachum, a role she knew well, having understudied it in the original Berlin production of the play in 1928. The production had the misfortune of opening on 26 May 1940, coinciding with the British government's introduction of mass internment of 'enemy aliens', leading to the production's rapid cancellation. This cancellation did not involve any financial sacrifice for Lilly Kann. Actors at the Laterndl, as at other refugee theatres, performed unpaid. All they could hope for was a share of the box-office takings, once the costs of the production had been met, although any such payments would barely have covered the cost of attending rehearsals.

In October 1940, at the height of the Blitz, Lilly Kann left London to live in Whitchurch, a small market town in Shropshire, at the instigation of her friend Li Nolden. Kann remembered it as 'a miserable small provincial town', but it did have a public library and she set about improving her knowledge of English by reading novels and short stories, particularly those by Somerset Maugham: 'my teacher and friendly guide into the English language'.[118]

While in Whitchurch, she also wrote to Heinrich Fischer, whom she had first met during the original Berlin production of *Dreigroschenoper,* and who was then working as a writer and producer for the BBC. He sent a prompt reply, inviting her to contribute to a BBC broadcast. She borrowed the money to get to London and took part in the broadcast, the first of many.

Kann finally returned definitively to London a year after leaving and in January 1942 was even able to resume acting at the Laterndl in the revue *Here is the News*, appearing in two of the short plays which were often used to punctuate the satirical sketches of Austrian cabaret. The first of these was *Brennende Erde* [Scorched Earth], in which she played 'a German woman'; the second was *Höchste Eisenbahn* [Highest Railway], in which she played the equally representative role of 'a Jewish mother'.[119]

She was to play only one other role at the Laterndl, making a guest appearance in December 1942 in Egon Erwin Kisch's *Die Galgentoni* [Gallows Toni], directed by the Czech-born actor Arnold Marlé, who praised Kann's performance in the title role as 'perhaps the best stage performance that the refugees have witnessed here'. It was a triumphal farewell to refugee theatre; by then Kann had already made her mark on the English stage.

---

116 *Picture Post*, 27 April 1940.
117 'Über weitere Mitwirkenden keine Angaben': Erna Wipplinger, 'Österreichisches Exiltheater in Großbritannien 1938–1945' (unpublished doctoral dissertation, University of Vienna, 1984), p.108.
118 Kann, p. 100.
119 See *Zeitspiegel*, 7 February 1942.

When she had first arrived in Britain, Lilly Kann had had little hope of continuing her acting career. In a short autobiographical account from 1957, she wrote that she had arrived in London 'not dreaming that I would ever find my way to the English stage'.[120] However, an undreamed-of opportunity occurred early in 1942, when she was unexpectedly invited by Alec Clunes, the director of the Arts Theatre, to audition for the role of Bessie Berger in *Awake and Sing*.

As previously described, *Awake and Sing* is a family drama set in an apartment in the Bronx district of New York which is home to three generations of the Bergers, an impoverished Jewish immigrant family. But the Bergers are a family at war; each scene of the play is a new battle. The central figure of the drama is Bessie Berger, a plum part for any actress. Bessie is a Jewish matriarch who controls and directs her family, aiming to ensure its survival with a modicum of respectability. She pushes her daughter Hennie to marry the poor immigrant Sam Feinschreiber, who is boarding with the family, in order to provide a father for her illegitimate child. She breaks up the love affair of her son, an idealistic young man for whom life will always begin tomorrow, but whom she wishes to force into a poorly-paid job as a clerk. Also living with the Bergers is Bessie's father Jacob, a defeated idealist who has never become accustomed to the ways of the New World.

Kann knew little about the play and probably even less about the Arts Theatre. She was certainly surprised to be invited to audition for a role she had neither performed nor read, but, after a rather perfunctory audition, she was offered the part. Only much later did she learn that she had been recommended for the role by the German dramatist Hans José Rehfisch, then also exiled in London, in whose play *Razzia* [Police Raid] she had appeared some fifteen years earlier in Düsseldorf. *Awake and Sing* gave Kann her breakthrough on the English stage, but during rehearsals for the play she found herself little better off, since rehearsals were at that time still unpaid, something she had not encountered in the German theatre. She managed to survive only through further work at the BBC.

In casting Miller and Kann in their respective roles, Clunes had made a shrewd, if risky choice. Neither spoke fluent English, neither had acted before on the English-speaking stage, and Kann later admitted she had had no idea whether an English audience would even be able to understand her. They not only understood — they applauded loud and long.

The critics, starved of good plays and good acting, were equally enthusiastic. Alan Dent, in the *Sunday Times* declared that 'this is certainly one of the three best and best-acted plays in London at the moment', noting particularly the outstanding performances of Martin Miller and Lilly Kann: 'Mr. Martin Miller plays the old man with an extraordinary poignancy. [...] Best of all, Miss Lilly Kann, an actress new to this country, fulfils the mother with remarkable power and passion'.[121] The *Times* also praised Kann's 'outstanding performance', while *Theatre World* declared that 'Lilly Kann, as the dominating Jewish mother, gave a not-to-be forgotten performance of great brilliance'.[122]

120 Lilly Kann, autobiographical outline, dated 13 January 1957, Lilly Kann Papers.
121 Alan Dent, 'Paradise Ungained', *Sunday Times*, 24 May 1942.
122 *The Times*, 21 May 1942; *Theatre World*, December 1942.

However, the most perceptive review of all appeared in the *Spectator*:

> The play is dominated (whether Odets intended it or not) by the matriarch Bessie Berger, who has accepted her unhappy world on its own terms and is determined to conform to them. She dominates and directs her family. And when all her plans collapse it is with unbowed head that she retires to bed, defeated perhaps but never subdued. Lilly Kann's performance in this rather difficult part is one of the finest pieces of naturalistic acting we have seen in years.[123]

Kann drew particular admiration for her handling of the crucial scene in which, in a fit of uncontrollable rage, she breaks Jacob's treasured collection of gramophone records, a wanton action leaving him in such despair that he commits suicide. Kann herself recalled her performance in *Awake and Sing* as 'the decisive turning-point in my life in England. [...] The role was a sensational success for me. One colleague told me: "You can't open any newspaper or magazine without seeing a picture of you or a review of your performance." '[124]

The role of the dominating Jewish matriarch was (as Kann herself observed) so well suited to her talents that it might almost have been written with her in mind.[125] It was the first of several such roles she was to play on the London stage. So great was the impact of her performance that she was invited to speak to Hugh ('Binky') Beaumont, of H. M. Tennent Management, then the most influential manager and producer in West End theatre. Beaumont asked her what role she would like to play next and after some reflection she suggested the title role in *Mrs Warren's Profession*, a part she had played to great acclaim in Germany. This suggestion was, as she later acknowledged, a miscalculation: Mrs Warren was an altogether too English character to be performed on the English stage by an actress with a foreign accent.

Kann would have been well advised, while her performance in *Awake and Sing* was still fresh in the memory, to seek the services of an agent. In the course of the play's run she was approached more than once by the theatrical agent Al Parker, hoping to represent her. Parker was well-known in this field, but Kann had initially refused to sign, not fully realising the comparative importance of the theatrical agent within the English theatre system. In Germany, the actor would audition to join a particular company for a season, and it was the theatre director who decided which roles in the repertory the actor was to play and who negotiated a fee with him or her, leaving the agent to draw up the final contract. Leading actors with any theatre ensemble would 'put out feelers' at the end of a season, if they wished to move to a new theatre. The agent would probably play a bigger role in the recruitment of actors for minor roles in the company. In the British theatre, by contrast, it was more likely to be the agent who secured an audition for the actor and who negotiated their fee. In this respect, Al Parker had one crucial advantage. He had

123   Basil Wright, *Spectator*, 28 May 1942.
124   Kann, p. 99.
125   Ibid., p. 86.

gained the reputation of driving a hard bargain and of securing the maximum fee for his actors. Kann would eventually sign with his agency.[126]

As it was, she ultimately failed to capitalise on her considerable success in *Awake and Sing*. She felt that, at her age, she could not revert to playing supporting roles, because to do so would have dispelled the aura of the leading actress. In retrospect she was prepared to accept that this too was a miscalculation, acknowledging that she was by then almost fifty years old, an age which greatly limited the number of roles she could play, a number restricted still further by her accent and appearance.

In fact, it was many months before she was offered another role in the theatre, a time of great personal uncertainty, during which she struggled to support herself with occasional work at the BBC and appearances at the Players Theatre. Kann makes little mention in her memoirs of the broadcasts she made at the BBC, describing them rather dismissively as 'BBC jobs'. In fact, she appeared regularly in 'features' (i.e. short dramatic sketches) for the BBC German Service, which were transmitted to Germany as part of broadcast propaganda. Records show that she also contributed to the BBC European Service, broadcasting to occupied Europe. Such 'BBC jobs' represented, together with appearances at the Players Theatre, her only source of income.

The Players Theatre, then located in Albemarle Street, had been founded by the actor Leonard Sachs as a theatre staging Old Time Music Hall. Despite the blackout and the difficulties of travel in London, the performances always played to a packed and responsive audience. Lilly Kann remembered the evenings for their atmosphere of warmth and conviviality, an atmosphere fostered by Sachs, as a genial master of ceremonies, with his elaborate introductions of the different performers. Kann remembered performing traditional songs in English, French, and German which helped to make her a popular performer at the Players — however strange it may seem at first sight that a German performer should prove so popular at a highly traditional British theatre in the depths of war. Leonard Sachs and his wife were to become Kann's life-long friends.

While still unable to find another role in the theatre, Kann did manage to secure a foothold in British cinema, appearing in two British war films. The first was *Escape to Danger*, released in July 1943.[127] The second was *The Flemish Farm*, a conventional spy thriller, in which Kann played a 'Flemish farmwife'. The film, principally notable for music composed by Ralph Vaughan Williams, has been described more recently as a 'tolerable wartime flagwaver'.[128] While both these parts were small, they were at least credited, and comparatively well paid.

Kann finally returned to the stage in July 1943 in *Blow Your Own Trumpet* by the twenty-two-year-old Peter Ustinov. The play was produced by the Old Vic Company in association with CEMA, and directed by Michael Redgrave, opening at the Liverpool Playhouse, which the Old Vic had helped to reopen after its closure in 1940. The production ran for two weeks in Liverpool before being transferred to London, where it ran for a further two weeks at the Playhouse Theatre.

126 Cf. Kann, p. 87.
127 More recently described as 'adequate propaganda hokum' (*Halliwell*, p. 254).
128 *Halliwell*, p. 284.

FIG. 8. Lilly Kann as Mother Superior in *The Cradle Song*, London 1944
(courtesy Rachel Ormerod)

Blow Your Own Trumpet is a comedy in two acts, set in an Italian restaurant in London 'sometime during the present war'. The theatre programme also reminded the audience that 'The Booking Hall, Piccadilly Circus station, is not an Air Raid Shelter. If you want to take shelter, see list in Entrance Hall'.[129] The play itself involved the agreements and disagreements of a stage Italian family who run the restaurant and its regular customers, consisting of several stereotypical foreigners. Lilly Kann played the part of Grandmother Bossi, the oldest member of the family, who 'has something inaudible to say about everything'. On stage almost throughout the play, she was seen but not heard: if her comments were inaudible, her reactions were intended to be. James Agate, while praising 'the highly imaginative production by Michael Redgrave', concluded that 'Mr. Ustinov possesses every quality of the first-class playwright except one. He cannot think of a story'. Re-reading *Blow Your Own Trumpet* today, one can only agree that the play is not really a play. How far Lilly Kann was able to exploit the dramatic potential of her mute role is uncertain: if reviewers had any opinions, they remained as inaudible as her performance.

Kann finally managed to reach the West End stage in January 1944. She received an invitation to call on the actor and director John Gielgud who, after a brief audition, offered her a leading role in *The Cradle Song*, an early twentieth-century Spanish drama.[130] Gielgud knew the play well, having acted in an Oxford production in 1924, at the beginning of his career. A short press notice reported that 'Since then he has waited for an opportunity to direct it himself'.[131] Set in a Dominican convent, the play required a predominantly female cast, causing the same press notice to suggest that 'the production had solved the manpower shortage in actors and native dramatists by reviving this charming Spanish play'.

Gielgud's production of *The Cradle Song* opened at the Apollo Theatre on 27 January 1944, with Lilly Kann in the leading role of the Mother Prioress, and Wendy Hiller as Sister Joanna, a young novice nun. Kann played her role with a calm authority which impressed the critics. The *Sunday Times* wrote that the play 'is exquisitely acted [...] Miss Lilly Kann's Mother Prioress might have sat for Rembrandt. There is something here that is utterly satisfying', adding that 'Mr. Gielgud's production is faultless'.[132] Despite the near-perfect pitch of Gielgud's direction and sensitive performances from the entire cast, the production was not a box-office success. Kann herself blamed the play, which she considered essentially undramatic, 'a poem rather than a play', but it ran for seventy-six performances, enjoying a certain *succès d'estime*.[133]

Gielgud was clearly much impressed by Kann's performance, remaining in touch with her for some years. She for her part was always grateful for his support and encouragement, and struck by the fact that such a distinguished actor ('a prince of the English stage', as she called him) should show such kindness to another actor.

129   Theatre programme, Playhouse, London, 11 August 1943. The play ran for thirteen performances, 11–21 August 1943.
130   Gregorio and Maria Martinez-Sierra, *The Cradle Song* (London: Samuel French, 1945).
131   *Evening Standard*, 29 January 1944.
132   *Sunday Times,* 30 January 1944.
133   *The Cradle Song*, Apollo Theatre, 27 January–25 March 1944.

She recalled that he was unfailingly kind and considerate in rehearsals, and later went to great lengths to put her in touch with people of position and influence who he thought might help her career, a gesture which she always remembered.

Although she was ready to concede that the role of Bessie Berger had suited her talents perfectly, Kann attempted to resist type-casting. Following her success in *Awake and Sing*, it had been suggested that she could play only Jewish roles, a question she was asked directly by John Gielgud — and which she impressively refuted with her performance as the Mother Prioress in *The Cradle Song*. She excelled in the role of the Jewish matriarch, which she had performed in *Awake and Sing* and subsequently played again in *The Golden Door*, though she also played several domestic roles as maid or housekeeper, nurse or nanny. These were always supporting roles, but were usually those that significantly affected the action and outcome of the play.

Following *The Cradle Song*, Kann's next West End appearance was in *Tomorrow the World*, an American play which had already enjoyed a long run on Broadway.[134] In London, the play opened at the Aldwych Theatre on 30 August 1944, running for almost twelve months; the magazine *Theatre World* called it 'one of the biggest successes in Town'.[135] This success was due partly to the play's topical theme: the re-education of Emil, a German boy who is sent by his parents to live with his uncle in the USA. He has, however, been deeply indoctrinated by the Nazis. The re-education of German youth was a key element of Allied policy as the war neared its end. It was also a theme of particular significance for Kann herself and her performance as Frieda, the family's German maid, was deeply felt and well noticed: 'Miss Lilly Kann and Mr Julien Mitchell are precisely right as the German-American maid (Miss Kann at her most expansive) and a shifty janitor', declared the critic of the *Observer*, while *The Times* agreed that Mitchell and Kann played minor parts admirably.[136]

German air raids on London continued during the final months of the war. Kann remembered that when the air raid alert sounded she would frequently leave the theatre and walk out onto the street; on one occasion she encountered Martin Miller, sitting on the steps of the nearby Strand Theatre, where he was appearing in *Arsenic and Old Lace*. Their paths were soon to cross again. Meanwhile, *Tomorrow the World* continued its long run through the final months of the war, proceeding seamlessly into peace-time.

134 *Tomorrow the World*, by James Gow and Arnaud d'Usseau, opened on Broadway, 14 April 1943; a film version was released in December 1944.
135 *Theatre World*, October 1944. The production ran from 30 August 1944 to 11 August 1945.
136 *Observer*, 3 September 1944; *The Times*, 31 August 1944.

ENTR'ACTE

CHAPTER 14

Calling Germany:
Lucie Mannheim at the BBC

Early in 1940 Lucie Mannheim's career changed direction, as she joined the German Service of the BBC, a move that effectively put her stage career on hold: in fact it was several years before she appeared again on the London stage. The BBC German Service had begun in 1938 as an ad hoc arrangement for broadcasting to Nazi Germany at the height of the Munich crisis, but it soon developed into a permanent service, which was responsible in wartime for broadcasting propaganda to 'the enemy', becoming, particularly after the fall of France in May 1940, a crucial part of the British war effort.

Early in the war, the government took effective control of broadcasting and the BBC. It exercised control through the Political Warfare Executive (PWE), a clandestine section of the Foreign Office, working under the cover of the non-secret Political Intelligence Department. The basis of broadcasts to Germany was the weekly policy directive, drawn up by Richard Crossman of PWE in line with intelligence information and German press and radio reporting. The directive usually stipulated both particular topics and the way in which they should be treated.

Broadcasting to 'the enemy' was far from straightforward. There were various technical problems, including difficulties of reception in some parts of Germany. Austria, for example, though now part of the German Reich, was on the very margin of audibility, according to advice given to Sir Robert Vansittart at the Foreign Office in 1940.[1] The technical difficulties of reception were magnified by enemy jamming. Even where reception was good, there were other factors which deterred potential listeners, above all the severe penalties facing anyone caught listening to 'enemy stations' like the BBC, an offence that could be punished by imprisonment or even death. People did listen nonetheless, but the typical listener might well be listening at low volume or with their head under a blanket.

During the early months of the war Mannheim played several leading roles in radio drama, often roles she had already played in the theatre, such as Nora in Ibsen's *A Doll's House*, which was broadcast on the Home Service at the beginning

---

1   See Charmian Brinson, 'Patrick Smith bei den Österreichern: The BBC Austrian Service in Wartime', in *Stimme der Wahrheit*, ed. by Brinson & Dove, p. 3.

of 1940 and for which she was paid a standard fee of 35 guineas (£36.75). She also took part in a broadcast of Act 1 of Shaw's *Arms and the Man*, receiving the same fee, as well as expenses for third-class rail travel to Manchester in order to make the recording. Mannheim was a versatile actress who had also played comedy parts on the German stage. In April 1940, she played the title role in *Ninotchka,* a radio adaptation of the Hollywood film in which Greta Garbo had famously made her comedy debut. All three plays were broadcast in 'Curtain Up', a regular part of the drama output of the BBC Home Service.

Although Mannheim was shortly to become more involved in propaganda, she continued to perform in radio drama throughout the war: in 1942 she was invited to play Hilde Wangel in a radio version of Ibsen's *The Master Builder.* The role of Hilde Wangel was written for a woman younger than Mannheim then was, but this was no impediment to casting in a radio play. The fact that she was the first choice for the part is both a tribute to her acting abilities and an acknowledgement of her long-standing efforts to introduce British audiences to Ibsen and Strindberg.

In the same year, she played Sophie de Courvoisier, the leading role in Romain Rolland's *The Game of Love and Death*, already known to London audiences through its West End run some years earlier. The radio version, aired in December 1942, was produced by Val Gielgud, head of drama at the BBC who also chose Mannheim to play the leading role: proof, if any were needed, of her professional standing.

Mannheim was well aware that she was acting in a non-visual medium, and anxious to realise the full potential of her role. In a later letter to the drama booking manager, she asked him to send her in advance the script for a forthcoming drama production: 'I am so utterly lost, when I have to read the part in the first rehearsal, without having looked at it before. English is still a difficult language for me'.[2] Mannheim's request shows that she was well aware of the increased importance of language in a non-visual medium, but it is also a comment on the practice of some radio producers, noted elsewhere by Lilly Kann, of letting the actor see the script only shortly before they were due to perform it. It also confirms her relative unease with English as a language of performance.

Long before then, in fact, she had moved the main focus of her work to the BBC German Service, which she had joined early in 1940, at a time of its rapid expansion, and continued to work for until 1946. She had an excellent speaking voice, which would have served well as an announcer/newsreader, but women were not then considered acceptable in such roles, the prevailing opinion being that they lacked the required gravitas and authority. She was however chosen to read various talk scripts, which provided commentary on the news, for example a so-titled 'Dream Talk' (subject unknown) written by the German author Grete Fischer which was broadcast on 13 August 1940.[3]

In the first few months of the war, Mannheim was, like other refugees, distracted by questions of nationality. Having failed to apply for naturalisation before the

2   Lucie Mannheim to Sidney Attwood, drama booking manager, 10 October 1944. See Lucie Mannheim, Contributor file, BBC WAC, RCONT 1, Lucie Mannheim.

3   See Jennifer Taylor, 'Grete Fischer: Outside Writer for the BBC', in *'Stimme der Wahrheit'*, ed. by Brinson & Dove, pp. 43–57.

outbreak of hostilities, she had automatically become an 'enemy alien': a precarious status, particularly after the government implemented its policy of internment in 1940. In fact, Mannheim, became a 'British subject' early in 1941 through her marriage to the English actor Marius Goring, who was already her partner in the theatre. Goring was thirteen years her junior, but it was he who was the guiding influence on her career in the war years.

The question must arise whether this was, like some other marriages at this time, a marriage of convenience, intended to give Mannheim British nationality, but it seems unlikely that was the main purpose. Goring had divorced his first wife in order to marry Mannheim and might well have married her earlier, if he had not been obliged to wait for his divorce to come through. It was not a short-lived marriage, lasting thirty-five years and ending only with Mannheim's death in 1976; only after that did Goring marry for a third time.

Goring became a key figure in British wartime propaganda, joining the BBC as head of German features in September 1941. An actor of charm and conviction, he is now best remembered for his roles in various films made by the legendary partnership of Michael Powell and Emeric Pressburger, most notably *A Matter of Life and Death* (1946) and *The Red Shoes* (1948), but he had made his mark on stage during the 1930s, performing a variety of Shakespearean roles with the Old Vic, including Romeo (to Peggy Ashcroft's Juliet), Macbeth, and Feste in *Twelfth Night*. Goring was a fluent speaker of French and German who had also acted in Germany, acquiring a first-hand knowledge of European drama that most of his stage contemporaries lacked, qualities which had drawn him towards Mannheim. He was also a budding director who, as we have seen, had directed her in *A Doll's House*, winning critical plaudits but failing to attract audiences in sufficient numbers. Even as an actor, Goring was anxious to contribute to the British war effort. During 1940, he acted in *Pastor Hall*, a British film version of an anti-Nazi play by Ernst Toller, in which he played the role of a Nazi opportunist — the first of several such roles.

Early in 1941 Goring joined the army, serving briefly as a soldier before being seconded in September to the BBC German Service. As well as regular news bulletins, the German Service had also begun broadcasting so-called 'features'. These were dramatic sketches or series, usually of a satirical nature, which were introduced to add colour and variety to the basic diet of news and commentary — and which, as already stated, provided a rich source of employment for German-speaking actors. Goring was appointed head of the features section, replacing the German actor Walter Rilla, an appointment that clearly signalled the government's determination to bring propaganda to Germany under its own immediate control. In his new post, Goring feared that his name, although perfectly English, might be confused with that of Nazi leader Hermann Goering; while he kept his own name internally at the BBC, he took the precaution of broadcasting to Germany under the pseudonym of Charles Richardson. Mannheim indeed took part in a short series of programmes in December 1942, listed as 'Discussions with Charles Richardson', in which she and Goring discussed current political issues.

Mannheim was also heard occasionally in the feature series 'Kurt und Willi', which became one of the legendary feature programmes of the wartime German Service. The sketches, containing frequent reference to political events, contrasted the politically gullible schoolmaster Kurt Krüger with the cynical Willi Schimanski, an official in the Ministry of Propaganda — the former willing to believe almost everything and the latter knowing too much to believe anything at all. The programme was essentially a dialogue: in fact early episodes of the series were subtitled 'a propaganda dialogue'. Mannheim acted occasionally on the programme, in the role of Willi's secretary, though only on special occasions, such as 'Kurt and Willi on Hitler's Birthday Celebrations'.[4]

While Mannheim had found success in London as a dramatic actress, her popularity in Germany had rested equally on her performances as a singer in cabaret and musical theatre and it was particularly this side of her talent which the BBC now set out to exploit more fully. The German Service had begun life as a spoken word programme, but like other sections of the BBC, it began increasingly to use music as an introduction or accompaniment to speech. In 1940 it commissioned the composer Mischa Spoliansky to write songs with German lyrics which could be used for propaganda purposes. As a Russian émigré, Spoliansky had lost no time in leaving Berlin in 1933. Arriving in Britain the same year, he had quickly made a name as a film composer, writing for example, the score for the film *Sanders of the River*, including the songs so memorably performed by Paul Robeson. The songs he wrote for inclusion in German Service broadcasts in 1941, such as 'Wir fahren immer hin und her' [We're Always Going To and Fro] and 'Heim ins Reich' [Home to the Reich], were sung by Lucie Mannheim, ironically reuniting her, however tenuously, with the audiences who had once lionised her on the Berlin stage. According to one source, they were 'very successful with listeners and were broadcast frequently'.[5]

These were the first of many songs that Mannheim sang for broadcast to 'the enemy'. In March 1943, in a feature directed by Marius Goring, she sang a selection of familiar German songs, including renderings of the popular wartime songs 'Lilli Marleen' and 'Es geht alles vorüber' [Everything Passes].[6] The lyrics of 'Everything Passes' were ostensibly the feelings of a young soldier thinking of his girl back home, but in 1943 could equally be taken to apply to the war — or to the Führer and the Third Reich:

> Everything passes
> There's an end to it, okay
> For every December
> Is followed by May.

4 Broadcast on 25 April 1944. See BBC WAC, RCONT I, Lucie Mannheim.

5 Toby Thacker, 'Liberating German Musical Life', in *Stimme der Wahrheit*, ed. by Brinson & Dove, pp. 83–84. He presumably means that they were well received by German emigrés in Britain, since there was no reliable way of checking on their reception in Germany itself, although such questions *were* later asked during the interrogation of German prisoners of war.

6 'Es geht alles vorüber', written by the operetta composer Fred Raymond in 1942 and sung by Lalle Anderson, was a popular song used to sustain military morale in Germany.

'Everything Passes' was broadcast several times on the German Service, but not every song Mannheim had to sing was so easy, or so easy on the ear. Other songs such as 'Lied der S.S. Brigaden' [Song of the SS Brigades], highlighted the aggression and brutality of the SS or other German units; it was sung in a feature produced by Julius Gellner and broadcast on 28 May 1942. An internal note on this transmission in Mannheim's file gives some indication of its structure: 'Miss Mannheim sang an extremely difficult political song which was interspersed with spoken comment. The production was so difficult that two rehearsals were necessary'. A further programme, entitled simply 'Terror', earned a similar comment: 'Miss Mannheim took part in the above mentioned feature and sang a song to conclude the feature', once more stating that 'this was a rather difficult production' which required further rehearsal.

May 1942 was a busy month, in which Mannheim also appeared in a series of six programmes entitled 'Germany Awakes', a pointed reference to the Nazi election slogan 'Deutschland erwache!' [Germany Awake!]. The programmes were produced by Goring, but what Mannheim said or sang is not recorded. Propaganda to 'the enemy' continually developed, following the course of the war itself. As the Russian campaign proceeded, reaching stalemate and then German retreat, there were regular programmes aimed at young soldiers and their families. Mannheim was heard, for example, in features such as 'He Died for the Führer' and 'The Girl You Left Behind You', as well as others, like 'German Casualties' or 'Casualties in Russia', aiming to exploit the appalling losses suffered by German forces there. Such broadcasts were unable of course to reach Russia itself, but the threat of being posted to the Eastern front was used regularly in BBC news and feature programmes as a bogey to frighten German soldiers in the West. Mannheim played a regular part in such programmes, usually produced by Goring or by Julius Gellner, the German theatre director whose work for the Old Vic was described elsewhere.

Despite the intensification of propaganda in German Service broadcasts, Mannheim also found time to play occasional dramatic parts. In 1942, she was heard in Goethe's tragedy *Egmont*, enacting the Dutch struggle for freedom from Spanish rule: a historical play evidently chosen for its contemporary relevance. Mannheim played the leading female role as Egmont's lover Klärchen who, after committing suicide over his impending execution, returns during the final scene, appearing to Egmont in a dream as an allegory of freedom.

On 6 June 1942 Mannheim took part in a fifteen-minute German feature programme to mark the occasion of 'Thomas Mann's Birthday' (his sixty-seventh), produced by Goring, who made the comment on Mannheim's file that she 'took a very important and difficult part in the above feature programme', though somewhat frustratingly no details of the part were given. Such literary occasions were infrequent, but on 2 July 1943, she gave a 'Recital of Rilke Songs', also produced by Goring, though once again the file gives no details of the programme. She also read a Christmas poem (title unknown) which was transmitted on Christmas Day 1943.

Mannheim's crowning achievement came in March 1943, when she first performed an anti-Hitler parody of the internationally popular 'Lili Marleen'. The original song had had an extraordinary rise to popularity. When the Germans occupied Yugoslavia, Radio Belgrade became the German forces radio station, its broadcasts heard by troops from the Russian front to North Africa. 'Lili Marleen' was played frequently, the sentimental lyrics and haunting refrain proving so popular with German soldiers in Rommel's Afrika Korps that it became the signature tune for the regular evening programme broadcast to troops in the front line. The song quickly crossed the battle lines and was adopted by the British soldiers of the Eighth Army before being taken up by soldiers of other countries, becoming the most popular song of the entire Second World War.

The BBC quickly turned the song's universal appeal to propaganda advantage. Lucie Mannheim was asked to sing a parody version with anti-Hitler lyrics which was first broadcast on the German Service in March 1943 and repeated thereafter. It was clearly aimed at undermining the morale of the very German soldiers who so loved the song, aiming to encourage disaffection and even desertion:

> Perhaps you'll die in Russia
> Perhaps in Africa
> But somewhere die you must
> For that's the Führer's will.

According to BBC estimates in 1944, there were between ten and fifteen million listeners to BBC broadcasts in Germany: how many heard Mannheim's subversive version of 'Lili Marleen' can only be a matter for speculation.

The original version of the song remained popular after the war, being recorded, and frequently performed, by both Vera Lynn and Marlene Dietrich, recordings which still survive today. Fortunately, Mannheim's performance of the anti-Hitler parody has also survived and can still be seen in the short documentary *The True Story of Lili Marlene* [sic]. Made in 1944 by the Crown Film Unit and directed by the leading documentary film-maker Humphrey Jennings, the film is a documentary only in name. It is first and foremost a propaganda film, produced by the Ministry of Information. The song's story is narrated by Marius Goring, who strikes a suitable note of propaganda by describing 'Lili Marlene' as 'the song of the Eighth Army', dubbing it 'a trophy of war'. The film does feature Lale Andersen, singing the song that made her famous — but by deliberate contrast it also features Lucie Mannheim's performance of the anti-Hitler parody, sung with fierce conviction:

> The Führer is a scoundrel
> As we can clearly see
> He turns children into orphans
> And women into widows.

In the final refrain, Mannheim abandons the haunting melody altogether to shout her final message; 'String him up, the Führer | Hang him from the lantern'. While it is impossible to judge the effect of Mannheim's anti-Hitler version of *Lilli Marlene*, it certainly represents her most forceful contribution to the British war effort.[7]

---

7   *The True Story of Lili Marlene* is available online, <https://www.youtube.com/watch?v=AopClfB-5rg&list=PLyeO6OXuQoocUf6bBigvx4wpXSpItiv8R> [accessed 11 February 2016]. Mannheim sings the anti-Hitler version in English, confirming of course that the film was made for a British

In 1943, after an absence of almost five years, Mannheim returned to the British cinema. Her resumption of film acting no doubt offered a break from the inherent limitations of radio propaganda, but it was really no more than a move sideways. British film-making during the war years was strongly influenced by the Ministry of Information, which was determined that cinema, as the most important medium of popular entertainment, should be used to help maintain morale on the home front. Each of the three feature films Mannheim was involved in, beginning with *Yellow Canary*, contained elements of wartime propaganda.

Released in October 1943, *Yellow Canary* is an entertaining piece of spy fiction: a good example of popular entertainment as propaganda. Herbert Wilcox directed a strong cast, featuring the popular star Anna Neagle (who was also his wife) as a socialite suspected of being a Nazi sympathiser, but who, it turns out, is really a British agent. In fact, nobody in the film is quite what they seem. There was a strong émigré presence in the cast, including the German actor Albert Lieven as Jan Orlock, a Nazi spy, and Mannheim as Madame Orlock, Jan's mother, who is ostensibly an invalid, confined to a wheel chair, but is in fact the active head of a Nazi spy ring. Lieven had been a film actor in Germany in the 1920s and early 1930s, surviving the end of the silent era and making the transition to sound films. Although not a Jew, he had been forced into exile because of his reluctance to divorce his Jewish wife. He had made his debut on the British stage in June 1937 as Prince Ernest in Laurence Housman's play *Victoria Regina*. Later, on tour, he had taken the more substantial role of Prince Albert. During the war he had, like Mannheim, joined the BBC German Service, lending his voice to the anti-Hitler campaign as an announcer. Their appearance in *Yellow Canary* was the only time they ever acted together.

In the same year, Mannheim also appeared in *Hotel Reserve*, co-starring with James Mason, with whom she had first starred five years earlier in *The High Command*. She played the role of Madame Koch, the proprietor of the hotel around which the action revolves, while other émigrés, such as Frederick Valk and Martin Miller, also played leading roles. Valk played Paul Heimberger, a member of the anti-Nazi resistance in Germany who has escaped to France. The plot hinges on a short, but crucial scene in which a suspicious conversation between Heimberger and Madame Koch is overheard — and misunderstood, leading to an action-packed denouement. It was not the first time that Mannheim had appeared with Frederick Valk. They had first acted together at the Prussian State Theatre in 1929, but this remains their only film scene together, and the only record of their careers intersecting in Britain.

In 1944 Mannheim appeared in *Tawny Pipit*, which can best be described as a *very* British war film. It was directed by Bernard Miles, who also played a leading role as the retired army officer, Colonel Barton-Barrington. The plot revolves around the discovery by a former RAF pilot that a pair of tawny pipits, a breed of bird rarely seen in England, are nesting beside a field which is due to be ploughed up for

audience, whereas the original transmission in the German Service had naturally been sung in German.

agricultural use, a proposal that unites the whole village in opposition. The film's propaganda value lay in its portrayal of a close-knit village community acting in defence of the English countryside, a message reinforced through the camera-work, which included location shots in the Cotswolds.

There was also a significant sub-plot, paying tribute to the heroism of the Red Army, as personified by Corporal Bokalova, a Russian sniper making a goodwill tour of Britain — a role played by Lucie Mannheim. The fiery British colonel presents her with his treasured Browning automatic rifle, making a powerful speech about some foreigners (obviously including Mannheim) being 'jolly good chaps'. Propaganda is of necessity short-lived. Such fulsome affirmation of the Soviet Union as a war ally quickly became an anachronism, abandoned after 1945 in favour of the new orthodoxies of the Cold War.

ACT IV

Five Actors in Search of a Stage

CHAPTER 15

Post-war Developments in
British Theatre and Film

In the aftermath of war, the British theatre was still in a state of decline. Freed from the blackout and the threat of enemy bombing, London theatres switched back to late evening performances and began to play to full houses. But there was no immediate recovery: the scars of war ran too deep. About a fifth of London's theatres had been destroyed or severely damaged by enemy bombing, others had become redundant and had been closed or converted into cinemas. In addition, some theatre management companies had gone out of business, notably the Stoll Theatre Company which owned several London theatres and was sold in 1942 after the death of its founder Sir Oswald Stoll. It was acquired by the Prince Littler organisation which already controlled numerous London theatres.

Along with a lack of theatre space, there was a shortage of actors, many of whom were still serving in the forces or touring with ENSA, a shortage which provided continuing opportunities for foreign actors. And most significantly there was a dearth of new dramatists. It is therefore scarcely surprising that the end of the war did not bring any immediate surge of recovery. Indeed, fewer productions were staged in the West End during 1945 than in 1944 and almost exactly the same as in 1941, when the country had faced a serious threat of invasion. Theatre activity did increase thereafter: by 1948 this figure had almost doubled.[1]

Among those theatres badly damaged during the war was the Old Vic. The company itself had returned to London in 1944, performing at the New Theatre until its historic building was ready to re-open in 1950. The two seasons which bridged the end of the war, 1944–1946, when the company played under the direction of Laurence Olivier and Ralph Richardson, have now become a legendary part of the company's history. In fact, in the early post-war years, Shakespeare was in the ascendant, continuing to play the role of national dramatist he had assumed during the war.

Meanwhile, the commercial West End theatre continued much as before, its repertoire consisting largely of plays offering the best guarantee of success at the box-office: comedies, farces, and 'whodunnits'. 'Straight drama' was dominated

---

1 Figures of West End productions were obtained from J. P. Wearing, *The London Stage 1940–1949* (Metuchen, NJ, & London: Scarecrow, 1991).

by the fashion for the naturalistic 'well-made play', a convention with which such serious dramatists as Shaw and Ibsen had had to compromise. However, the escapist entertainment of Coward and Novello was still popular. Coward's *Present Laughter*, first produced in 1943, was revived for a much longer run in 1947, while his *Peace in Our Time*, depicting the alternative reality of a Britain occupied by Nazi Germany, was also staged in the same year. Meanwhile, Novello had renewed success in 1945 with *Perchance to Dream*, starring himself, which ran for over a thousand performances, and *King's Rhapsody* (1949) in which he also appeared, indeed collapsing and dying shortly after completing a performance of the play in 1951. Both men have a continuing presence in the West End: in 2005 the Strand Theatre was re-named the Novello and a year later, the Albery (originally the New) Theatre became the Noel Coward Theatre.

The most striking change during the early post-war years was the arrival of the American musicals which were to dominate the West End stage over the next decade and a half. The first of these, *Oklahoma*, opened at the Drury Lane Theatre in April 1947, earning rave reviews and playing to full houses for well over a year. Hard on its heels came *Annie Get Your Gun*, which opened at the Coliseum in June 1947, and ran for even longer, followed by *Brigadoon* (1949), *Carousel* (1950), and *South Pacific* (1951). Their success became a financial prerequisite of the survival of the West End theatre.

There was one other growing trend. The continued post-war activity of CEMA, which in 1946 was renamed the Arts Council, reaffirmed the idea of public subsidy of the arts, not least theatre. More specifically, it underwrote the production at smaller London theatres, like the Arts and the Lyric, Hammersmith, of European classics by Chekhov, Ibsen, and Strindberg, which might otherwise have been commercially unviable. Chekhov proved particularly popular with post-war British audiences: there were, for example, three different productions of *The Cherry Orchard* in 1948.[2] Samuel Beckett also proved surprisingly popular: *Waiting For Godot*, the first play of Beckett's to be produced in London, opened at the Arts Theatre in August 1955, directed by the twenty-four-year-old Peter Hall. The translation was Beckett's own English version of his original French text. At the time, British theatre was still subject to censorship by the Office of the Lord Chamberlain, which insisted — much to Beckett's amazement — on several linguistic omissions and changes; the word 'erection' had to be removed, the name 'Fartov' was replaced by 'Popov' and so on. The early reviews were mostly scathing, but the atmosphere changed completely on the following Sunday, when the influential critics Kenneth Tynan and Harold Hobson both championed the play, turning it into a cult success. Less than two years later, Beckett's one-act *Endgame* was actually premiered in a French-language production in London (at the Royal Court Theatre). But the so-called Theatre of the Absurd did not take London by storm.[3] Ionesco's *The Bald Prima Donna*, for example, though written in 1950, did not reach London until 1958 and

2 These were at the New Theatre, with Edith Evans as Madame Ranevskaya, the Aldwych Theatre, starring Googie Withers, and the Arts Theatre with Daphne Slater.

3 The term was coined by the critic Martin Esslin in his book *The Theatre of the Absurd*, published in 1961.

was then dismissed by Tynan, who, as a recent convert to Brecht, sought to compare Ionesco unfavourably to the work of his new modern master. It is questionable how far such modernist plays helped to provide suitable parts for foreign actors.

Even without the war, theatre would have faced increasing competition from other forms of entertainment, notably cinema. During the war, the cinema had become by far the most popular public entertainment, a position it only consolidated in the post-war years.[4] In fact, the post-war British film industry enjoyed a brief Golden Age, lasting roughly a decade, as film production expanded and cinema admissions increased, before both went into decline, as television began to eclipse cinema as the dominant medium of popular entertainment.

Many films of this period were routine spy thrillers, or costume dramas, calculated to relieve the drabness of post-war reality. Between 1945 and 1955, however, a number of outstanding British films were produced, including David Lean's *Brief Encounter* and *Oliver Twist*, Powell and Pressburger's *A Matter of Life and Death* and *The Red Shoes*, and Carol Reed's *The Third Man*, while Ealing Studios produced a succession of celebrated comedies, ranging from *Kind Hearts and Coronets* to *Passport to Pimlico*. In the early 1950s, the industry began to produce a series of war movies such as *The Cruel Sea* and *The Dam Busters*. Not all British films were of such high quality, let alone originality; some were low-cost productions, made to satisfy the British film quota, which stipulated that cinemas should show a certain percentage of British films.[5]

Nonetheless, even such 'quota quickies' provided lucrative employment in a notoriously unreliable profession. The trends and fortunes of the British entertainment industry in the post-war decade helped to shape the careers of many actors. The spate of war films, for example, ensured a number of 'foreign accent roles'. Frederick Valk appeared (in an uncredited role) in *A Matter of Life and Death*, and as the camp *Kommandant* in *The Colditz Story*, Gerard Heinz played a Polish ship's captain in *The Cruel Sea*, while *The Third Man*, set against the atmospheric ruins of post-war Vienna, featured various German-speaking actors in uncredited (and non-speaking) roles, including Lilly Kann and Martin Miller. Even the Ealing comedies, internationally recognised as the face of British cinema, offered a few 'foreign accent' parts. A relatively small number of Austrian and German actors, perhaps as many as fifty, became part of this post-war boom, making a career on the British screen which they could scarcely have imagined five or six years earlier.

Cinema admissions reached a peak in 1950, before beginning to fall away in the face of further changes in the entertainment industry. In 1953 the coronation of Queen Elizabeth II was televised by the BBC, creating the first mass audience for a public event on television. This beginning was consolidated the following year with the passing of the Television Act which established commercial television in Britain, in direct competition with the BBC. The first commercial broadcasts were made in 1955, expanding the growing audience for television which superseded cinema as the dominant medium of mass entertainment, sending cinema audiences into decline.

4 See Angus Calder, *The People's War* (London: Pimlico, 1992), p. 367.
5 The British screen quota was started in 1927 through the Cinematograph Films Act.

The rise of television also had a profound effect on the theatre, hastening its post-war decline. Falling audiences and rising maintenance costs forced many provincial theatres to close. Some were converted to other uses, becoming bingo or dance halls; others were simply demolished, often in the course of 'urban redevelopment'. Theatre management companies clearly recognised the competition posed by television: the leading London theatre impresario, Prince Littler, also became a major shareholder in Associated Television. Although the West End theatre played on during the 1950s, it did so against the background of an ever more precarious financial situation.

CHAPTER 16

Gerhard Hinze:
Alias Gerard Heinz

Gerhard Hinze never commented publicly on his reasons for staying in Britain, though they were clearly a mixture of the personal and the political. By 1945 his personal life had changed with the possibility that Joan Rodker and their son Ernest could rejoin him. When she finally returned to London in 1947, she certainly hoped to be reunited with him. Hinze eventually preferred to live apart, though Special Branch, which continued to keep him under surveillance, noted that he 'still contributes to the maintenance of his son', with whom he also kept regular contact.[6]

However, the main reason he chose to remain in Britain undoubtedly lay in his faltering political commitment. According to Hans Flesch, who got to know him well in the months after the war, Hinze's basic political convictions remained unchanged, though he had lost faith in the Communist Party as the best vehicle to achieve them. Joan Rodker confirmed that he was no longer a committed communist: 'He just wanted a quiet life. I called him a traitor to the cause'.[7] MI5 later noted, citing an unidentified source, that 'Gerhard Hinze [...] is now telling everyone that he has changed his political views and is now an anti-Communist'.[8]

There were also professional reasons for Hinze's decision. His early success on the London stage offered him the chance of making a post-war career there, an opportunity not available to many of his fellow-exiles. If the difficulties confronting a German-speaking actor in post-war Britain were considerable, they may have seemed less daunting than the prospect of returning to a country which was materially and morally in ruins. However, he was torn by divided loyalties: in turning his back on his native country, he was also losing the comrades who had shared his exile.

Hinze's post-war career was made initially on the London stage, but he went on to play numerous film and television roles. In 1946 he changed his stage name to Gerard Heinz, the Home Office raising no objections to his adoption of the

6 See extract from Special Branch report to MI5, TNA, KV2/2365/ 81a.
7 Conversation with Joan Rodker, 5 August 2009.
8 MI5 source report, 4 March 1950, TNA, KV2/2365/82a.

name 'for professional purposes'.[9] Two years later he became a British citizen.[10] By the end of the war, Hinze had secured a firm foothold on the London stage. In the course of 1945 he appeared in two further productions: as Dr Gerard in Agatha Christie's *Appointment With Death*, at the Piccadilly Theatre, and as Kurt Sigrist in *The Shouting Dies*, at the Lyric, Hammersmith. However, despite this apparently smooth transition to the English stage, the second act of his career was fundamentally different from the first, involving both a change of language and of theatre culture. In other respects too, the second act represented a clean break with the first. Up to 1945 he had placed his career at the service of his political ideals; after 1945 he pursued a more conventional career, in which politics was no longer centre stage.

His new career was of course shaped by performing in a new language, one in which he would never attain the perfection of his German stage diction. Ernest Rodker confirmed that his father spoke English with a slight accent, though when he had actually learned English is something of a mystery. Joan Rodker recalled that during their time in the Soviet Union and even after he rejoined her in Britain, their common language was German. The transcript of his interview with the Aliens Tribunal confirms that by the time of his return from Canada he spoke English competently, if rather slowly. Indeed the letters he sent Joan from internment in Canada, penned in his own small and meticulous handwriting, were all written in English, a language used for reasons of censorship. By the time of his appearance in *Flare Path* in mid-1942, he was obviously well able to deliver stage lines, even turning his accent to his own advantage. However, acting in a new language inevitably limited the range of parts available to him: he was often restricted to 'foreign accent' roles, a form of type-casting which affected all foreign actors on the British stage. Language was not the only difference. The second act of his career took place within a new theatre culture. The West End theatre was commercially driven, offering a relatively conventional repertoire. A brief examination of London theatre productions in 1945–1946 reveals little evidence of experimental theatre or of plays with a social or political theme.[11]

Some of the post-war productions in which Gerard Heinz appeared were mediocre, even for the West End, although his performances often won praise. Agatha Christie's *Appointment With Death*, for example, drew the comment: 'all the polish of the acting and the production cannot disguise the artificiality of the characters', though 'Gerard Hinze' was said to 'prose away happily as a mad psychiatrist', a profession then always cast as a 'continental' role.[12] Ten years later, he was to return to the West End in another Christie play, *Verdict,* in which he played yet another psychiatrist, a role which had by then already become a stage cliché.

However, there were also opportunities for more demanding roles, though mainly

---

9   See letter from Home Office (Nationality Division) to Hinze, 4 June 1946, TNA, KV2/2365, no. 76a.

10   The certificate of naturalisation, dated 8 September 1948, was granted to 'Mr. Gerhard Hinze, known as Gerard Heinz', TNA, KV2/2365/78a.

11   London theatre productions for 1945–50 are listed, for example, in *Who's Who in the Theatre*.

12   *The Times*, 2 April 1945.

at smaller 'try-out' theatres testing productions for the West End. In October 1945, for example, he made his first post-war stage appearance in *The Shouting Dies* by the American writer Ronda Keane at the Lyric, Hammersmith. The plot concerned a soldier returning to a small American town — only to find that his rival in love is a committed Nazi. Hinze was outstanding in the role of the Nazi, but the play itself was found wanting: 'A play of good intentions but of less substantial achievement, it is acted simply and well by Mr Gerard Hinze and Mr John Slater, as the rivals'.[13]

A year later Hinze — or Gerard Heinz, as he had now become — appeared at the Embassy Theatre in *The Day of Glory,* a play by the popular novelist H. E. Bates, enacting the impact of war on the individual. It portrays a single day of action as it affects the family of a young and successful fighter pilot. Though written during the war, the play was not performed until 1946. Heinz played the part of Pilot Officer Radwanski, reprising the role of a Polish RAF pilot he had played in *Flare Path*, though without the same success. *The Day of Glory* did not transfer to the West End, a fact the author himself attributed to post-war indifference to the play's wartime theme.

In March 1948 Heinz appeared in John van Druten's play *I Remember Mama,* produced at the Aldwych Theatre. Adapted from Kathryn Forbes's novel, *Mama's Bank Account,* the play portrayed, in a series of short vignettes, the ups and downs of a Norwegian immigrant family in the 1910s in San Francisco, offering various character roles that might have been written with émigré actors in mind. Hinze was cast as 'Papa', acting alongside his compatriots Frederick Valk and Lilly Kann.

The play had been a resounding success on Broadway, opening in October 1944, and running for 713 performances with a cast that included Mady Christians as 'Mama' and Marlon Brando, making his Broadway debut, as 'Nels'. In view of the success of the Broadway production and the presence of Mady Christians, reprising her leading role, the producers must have anticipated, and the actors must have hoped, that the play would have a long run in London, but it did not, closing after only fifty-four performances.

The reason for this relative failure lay partly in the play's lack of dramatic structure — one critic described it as 'a charming play with no plot'[14] — and partly in the subject-matter itself: American audiences identified far more readily with the immigrant experience than British audiences. Reviewing the play in terms which are eloquent of post-war British perceptions, Harold Hobson seems to have foreseen why it ultimately failed:

> The heart of the play is a colony of foreigners. But to Englishmen and to Americans, foreigners come with a very different impact [...] Every American knows and values some foreign family. Every American is, in some sense himself a foreigner. Consequently, to an American audience, this kindly crowd of Norwegian Hansons has an emotional appeal that an Englishman can only vaguely appreciate. [...] In London then, *I Remember Mama* has to meet the difficulty that it is hard to be moved by the recollection of what one hasn't experienced.[15]

13   *Observer,* 7 October 1945. The play ran from 5 October to 3 November 1945.
14   W. A. Darlington, *Daily Telegraph,* 2 March 1948.
15   Harold Hobson, 'Temps perdu', *Sunday Times,* 7 March 1948.

FIG. 9. Gerard Heinz in the 1950s (courtesy Ernest Rodker)

Hobson's judgement proved correct. While the New York production had run for two years, its London counterpart closed after less than two months. For Heinz this was certainly a disappointment, though his role as Papa, 'who for some reason never stops smiling, however bad the news' was certainly overshadowed by an exuberant performance from Frederick Valk, as the redoubtable Uncle Chris: 'the uncle of beetling brow and bullying tongue'.[16]

In his new persona, Heinz also played light comedy, something he would hardly have countenanced during the first act of his career. This transition was not easy. His first appearance in comedy in the West End was in 1947 as Laszlo Vertes in *Honour and Obey*, by the American writer Hagar Wilde, together with Ursula Howells, as a fractious fiancée. Unfortunately, the critics savaged the play. The *Daily Telegraph* called it 'a trivial comedy of manners' and *The Times* dismissed it as 'almost from beginning to end, sad stuff'.[17] The production ran for only a month.

Heinz had much better luck in 1952 with *Dear Charles,* a comedy by Alan Melville, based on a French play, *Les Enfants d'Edouard*, which had recently enjoyed a run of over five hundred performances in Paris. The plot was highly contrived. A middle-aged Frenchwoman suddenly tells her three grown-up children that the oil painting of 'dear Charles', their late father, hanging over the fireplace, is not of their father at all. In fact, each of her children has a different father. She then decides — a decision satisfying no demands except those of the plot — to invite all her three former lovers to the house in order to decide which one will be the best father to her children. This implausible situation had of course great comic potential which the production fully exploited. The play had made a pre-London tour in the autumn of 1952, starting in Hull and arriving in London shortly before Christmas. The first night was greeted by the critics as a 'triumph', particularly for the leading lady, Yvonne Arnaud, a French actress who had long been a permanent visitor on the London stage, who gave 'a wholly delightful performance'.[18]

Among critics who called it a triumph was the *Daily Telegraph's* W. A. Darlington who forecast a long run:

> I think I am speaking the exact truth when I say that *Dear Charles*, at the New, will run for at least a year. How can it help it? It has about the best part for Yvonne Arnaud ever written. It is artfully concocted by Alan Melville out of a French original. It is perfectly cast.[19]

The *Manchester Guardian* gave a more sober but equally positive appraisal: 'If this is not a delightful and witty comedy on paper, it is just that when seen on stage'.[20]

Gerard Heinz was cast as one of the three lovers, Dominique Lecler, who was variously described as 'a dubious financier', 'a questionable French business-man', or 'a personable Frenchman with a past'. Although casting Heinz as the French lover might have seemed counter-intuitive, his performance, like those of his fellow-

16 Ivor Brown, 'Mum's the Word', *Observer*, 7 March 1948.
17 W. A. Darlington, *Daily Telegraph*, 20 November 1947; *The Times*, 20 November 1947.
18 'Criticus', *Tatler and Bystander*, 7 January 1953.
19 W. A. Darlington, 'Triumph for Yvonne Arnaud at the New', *Daily Telegraph*, 19 December 1952.
20 Philip Hope-Wallace, 'Yvonne Arnaud in a new Comedy', *Manchester Guardian*, 20 December 1952.

actors, was widely praised. The critic of *The Times*, remarking on 'the absurdity and gaiety of it all', particularly admired 'the touching simplicity with which Mr Gerard Heinz's bad lot hears of his son's confident pride in him'.[21] Darlington's prediction proved correct and the play ran for well over a year, Heinz acting the role of Dominique Lecler in 468 consecutive performances. Some considered it his best stage role.[22]

Heinz also enjoyed success as a film actor, his career roughly following the trajectory of the post-war British cinema. During the boom years of the first post-war decade he became a prolific supporting actor, appearing in no fewer than twenty films, many produced by leading British studios, such as Gainsborough Pictures and Ealing Studios, and made by accomplished directors, including Carol Reed, Ralph Thomas, and J. Lee Thompson. One critic has suggested that his 'screen characters often had an austere and intense demeanour that either suggested ruthless fanaticism or moral authority'.[23] Certainly his face became familiar to cinema-goers, though few of them could probably have put a name to it.

Post-war British films were made very much as popular entertainment, a diversion from the somewhat drab reality of post-war society. Heinz made his first post-war film appearance, for example, in the costume melodrama *Caravan* (1946), one of the last in the series of costume extravaganzas produced at the Gainsborough studios. Heinz played the role of Don Carlos, in what has been described as 'artificial, romantic, high-flown period tosh'.[24] However, his next role was in a film with an altogether more challenging agenda: *Frieda* (1947) addressed the question of 'enemy' war brides and the inevitable prejudice they encountered. Heinz played a small role as a Polish priest. Thereafter he appeared in several notable films, such as *The Fallen Idol*, *The Clouded Yellow*, *State Secret*, *The Cruel Sea*, and *The Prisoner*, some of which deserve further elaboration.

Heinz appeared in four films in 1948, the best-known being his niche role in *The Fallen Idol* (1948), directed by Carol Reed and with a screenplay by Graham Greene, based on his own short story. The film is a coming of age drama: a child's eye view of adult deceit. Heinz made a brief but effective appearance as the Ambassador, a character whose significance lies largely in his absence and who appears only at the beginning and end of the film. Carol Reed was a director then at the height of his powers. *The Fallen Idol* was named the best British film of 1949, and remained Greene's favourite film of his own work.[25]

Many of Heinz's appearances were inevitably in 'foreign accent roles'. Also in 1948, he appeared in another Gainsborough production, *Portrait from Life*, starring Mai Zetterling and Robert Beatty, and featuring several émigré actors such as

---

21 'Dear Charles by Alan Melville', *The Times*, 19 December 1952.

22 See Heinz's obituary in *The Stage*, 30 November 1972, p. 21.

23 Brian McFarlane (ed.), *The Encyclopedia of British Film*, foreword by Philip French (London: Methuen, 2008), p. 334.

24 *Halliwell.*

25 Among recent reviews of the film, see Philip French, *Observer*, 30 July 2007. The film received a BAFTA award as 'best British film' of 1949. It also received two Academy Award nominations for Best Director and Best Screenplay.

Arnold Marlé, Sybille Binder, and Herbert Lom. The film, scripted by Muriel and Sydney Box, was located in occupied Germany, and included various sequences in a displaced persons camp. Heinz appeared as a 'displaced person' called Heine, a name he may even have suggested, as it was the name of one of his forbears.

Though Heinz was now a British subject, and making regular appearances on stage and screen, he remained under surveillance by the security service. It is perhaps eloquent of the prevailing suspicion of the 'cold war' period that the star of *Portrait From Life,* the young Swedish actress Mai Zetterling, was also under MI5 surveillance, as was Heinz's fellow-émigré Herbert Lom. To MI5, Heinz always remained Hinze; his file was not finally closed until 1954.

While film work had previously been a useful source of income for Heinz, it became for several years the main focus of his career. After acting in no fewer than four films in 1949, Heinz appeared the following year in *The Clouded Yellow,* a film with a minor place in British cinema history. Produced at Rank's Pinewood studios, the film was notable as Betty Box's first independent production: indeed she had to mortgage her house in order to keep the production afloat. Scripted by Eric Ambler, and featuring major British stars such as Trevor Howard, Jean Simmons, and Kenneth More, the film was a thriller in the Hitchcock vein, culminating in some spectacular chase sequences across the Lake District. Heinz appeared in the role of Dr Karl Cesare, playing alongside his fellow-émigrée Lilly Kann. Also in 1950, he appeared in *State Secret,* a political thriller, in which an eminent surgeon is summoned to operate on the president of an unnamed Balkan state. When the president dies, the surgeon has to go on the run. Scripted by Sydney Gilliat, the film won an award at the Venice film festival.

In 1951, Heinz appeared in *White Corridors,* a film starring Googie Withers, James Donald, and Moira Lister. Heinz played a small but important supporting role as Dr Macuzek, a Czech assistant surgeon. Portraying daily life in a hospital, the film was credited with pioneering a documentary approach, later much used in television plays and serials. The film was both a popular and critical success. In 1952 Heinz performed in the major British war movie *The Cruel Sea.* Made by Ealing Studios, and adapted by Eric Ambler from a best-selling novel by Nicholas Monsarrat, the film was a landmark in post-war British film production. Heinz appeared as a Polish ship's captain: one of the 'continental' roles which had become his trade-mark. In 1955, at the end of this extraordinarily productive decade, he appeared in *The Prisoner,* based on the real-life case of the Hungarian Cardinal Mindszenty, who was falsely accused of treason and, in the course of a show trial, confessed to everything he was accused of. The part of the unnamed cardinal in an unnamed totalitarian state was played by Alec Guinness, that of his interrogator by Jack Hawkins, with Gerard Heinz playing the part of the prison doctor.

As television rapidly superseded cinema as the main medium of popular entertainment, Heinz began to appear regularly in television drama, making his first appearance in the ITV series 'Douglas Fairbanks Presents' in 1953. He also appeared more than once in the BBC's 'Sunday Night Theatre', most notably in Zuckmayer's *The Captain of Köpenick* (1958) playing the role of Chief of Police. He was indeed often cast as a figure of authority, playing a variety of roles as professor, doctor, ambassador, or ship's captain. Thereafter he played a number of small roles in popular television series, such as *Fabian of the Yard*, in which he played an ambassador, *The Count of Monte Cristo* (another ambassador), *Emergency Ward Ten*, playing the improbably named Mr Mozart in three episodes, and *The Saint*, in which he played three or four different roles in 1966. During the 1950s he was also a regular contributor to the BBC German Service, a steady source of income in the interludes between film and theatre parts. (Ernest Rodker remembers having lunch with his father in the impressive surroundings of Bush House, on the occasion of one of his broadcasts.)

Heinz was often unlucky in love. His relationship with Joan Rodker, though strong enough to resist the shock of expulsion from Soviet Russia, and subsequent months of separation, was destroyed by the shifts and contradictions of war. His subsequent marriage to Miriam Landsberger, a fellow-refugee working for the BBC German Service, ended tragically in November 1954, when she committed suicide — such at least was the verdict of the inquest, though Joan Rodker maintained that Miriam's action was not suicide, but a cry for help which went tragically wrong. Only in his later years did Heinz find real happiness with the actress Mary Kenton, who became his second wife. The couple first met on stage in 1952 and married a few years later, appearing together as Mr and Mrs Serafin in one episode of the television series *The Cheaters* (1961) and in *The Sullavan Brothers* in which she appeared regularly as Beth Sullavan, while he appeared as Professor Karsch in an episode written by the popular playwright Ted Willis in 1964.

Despite his growing list of television credits, Heinz continued to play film roles during the last fifteen years of his life. In 1958 he appeared in *The Man Inside*, which concerned a jewel thief who is pursued across Europe. With an international cast including Nigel Patrick, Sid James, Jack Palance, and Anita Eckberg, the film was obviously aimed at an international audience — which it singularly failed to achieve. Heinz played another supporting role. Only once did he play the leading role in a film. In *Highway to Battle* (1960), set on the eve of the Second World War, he played the German ambassador who falls under suspicion when one of his envoys fails to return to Berlin. The arrival of two Gestapo agents in pursuit of the missing man forces the ambassador to re-think his Nazi allegiance.

During the 1960s Heinz appeared in several major films, though only in minor supporting roles, occasionally in 'bit parts'. In 1961, for example, he appeared in the classic British war film *The Guns of Navarone*, though his role was uncredited. In 1965, he played a supporting role as a Norwegian partisan in another Second World War drama, *The Heroes of Telemark*. In 1967 he appeared in the highly successful film *The Dirty Dozen* which featured such well-known actors as Lee Marvin and John Cassavetes, making a brief appearance, uncredited, as a German officer playing cards. His final screen appearance was in *Venom* (1971), a low budget horror film from an independent producer, in which a Nazi scientist and a woman known as a 'spider goddess' try to develop a nerve gas made from spider venom in rural Bavaria: a bizarre and down-beat finale to Heinz's long film career.

Despite his long list of credits in cinema and television, Heinz's first love remained the theatre. During the 1960s he was able to show his versatility as an actor in two sharply contrasting roles. In 1964 he appeared in *Amber for Anna*, described as 'a new murder thriller', in which he played the role of Herman Voss, a refugee from Nazi Germany who is the subject of a nasty rumour that he might once have been the *Kommandant* of a concentration camp, though critics agreed that he was far too charming to have been anything of the kind. The *Tatler* commented that 'Both actors and audience are early and rightly convinced that he is exactly what he purports to be — a grateful refugee from Nazi oppression'.[26] None of the critics noted the parallels of the character with Heinz's own biography. The *Tatler* critic also found the play 'an extremely pleasant evening' and Philip Hope-Wallace in the *Guardian* even thought that '*Amber* may well keep the lights on at the Vaudeville (a boneyard of theatrical endeavour of late days)'.[27] A year later he appeared in *Oh Dad, Poor Dad*, a surreal black comedy which had enjoyed success in America.[28] Repeating the role she had played on Broadway, Hermione Gingold was 'in splendid, relishing form' as Madame Rosepettle, a widow who visits successive luxury hotels, accompanied by her son and a coffin containing her late husband.[29] Heinz had the daunting task of playing her would-be suitor, the drunken millionaire Commodore Roseabove. Despite enthusiastic reviews, particularly for Hermione Gingold, the production ran for only six weeks.

Thereafter, Heinz was long absent from the London stage. Between 1965 and 1972, his only British stage role was in Pirandello's *As You Desire Me*, at the Yvonne Arnaud Theatre, Guildford, in 1968, playing the role of Carl Salter, with Barbara Jefford as the Unknown Woman. One reason for this lengthy absence was that he had begun to appear in television plays and films in West Germany. He confessed he did not always feel comfortable in his native country where, despite the passage of time, he still heard disturbing echoes from the past. He did not return to the German stage. During his final years, Heinz's career was also interrupted by ill health; he suffered at least one heart attack during the 1960s, perhaps unsurprisingly since he had been a smoker for many years. (His son remembered his characteristic mannerism of always tapping a cigarette on the packet before lighting it.)

Heinz made his final stage appearance in Elleston Trevor's *Touch of Purple* which opened in London at the Globe Theatre in October 1972, after a brief provincial tour. Heinz was in a positive mood, telling his son that he was looking forward to being in the West End again. He played the part of Max Weiner, a Czech refugee painter who inadvertently discovers a murder, but is at first afraid to go to the police. Although critics dismissed the play as 'a lamentable thriller' (*Punch*) or 'a waste of everybody's time' (*The Times*), they reserved high praise for Heinz's performance, noting his unusual identification with his refugee character: 'a man

---

26 Pat Wallace, *Tatler and Bystander*, 27 May 1964.
27 Phillip Hope-Wallace, *Guardian*, 29 April 1964.
28 The play's full title is *Oh Dad, Poor Dad, Mama's Hung You in the Closet, and I'm so Sad*. It had already been staged in London at the Lyric, Hammersmith, in 1961 and was obviously brought back because of Hermione Gingold's willingness to repeat her Broadway role.
29 Phillip Hope-Wallace, *Guardian*, 7 October 1965.

who has searched the ground for his shadow to confirm that he existed (one of the play's few compelling statements of character, feelingly played by Gerard Heinz)'.[30] Days after the preview, Heinz suffered a heart attack and was unable to continue the play's run. An initial operation was thought to be a success. He told his son, who visited him in hospital,that he felt much better and would be back on stage before long. In fact, he never left hospital, dying of stomach cancer in London on 22 November 1972.[31]

Hinze's career was therefore highly productive, although untypical, even of the actor in exile, its most striking feature being the extraordinary dichotomy between its two halves. At first sight, the first act of his career, in which he lived a life more dramatic than any of his stage roles, is of greater interest than the second, which followed a less adventurous and more conventional path.

Certainly, the second act of his career limited his options in several ways, most obviously by restricting the range of stage parts he was offered. However, though some of his roles were insubstantial, he was often able to transfigure his material, proving himself a versatile actor, who was frequently commended for the conviction he brought to his performance. When he arrived in Britain, Hinze described himself as an actor and producer, but the English theatre never gave him the opportunity to show his undoubted talents as a stage director. Hinze had always spoken of his great love of German classical theatre, but this love was to remain unfulfilled in his later career as Gerard Heinz. The post-war English stage had little room for plays from continental Europe, least of all from Germany.

The balance of his career also shifted from stage to screen. As a film actor, he was often typecast, but he was remarkably prolific: in a well-established British career spanning thirty years, he appeared in some forty films, as well as numerous television dramas. Indeed, considering that he was nearly forty before he began acting in English, the achievements of the British actor Gerard Heinz may well equal those of the German actor Gerhard Hinze.

30   *The Times*, 19 October 1972.
31   See biographical note by Joan Rodker, Gerard Heinz Papers.

CHAPTER 17

Frederick Valk:
'The Best Actor in England'[32]

When the war finally came to an end, German-speaking refugees had to face the decision which eventually confronts any exile: whether to stay or return. For Frederick Valk, the decision was clearly a troubling one. He had originally planned to resume his career in Germany at the earliest opportunity and in 1946 had already accepted the offer of a contract at the Schauspielhaus in Düsseldorf. Shortly before his planned departure, he changed his mind. The problem was not a matter of location — he was well acquainted with Düsseldorf, where he had made his last appearance on the German stage in 1932 — nor was it a question of salary, still less of star billing. His change of mind went to the very heart of his own identity. He told his friend Hans Fladung that, as a Jew, he felt emotionally unable to go back to a country which had systematically planned the extermination of European Jewry.[33]

Nevertheless, he did return briefly to Germany in 1947, when he was invited to speak the part of Galileo in a radio version of Brecht's famous play, to be broadcast on North-West German radio in Hamburg, at that time still under the supervision of the BBC. Revisiting his home city, and even sitting in the theatre where he had spent his apprentice years (and which had miraculously survived British bombing) only strengthened his resolve not to return permanently: 'It is all too much — sad and exciting, but I am happy above all that I live in England. My first impression was: pack your bag and leave this country by the next train'.[34] Valk never did return to the German stage, but Germany's loss was Britain's gain, as Valk went on to consolidate his reputation in London in a number of major roles.

Within a week of the war ending, he was back on stage, playing the Hannoverian King George III in *The Gay Pavilion* at the Piccadilly Theatre.[35] It was a role for which his German accent was a recommendation, so much so that he played the

32 Kenneth Tynan, *He That Plays the King* (London: Longman, 1950), p. 94. ('I name him [Alec Guinness] the best living English character actor. But not, while Mr. Valk is here, the best actor in England'.)

33 See Hans Fladung, *Erfahrungen: Vom Kaiserreich zur Bundesrepublik* (Frankfurt am Main: Roderberg 1986), pp. 278–79.

34 Valk, p. 12.

35 *The Gay Pavilion*, by William Lipscomb, Piccadilly Theatre, 15 May–2 June 1945.

same role two years later in the film *Mrs Fitzherbert* (1947). The plot of *The Gay Pavilion* concerned the relationship of the Prince of Wales (and future King George IV) with Mrs Fitzherbert, presenting it as a story of love renounced for reasons of state. The critics dismissed the plot as feeble, and the play was redeemed only by an outstanding performance from Valk, but even this was a double-edged sword:

> Mr William Lipscomb's play also has a perilous decoration. That is a tremendous performance of George III by Frederick Valk, a piece of acting so large, loud, vibrant and compelling that everything else is made to look two sizes smaller [...] Mr Valk overwhelmingly dwarfs Mr John Byron's Prinny and when he is gone, one is tempted to withdraw the mind.[36]

The production lasted only three weeks and twenty-three performances.

Valk had better luck with his next role, in an American play, *A Bell for Adano*, which ran at the Phoenix Theatre for two months and sixty-nine performances.[37] In a cast including his fellow-refugee Milo Sperber, Valk played the role of Tomasino, the head fisherman in a Sicilian village occupied by American troops. His performance was suitably restrained: 'Mr Frederick Valk is in his best (not too vibrant or vehement) form'.[38]

The year 1946, in which he married the actress Diana Quirk, was also one of intense professional activity for Valk. He began the year playing Nick, the barman in William Saroyan's *The Time of Your Life*, a role he had first played on tour with the Old Vic. The production at the Lyric, Hammersmith, ran for twenty-five performances in February-March 1946.

The run had hardly finished before Valk was thrust into a reprise of his role as Othello. The play was performed at the Winter Garden Theatre, Drury Lane, as part of a Shakespeare season, produced by Donald Wolfit.[39] Wolfit's production of *Othello* was something of an oddity. It had opened in February 1946 with Wolfit himself playing Othello, but after some rather tepid reviews, Wolfit, while continuing to direct the production, had switched to playing the role of Iago, and had engaged Valk to play Othello. The experiment was seemingly successful:

> Mr Donald Wolfit's enterprise in taking on the role of Iago and engaging Mr Frederick Valk to play Othello, provided London with a thoroughly exciting evening. [The audience] was so entranced by the violence and the verve of the acting that not a cough could be heard.[40]

Later that year, Valk won widespread acclaim for his role as old Karamazov in a stage adaptation by Alec Guinness of Dostoyevsky's *The Brothers Karamazov* at the Lyric, Hammersmith. The play was directed by the precocious Peter Brook, then in his mid-twenties and a rising star of British theatre. While most critics were ready to accept that the great Russian novels could not be condensed into great plays, they viewed Guinness's experiment with interest. It was above all Valk who

36 *Observer*, 20 May 1945.
37 *A Bell for Adano*, by Paul Osborn, Phoenix Theatre 19 September-17 November 1945.
38 'A Bell for Adano', *Observer*, 23 September 1945.
39 The Winter Garden Theatre opened in 1919, closed in 1959, and was demolished in 1965.
40 *Evening Standard*, 6 April 1946.

caught the eye. The *Observer* critic wrote that 'Valk, as old Karamazov, commits the fault of acting his neighbours off the stage, such volume has his work. But what a magnificent solo it is, a flux of humours and passions, gross, oafish and grotesque'.[41]

James Agate in the *Sunday Times* was at his most magisterial:

> This week's performance has put an end to any shilly-shallying I have entertained on the subject of Mr Valk and I announce my intention — in case it should interest anybody — of henceforth alluding to the player who filled the role of old Karamazov as 'that great actor Frederick Valk'. [...] I, who saw Irving, say that Valk is a great actor.[42]

Valk's performance also elicited a review, written for an Oxford magazine, by a nineteen-year-old undergraduate called Kenneth Tynan:

> Valk, as the lousy boorish old patriarch, was shattering. His bull neck, thrust out defiantly as he drove home some crapulous jest, his colossal stride of feet, his laborious guttural voice, his thunder-darting eyes — Valk is pre-eminently an actor in whom physical attributes obtrude to the extinction of all other values. Yet he is subtle: the timing of his interminable pauses, which defy interruption, is uncanny. He is the most insidious of battering-rams, the most persuasive of earthquakes, he burns like a hard, gem-like holocaust. [His performance] temporarily blinded me to the rest of what was going on.[43]

Tynan's review was, as usual at this time, both self-dramatising and perceptive, identifying the attributes of an outstanding performance. Early in 1947, Valk was awarded the Ellen Terry Prize as the best actor of 1946 for his role as old Karamazov, a highly unusual, if not unique choice, given that he was ostensibly playing only a supporting role.

He had opened the year 1947 with an overpowering performance as Solness in *The Master Builder* at the Arts Theatre. It was his first performance in any Ibsen role on the English stage, but he had already played major Ibsen roles regularly during his career in Germany. He had first played Solness as a young actor in Lübeck in 1920, repeating the role a decade later in Düsseldorf in a production co-starring, as Hilda Wangel, the twenty-year-old Luise Rainer, who shortly after left Germany on her way to becoming a Hollywood star.

There was critical acclaim for the production and for Valk's performance in particular. W. A. Darlington in the *Daily Telegraph* called it the best performance of *The Master Builder* that he had seen, adding:

> As for Mr Valk, he was at his best, which is magnificent. It does not matter that Solness should speak English with a foreign accent and so his one disability is removed. His power is extraordinary in his quiet moments and shattering when fully unleashed. He achieves without difficulty the sense of a man possessed.[44]

The Times's critic agreed: 'Mr. Valk's superbly flamboyant playing of Halvard Solness

---

41 *Observer*, 9 June 1946.
42 *Sunday Times*, 9 June 1946.
43 Tynan, pp. 54–55.
44 'Ibsen at the Arts Theatre: Strong Acting', *Daily Telegraph*, 2 January 1947.

reminds us that the necessary basis of the Master Builder's destructive genius is a superabundant vitality', arguing that English actors were so concerned to convey the fear and remorse of the sick and aging artist that they underplayed:

> The spirit struggling to the last against retribution. Mr Valk brings Solness completely to life [...] His Solness is a man in whose genius and reckless charm we can believe; the remnants of those qualities are there, along with the remorse bred of age and introspection and the fantastic fear of youth, and the still more fantastic craving for it.[45]

Kenneth Tynan, still an apprentice critic, was equally unstinting in his praise:

> This performance is the most towering single thing to be seen in the West End for many months. It is also the strongest [...] Like everything Mr Valk does, it is inordinate [...] Mr Valk's Othello was like a great dam bursting [...] and now his Solness has made his star blaze red across all this continent and other lights are tapers. You felt at once that this man had built monuments, stone upon stone, and was capable of sheer muscle-tight toil. You could not consent to it as a mere stage presence. [...] He seemed an Alp. And when he fell from his crazy tower, the very fall of the House of Usher seemed like crackling matchwood. Mr Valk rules our stages, but not with the negligent assurance of a constitutional monarch. Mr Valk is a dictator.[46]

Despite such youthful hyperbole, Tynan's review shows a keen eye for a great performance and, above all, a recognition of Valk's ability, in portraying an individual character, to evoke the representative social role behind it.

Perhaps the most cogent comment came from Michael Meyer, best known as the English translator and biographer of Ibsen, who admired Valk's Solness as much as his Othello, recognising that Solness was 'among the most difficult roles to bring off', requiring a completely different approach from Othello or Shylock.[47]

In fact, Valk followed his role as Solness with a reprise of Othello in Donald Wolfit's production as part of a short Shakespeare season at the Savoy Theatre in April 1947, when he again played the Moor to Wolfit's Iago. Notably, although Valk was playing the title role, Wolfit still gave himself top billing. Wolfit's Iago indeed earned high praise, but his star was eclipsed by the acclaim that greeted Valk's performance.

James Agate, repeating his earlier praise, declared Valk to be 'an actor whose passion and power have not their like in this country', and, staking his reputation as a dramatic critic, concluded: 'If Valk is not a great Othello and if the duel with Wolfit is not magnificent throughout, then let me retire'.[48]

After seeing the same production, Kenneth Tynan sent Agate a copy of his own review, in which he declared: 'I have seen a public event of constellated magnitude and radiance. I have watched a transfusion of bubbling hot blood into the invalid frame of our drama'. He too acknowledged Wolfit's skilful contribution, but it was Valk's performance that he found overwhelming:

45   *The Times*, 5 June 1946.
46   Tynan, p. 95.
47   Meyer, p. 239.
48   James Agate, *Sunday Times*, 17 February 1947.

But this was Mr Valk's private adventure, no other near, and we were soon made to realise it. In appearance he was quintessentially teddy-bear [...] Yet temperamentally (and this is the unseekable key) there is no other such tragic player on our stages. The theatre was perturbed, but pin-still.[49]

In one respect Valk's performance surpassed even his earlier triumph with the Old Vic, when, according to one writer, he had been 'for long passages of the play, all but unintelligible'. Of his later performance with Wolfit, the same writer noted 'the obvious improvement' in the quality of diction: 'he has acquired far greater clarity and one loses the sense only in moments of rushing excitement'.[50]

Overall, 1947 was a memorable year for Valk, in which he also celebrated the birth of his first son. The year 1948 seemed to begin well: Valk was cast as Uncle Chris in the London production of the successful American play, *I Remember Mama*, a chronicle of a Norwegian immigrant family in San Francisco. Critics in London were agreed that this was not a great play, since it lacked a strong plot, but were quick to praise a parade of colourful character parts. Valk, who always regretted that he was not offered more comedy parts, demonstrated his comic talent as the bullying and disreputable Uncle Chris, who after terrifying and scandalising the family for years, is finally revealed to have had a heart of gold.

Harold Hobson, despite his reservations about the play itself, had no doubts about the acting, praising particularly 'the sham fury of Mr Frederick Valk's limping, black-moustached and wicked uncle, who [it turns out] has spent most of his money on operations for crippled children'.[51] It was not only Valk whose performance caught the eye. The *Daily Telegraph* noted that 'Frederick Valk presents a wonderful, intimidating outsize great-uncle'.[52]

The Times agreed: 'Mr Frederick Valk, with gleaming black eyes and an Osbert Lancaster moustache, is enormous fun as the family's disreputable despot and the two old frumps of Miss Lilly Kann and Miss Amy Frank are also great fun'. [53] Unfortunately, such strong acting could not save the show and it closed after just fifty-four performances.

Valk did not appear on the London stage again for another year. In 1949 he acted in one the most curious productions of the early post-war years: *The Power of Darkness*, Leo Tolstoy's harrowing play of Russian peasant life, which had proved contentious in Russia itself, having been banned for several years because of its earthy content, before being produced by Konstantin Stanislavsky in 1902.

The London production was unusual in featuring two stars of the British cinema, Stewart Granger and Jean Simmons, both of whom had momentarily forsaken the screen to return to the stage. Granger, an immensely popular leading man in British films, who had made his name with Gainsborough Pictures in melodramas such

49   Tynan, pp. 84–86.
50   Audrey Williamson, *Old Vic Drama: A Twelve Years' Study of Plays and Players* (London: Rockliff, 1948), pp. 154–56.
51   Harold Hobson, 'Temps perdu', *Sunday Times*, 7 March 1948.
52   W. A. Darlington, 'Charming Play with no Plot', *Daily Telegraph*, 2 March 1948.
53   *The Times*, 3 March 1948.

as *Fanny by Gaslight* and *Caravan*, had not been seen on stage for some eight years. Simmons, who began acting at the age of fourteen, was then still only twenty, but already a star in Britain, particularly after playing Ophelia in Laurence Olivier's *Hamlet*. The production of *The Power of Darkness* was clearly instigated by Granger, as a vehicle for himself to star with Jean Simmons. It was also an attempt to bring serious 'continental' drama to the West End stage, calculating that star names would attract big audiences. The play opened in London after an eight-week provincial tour to Manchester, Liverpool, Glasgow, and Edinburgh, where the play — and its two stars — had played to full houses. In London, however, it flopped expensively, closing after only twenty-eight performances following poor reviews.

Ivor Brown, reviewing the play under the mischievous title 'The Star-Lit Steppes', wrote: 'The disastrous weakness of the present performance is that throughout it is namby-pamby. None of the principals can conceal the tell-tale marks of civilization', adding caustically that Jean Simmons, as a Russian peasant, speaks 'with an accent that would become a Kensington drawing-room'.[54] The *Daily Telegraph* was even harsher:

> Tolstoy's play is a grim drama [...] Its people are Russian villagers of the late nineteenth century. They are alive and they are earthy. In Peter Glanville's production neither the life nor the earthiness was fully expressed. [...] The people on the stage were not peasants, but actors and actresses pretending to be peasants.[55]

Only the *Sunday Times* was more generous, deeming it 'an honourable failure' and praising excellent performances by Valk and Sonia Dresdel.[56]

In March 1950, Valk returned to the Arts Theatre to play the title role in *John Gabriel Borkman*, his second Ibsen role on the London stage. Under the continuing direction of Alec Clunes, the Arts Theatre had become, in one critic's striking phrase, 'a pocket-sized national theatre', praised for its 'intelligent unpretentious revivals and occasional innovations'.[57] Clunes had chosen to leave Shakespeare to the Old Vic, concentrating on neglected classics, particularly from the European repertoire. *John Gabriel Borkman*, Ibsen's penultimate play, was rarely seen on the English stage because few producers had the courage to tackle it. On this occasion, it was staged by John Fernald who had also translated it, together with his wife, the actress Jenny Laird. The *Daily Telegraph*, calling it 'a seldom-seen Ibsen play', praised 'Fernald's admirable production', as well as the 'excellent acting' of Valk as Borkman and Louise Hampton as his embittered wife.[58]

John Gabriel Borkman is a study of failure and disillusionment. Borkman is a disgraced banker, imprisoned after fraudulent investment, who had once attained wealth and status, but in order to do so, had sacrificed the woman he loved, marrying her sister. Valk had the advantage of having already played the role in

---

54 Ivor Brown, 'The Star-lit Steppes', *Observer*, 1 May 1949.
55 W. A. Darlington, 'Grim Russian Drama', *Daily Telegraph*, 29 April 1949.
56 *Sunday Times*, 1 May 1949.
57 Ivor Brown, *Observer*, 5 March 1950.
58 W. A. Darlington, 'A Seldom-seen Ibsen Play. Excellent Acting.' *Daily Telegraph*, 2 March 1950.

Prague, an experience which stood him in good stead. The *Sunday Times*, praising the acting as 'first-class', particularly admired Valk's performance:

> Mr Frederick Valk as Borkman is better than I have ever seen him before [...] with the craggy lines of Ibsen, he appears to have gained a new mastery of the intricacies of English. As he tramps up and down, waiting for the summons to renew his life that never comes, there is a brooding intensity about his performance that hovers on, but does not stray over, the borderland of madness. It is very impressive.[59]

Ivor Brown was equally impressed: 'Let nobody miss this magnificent product of Ibsen's last phase [...] I have not seen Frederick Valk and Louise Hampton in better control of their great powers'.[60]

While *John Gabriel Borkman* was a critical triumph for Valk and the Arts Theatre, it made little money for either. Like other plays at the Arts, it ran for just three weeks and twenty-three performances. In addition, the Arts paid all actors the same wage, in this case probably £10, a modest wage, accentuated by a short run. For Valk, however, the play was the thing. A year later, in June 1951, he performed his third Ibsen role in Britain, playing Pastor Manders in *Ghosts*, with Beatrix Lehmann as Mrs Alving, at the King's Theatre, Glasgow.[61] Just before that, he had repeated his role as Shylock at Glasgow Citizens Theatre with Douglas Campbell.[62]

By then Valk was firmly established as an actor of a (limited) range of classical roles, but he had some difficulty in broadening the scope of his career. He took a small step in this direction by playing the role of Messerschman, a melancholy millionaire, in *Ring Around the Moon*, a translation by Christopher Fry of Jean Anouilh's *L'Invitation au château*, which enjoyed great success in 1950–1951, running for 682 performances. Valk did not join the cast until the final months of the play's long run, replacing Cecil Trouncer, but he must have welcomed the chance to play a lighter role in a highly successful play.

In 1952 Valk played in *The Same Sky*, a family drama by Yvonne Mitchell, who was better known as an actress than a playwright (she was already acquainted with Valk, having acted with him in *The Master Builder*.) Originally written for television, *The Same Sky* was her first stage play. It was essentially a romantic drama, set in 1940: a young couple — Esther Brodsky who is Jewish and Jeff Smith who is not — meet and fall in love, but their families do not approve of the match and only when Jeff is killed in action, do both families become reconciled. Valk played the role of the Jewish patriarch, Poppa Brodsky: the play ends with his brief exposition of racial tolerance, a speech which Valk must have savoured. Despite the well-worn plot, the play was popular, running for eighty performances during March–April 1952, opening at the Lyric, Hammersmith, before transferring to the Duke of York's.

Kenneth Tynan, by then a professional critic, reviewed the play favourably, though he seemed to be in two minds about Valk's performance, tempering praise with heavy irony:

59 Harold Hobson, *Sunday Times*, 5 March 1950.
60 Ivor Brown, *Observer*, 5 March 1950.
61 See *Glasgow Herald*, 26 June 1951.
62 *The Merchant of Venice*, Citizens Theatre, Glasgow, 17–19 April 1951.

> And Mr Frederick Valk is there, like the Inchcape Rock, an immobile warning
> to lesser shipping, bulkily breasting the role of a Jewish patriarch like a man
> hacking his way through the Matto Grosso. Some of what he does is laboured,
> but Mr Valk can still make one jump. Witness his rage on discovering that his
> daughter has betrayed him by marrying outside the true God.[63]

Following *The Same Sky*, Valk's stage career began to falter, as offers of theatre parts
dried up. The reason was probably that he had become too identified with a narrow
range of parts: leading roles in classics or weighty parts such as the traditional Jewish
patriarch or foreign figure of authority. Casting directors had long since decided he
was not cut out for comedy, though he had always regretted that he was offered so
few comedy parts.

The result was a long lull of more than eighteen months before Valk appeared
again on stage. During this time, he played a series of (mostly undistinguished) film
roles, even revisiting the role of camp *Kommandant* in the routine prisoner-of-war
film *Albert R. N.* (1953). Valk returned to the stage in *The Big Knife,* Clifford Odets's
melodrama of success and integrity in the film industry. The play was directed by
the young American actor/director Sam Wanamaker, who had only recently moved
to Britain to re-establish his career after being blacklisted in Hollywood by the
House Un-American Activities Committee in 1952. Wanamaker not only directed
the play but also took the leading role as Charles Castle, a major Hollywood star
who feels so compromised by what he has become that he sees suicide as the only
way out. After a short provincial tour, the play opened in London at the Duke of
York's on 1 January 1954. Valk played the ruthless and tyrannical studio boss Stanley
Hoff, a part which might almost have been written with him in mind: 'The play has
moments of great passion and vigour in which Frederick Valk towers with massive
presence and thundering voice as the wicked magnate'.[64] Despite mixed reviews,
the production was successful, later transferring to the Westminster Theatre and
playing in all for 138 performances.

Following his success in this larger-than-life role, Valk endured another enforced
absence from the theatre, this time of almost two years. He had not been offered
a Shakespeare part for four years, since he had last played Shylock in Glasgow and,
since *The Big Knife*, no stage parts at all. As before, he used film work as a means
of survival. Throughout his career in Britain, Valk had to accept film roles which,
while relatively well paid, were unworthy of his talents. Unfortunately, the only
chance of rediscovering Valk today is precisely in such roles.

In 1954, he returned to Germany once more, visiting Munich to make a film
about the life of Richard Wagner, *Magic Fire*, in which he played Minister von Moll.
His feelings about Germany, a familiar yet unknown country, were unchanged:

> I have gone away from Germany. I don't feel at home here anymore. The
> people? What they say and do, it doesn't touch me. They are strangers.
> Strangers? I would look at strangers and at a strange country with more interest
> and feel more at ease.[65]

63   *Spectator*, 15 February 1952.
64   A. E.Wilson, 'Hollywood Drama', *The Star*, 2 January 1954.
65   Valk, p. 15.

His next film appearance, however, was as one of the German figures of authority which he was so often asked to portray. He appeared in *The Colditz Story* (1954), a prisoner-of-war film, in which he was part of a distinguished cast that included John Mills, Eric Portman, and Ian Carmichael. The film was set in the fortress prison of Colditz in Saxony, where the Nazis confined prisoners-of-war who had already tried to escape. Valk was cast once again as the camp *Kommandant*, this time wearing a monocle and an Iron Cross complete with swastika. Although the role made him a prominent point of focus in the film, it made few demands on his considerable acting talents. Interestingly, he appeared alongside Leo Bieber, credited as the 'German interpreter'. *The Colditz Story* was a well-made piece of work that became the fourth most popular film at the British box office in 1955. Offers of theatre parts remained rare and Valk's next job was yet another film, *I Am a Camera*, a flat and unconvincing version of Christopher Isherwood's stories of Berlin in the early 1930s.

Valk finally returned to the stage in 1955, when he was invited to perform at the fledgling Stratford Shakespeare festival in Canada, which the British director Tyrone Guthrie had helped to establish. It was Guthrie who, over lunch at his home in Lincoln's Inn Fields, invited Valk to appear at the festival in a production of *The Merchant of Venice*, once more playing Shylock, a role still strongly linked to his name. Guthrie, who was also to direct the play, had an abiding memory of Valk's performance as Shylock over a decade earlier at the Old Vic.

Valk had no hesitation in accepting the offer, which gave him the chance to return to the stage, and above all to his beloved Shakespeare. The production caused a considerable furore which began before Valk had even set foot in Canada. Jewish groups there denounced the play as anti-Semitic, questioning whether it should be performed at all. When Valk arrived for rehearsals, he was asked during an interview how, as a Jewish actor, he could even consider playing Shylock. He replied that it was as illogical for a Jew to resent the role of Shylock as for a Scot to object to the part of Macbeth. He insisted that *The Merchant of Venice* was a pro-Semitic play, citing the celebrated speech that includes the words:

> Hath not a Jew eyes? Hath not a Jew hands,
> organs, dimensions, senses, affections, passions [...]?
> If you prick us, do we not bleed?[66]

Before returning to Britain, Valk faced another challenge, playing Othello at the Crest Theatre in Toronto. In a letter to his wife, while the play was in rehearsal, he wrote that he had finally understood what the part entailed: '*Othello* develops into a marvel. I herewith say the proud word: I am able to play him now'.[67] This final performance of Othello, glowingly reviewed, may well have been the pinnacle of his stage career.

Frederick Valk's final stage performance was as the Russian ambassador in Peter Ustinov's Cold War comedy *Romanoff and Juliet*, which had opened on 17 May at the

---

66 'Jewish Actor Defends Role of Shylock', *Ottawa Citizen*, 21 May 1955, cf. 'Frederick Valk', <https://en.wikipedia.org/wiki/Frederick_Valk> [accessed 16 February 2014].

67 Valk, p. 108.

Piccadilly Theatre and was enjoying great popular success. According to Michael Meyer, who saw the play, Valk was delighted to be doing comedy again and pleased with the play's success. He had already accepted an offer to play in the American production on Broadway, when he died suddenly, following a stroke, on 23 July 1956 during the London run of the play. As usual in the theatre, the show went on, eventually running for 378 performances. Valk was sixty-one years old, leaving behind his wife Diana and two young sons. Diana Valk revealed that 'Freddie' had been planning to write a memoir, not to record the itinerary of an actor's career, but 'to draw the curve of a life, lived in shadow and sun, but lived with gratefulness'.[68] At the time of his death, the memoir remained unwritten.

For those who saw Valk act, his performances remained unforgettable; even many years later. Michael Meyer remembered him as the greatest actor he had ever seen, an opinion echoed by the author and broadcaster Bryan Magee; for James Agate, he was 'that great actor Frederick Valk'; for Kenneth Tynan, he was quite simply 'the best actor in England'.[69] Such unanimity across generations and temperaments is rare, but despite this lavish recognition of the power and passion of his acting, Valk is now virtually forgotten, remembered, if at all, only for his film roles.

---

68   Diana Valk, 'Author's Note', in Valk, p. ix.
69   Bryan Magee, *Wagner and Philosophy*, (London: Penguin, 2000), p. 372.

CHAPTER 18

Martin Miller:
A Man of Many Faces

For reasons of language, culture, or political conviction, many émigré actors returned to the German or Austrian stage after the war, but for Martin Miller and his wife Hannah Norbert there was no question of going back. They had both lost too many family members in the Holocaust. In 1947 they acquired British nationality. Miller was fortunate in that, unlike many of his fellow-refugees, he had already been able to establish himself in Britain. By 1945, he had appeared in several British films, and had become a notable character actor on the London stage, continuing to appear in *Arsenic and Old Lace* until the production finally closed in March 1946.

Following his success in *Arsenic and Old Lace*, Miller was rarely out of work. In 1947–1948 he appeared in the comedy *Mountain Air* as Dr Johann Hubermann, the owner of a Swiss boarding-house, struggling, and failing, to master the intricacies of English idiom. The play itself was insubstantial. Critics dismissed it as 'a Swiss trifle [...] a frothy little comedy', but singled out Miller for 'a superb comic performance'.[70] Appealing to a post-war need for light relief, the play ran for several months.

In 1949, Miller gave one of his most accomplished performances in *Daphne Laureola*, a new comedy by the successful dramatist James Bridie, which was staged at Wyndham's Theatre by Laurence Olivier in March 1949 and ran for a year. *Daphne Laureola* was described as 'little more than a glorious vehicle for one of the finest British actresses of her day' (Edith Evans), who in a drunken soliloquy recounts her life to the other customers in a Soho café, but there were other notable performances. The production launched the British stage career of Peter Finch, whom Olivier had encouraged to come to London from Australia and who was cast as a young Polish refugee. Miller played the part of George, the worldly-wise waiter, around whose café tables the drama unfolds. James Bridie had wanted the part to be played with a cockney accent and objected at first to Miller's central European intonation, but he eventually gave way — fortunately so, since Miller's performance was greatly admired. J. C. Trewin, writing in the glossy London magazine *The Sketch*, noted that 'Martin Miller's waiter keeps a grave fatherliness',

70 Cecil Wilson, *Daily Mail*, 24 January 1948; *Daily Mirror*, 24 January 1948.

while another critic acclaimed his performance as 'so life-like that it is difficult not to believe that he has been fetched from a little restaurant in an adjacent street'.[71]

The *Daily Telegraph*'s W. A. Darlington spoke of 'an exhilarating evening', reporting 'the roars of delighted applause at the end of last night's performance'.[72] *Daphne Laureola* went on to win the Best Play of the Year award for 1949. Once again, Miller was involved in a long-running production. He went on to give more than four hundred performances in this role, which he also played in New York at the Music Box Theatre, making his American stage debut, for which he received a salary of $250 a week for eight performances. On Broadway, however, the play failed to repeat its London success, closing after only six weeks. In 1968 Miller reprised his role as the waiter in a revival at the Edinburgh Festival, one of the last stage roles he played.

After such triumphs, Miller was in great demand, but he was also in danger of being typecast as a comedy actor. During the early 1950s he appeared in a succession of light comedies, both British and American, such as *Collector's Item* (1951), *Double Alibi* (1951), and *Stately Homes* (March 1952), none of which was particularly successful. Most of them were run-of-the-mill plays, but Miller usually managed to transcend his material, suggesting facets of a character which even the author might not have intended.

In the first post-war decade, productions of modern European plays on the West End stage were rare and attempts to produce German plays almost unknown. There were occasional exceptions, some of which punctuate Miller's career. He appeared, for example, in a stage version of Kafka's novel *The Trial* at the Winter Gardens, Drury Lane, playing the role of the Inspector. The play had reached London by an indirect route: the text was an English translation of a French adaptation by André Gide and Jean-Louis Barrault. Unfortunately, the production was an expensive flop, suffering uncomprehending reviews and coming off after just six performances. *The Stage* lamented the failure of the production, but said it was inevitable because 'the play proved almost unintelligible to the average playgoer', an opinion widely echoed.[73]

A year later (15 February 1951) Miller appeared in a production of Jean Giraudoux's *The Madwoman of Chaillot* at the St. James Theatre, which included musical arrangements by the émigré composer Walter Goehr. This, Giraudoux's last play, concerns the 'Madwoman's' discovery that ordinary Parisians are at the mercy of Big Business which plans to destroy the city to exploit the oil they believe lies beneath it. The periodical *Queen* noted: 'Martin Miller is a frighteningly sinister oil prospector'. One critic observed that Giraudoux had been strangely neglected in Britain.[74] In fact, British audiences found modern foreign plays difficult to fathom, and London critics did little to pioneer their acceptance.

Ten years almost to the day after his English stage debut in *Awake and Sing*, Miller

71   J. C. Trewin, *The Sketch*, 27 April 1949; *Morning Advertiser*, 26 March 1949.
72   W. A. Darlington, 'Exhilarating Evening', *Daily Telegraph*, 24 March 1949.
73   *The Stage*, 20 April 1950; see also *New Statesman*, 22 April 1950. The production opened on 12 April and closed on 15 April 1950 after only six performances.
74   *New Statesman*, 24 February 1951.

once again appeared with Richard Attenborough in the comedy *Sweet Madness*, a first play by the actor and broadcaster Peter Jones, which opened at the Vaudeville Theatre on 21 May 1952. Publicity for the play described it as 'a piquant and amusing comedy', but the critics were less than convinced, being virtually unanimous that it was only Miller who rescued the play from disaster with a dazzling comic performance. 'He saved the play', wrote the critic of the *Daily Herald*: 'Martin Miller, 52-year-old Czech-born actor, strolled on as a voluble psychiatrist and marriage adviser and saved us from an evening of semi-boredom with his twelve-minute part', a view endorsed by the *Daily Graphic*: 'When the play was at its last laugh, it was saved by a delightful comic performance by Martin Miller'.[75]

Later that year, Miller rejoined Richard Attenborough to play the voluble and mysterious foreigner Mr Paravicini in Agatha Christie's murder mystery *The Mousetrap* which opened in London at the small Ambassadors Theatre in November 1952. *The Mousetrap* has been running ever since and is now by far the longest-running theatre production in the world, having played continuously for well over sixty years, thereby confounding the original reviews, none of which thought the production would run longer than six months.

The Mousetrap arrived at the Ambassadors after a good, but unremarkable pre-London tour. The first night, 25 November 1952, was equally unremarkable. The West End critics, familiar with such fare, were not slow to observe the usual shortcomings of the author and the clichés of the genre, while acknowledging the merits of the production and the cast, not least Martin Miller.

The *Sunday Times* review was perhaps typical of many others, commenting:

> We are all aware of Mrs Christie's weaknesses. When it comes to creating atmosphere she is nowhere near the brooding and sinister Simenon and the country mansion turned guest house of this play is particularly banal [...] Her characters come out of the discards of exhausted drawing-room comedy [...] All the same, there is much pleasure in *The Mousetrap*. Mr Richard Attenborough's painstaking detective is a careful and intelligent portrayal worthy of close study, Mr Martin Miller's hysterically gay old man is properly trying to the nerves and Mr Peter Cotes's production is taut and exciting.[76]

The *Manchester Guardian*, borrowing a bon mot from Tallulah Bankhead, commented that 'Agatha Christie's comedy-thriller [...] "has less in it than meets the eye"', before continuing, 'Yet the whole thing whizzes along as though driven by some real dramatic force, as though the characters were not built entirely of clichés and the situations not all familiar'. But there was nonetheless also praise for the performance of Martin Miller as 'the suspiciously articulate foreigner' in 'a company which makes the most of a middling piece'.[77]

Cecil Wilson in the *Daily Mail* judged the play on its own terms, striking a more positive note:

75 *Daily Herald*, *Daily Graphic*, *Daily Telegraph*, all 22 May 1952.
76 Harold Hobson, 'Alas, Freud', *Sunday Times*, 30 November 1952.
77 '*The Mousetrap*: New Comedy-Thriller by Agatha Christie', *Manchester Guardian*, 27 November 1952.

> The play, tautly directed by Peter Cotes, has the expert merit of keeping us guessing to the very end. After years of screen crime, Mr Attenborough obviously finds the policeman's lot a happy one. His wife, Sheila Sim, copes charmingly with an uncharming houseful; and Martin Miller, that redoubtable saver of plays in distress, lavishes his usual violent energy on a play that in this case needs no salvation.[78]

Mr Paravicini was rather more than the stereotypical foreigner. According to a stage direction, he is 'foreign and dark and elderly with a rather flamboyant moustache. He is a slightly taller edition of Hercule Poirot which may give a wrong impression to the audience'. He is in fact a very shady character who uses make-up to make himself look older, whose tricks may include concealing illegally imported Swiss watches in the tyres of his car and who inevitably, though wrongly, becomes the prime suspect for the original murder. He was certainly a character that gave Miller scope for interpretation. Miller acted in the production for two and a half years, giving over a thousand performances.

Although Miller had mastered English perfectly, he never lost his Austrian accent, a fact which did not hamper his career on the London stage but effectively restricted the range of parts he was offered. In *Arsenic and Old Lace* he had played the eccentric foreign surgeon Dr Einstein. Subsequently he was often cast as a Central European doctor or psychiatrist, a stock character at a time when the tenets of Freudian psychoanalysis had become a cliché of Hollywood film production.

After *Awake and Sing*, Miller was also cast in a variety of Jewish roles, often in plays set in a specifically Jewish milieu, such as Thornton Wilder's *The Merchant of Yonkers* (1951) and, in the same year, *Magnolia Street Story*, an adaptation of Louis Golding's successful novel, in which he was reunited with Lilly Kann. In a production at the Embassy Theatre he performed the leading role, Mr Emmanuel, while she played his domineering sister, Millie. It was their last stage appearance together. At the end of 1959, Miller played in Wolf Mankowitz's musical play *Make Me an Offer*, set in London's Portobello Road antiques market, which opened at the Theatre Workshop Stratford before transferring to the West End at the New Theatre. Miller played a shady antique dealer, 'taking his place as the least scrupulous and the most amusing of the dealers with a somewhat lighter but entirely acceptable rendering'.[79]

The course of Miller's stage career in the 1950s provides an oblique commentary on British theatre at a time when the West End repertoire rested heavily on comedies and American musicals. During this decade, Miller was largely restricted to comedy roles, often typecast as the amusing, eccentric, or mysterious foreigner. If he was offered serious dramatic parts, they were in plays with an antifascist or anti-totalitarian theme, such as *Off the Mainland*, a play by the actor Robert Shaw, which opened at the Arts Theatre on 30 May 1956. Shaw's play, in which he also acted, was staged in the same month as John Osborne's *Look Back in Anger*, the play which famously changed the course of British theatre. Though *Off the Mainland* was nowhere near as successful, it did offer Miller a plum part: 'The best character

78   Cecil Wilson, 'A Scream — then Curtains', *Daily Mail*, 26 November 1952.
79   *The Times*, 17 December 1959.

is the doctor, amusingly played by Martin Miller'.[80] The play was set on an island ruled by a sinister, totalitarian regime, Miller playing a doctor 'who treats a state of chronic fear with regular doses of brandy'.[81] There were, however, few such parts available on the West End stage.

Only in the late 1950s did the London theatre begin to broaden its horizons, the visit of the Berliner Ensemble in 1956 helping to transform attitudes and enlarge perceptions. One obvious consequence was a greater willingness to experiment with foreign plays. In April 1957 Miller appeared in Tennessee Williams's *Camino Real*, directed by Peter Hall, who had just established his own company, the International Playwrights' Theatre. Williams had completely rewritten the play after it had flopped in New York four years earlier, but though London critics praised Hall's direction, they found the play itself obscure and confusing, and it was taken off after a short run, having failed to attract large enough audiences.[82]

Nonetheless, Miller continued to attract the attention of leading directors. Later in 1957 he was cast by George Devine in a production of Sartre's *Nekrassov* for the English Stage Company, one of three productions in which he acted at the Royal Court Theatre. He also appeared in *Shadow of Heroes*, a documentary play by Robert Ardrey, based on the show trial in Hungary of Laszlo Rajk. The subject-matter of the play (sub-titled 'A Play in Five Acts From the Hungarian Passion') illustrated once again Ardrey's ability to grasp the dramatic potential of a particular political moment. The play was first performed to critical acclaim at the Piccadilly Theatre on 7 October 1958, once again in a production by Peter Hall. In an outstanding cast, which included Peggy Ashcroft and the actor-playwright Emlyn Williams, Miller played the Hungarian dictator Mátyás Rákosi, described briefly in the stage directions as 'bald, fat, cheerful and dressed immaculately', giving such an authoritative performance that he was asked to repeat the role soon after on television. *Shadow of Heroes*, staged in 1958, was filmed the following year for the BBC's 'Saturday Night Theatre', with Peggy Ashcroft as Julia Rajk and Miller as Rákosi. The television version was perhaps not entirely successful: Irving Wardle in *The Listener*, for example, considered that 'too much rhetoric' had been retained in some of the main characters' performances, including Miller's.[83]

Miller also had a highly prolific film career. Between 1943 and 1968 — twenty-five eventful years in the history of the British cinema — he appeared in over fifty films, a total which does not include his numerous television appearances. The figure becomes all the more remarkable considering that most of his film appearances were made alongside his successful stage career. He made his mark in British films as a character actor, playing a succession of cameo roles, often as a doctor, psychiatrist, or professor, but also as a waiter, shopkeeper, or rabbi. He was nearly always cast as the foreigner, alternating between the sinister and the comic.

Miller shared in the post-war boom years of the British film industry, appearing

80 Eric Keown, *Punch*, 6 June 1956.
81 *The Times*, 31 May 1956.
82 See *Daily Mail*, 17 May 1957.
83 Irving Wardle, 'Critic on the Hearth', *The Listener*, 23 July 1959. The play was transmitted on 19 July.

in various films — the good and the bad, the light and the dark, the comic and the serious. In 1947, for example, he appeared in Vernon Sewell's *The Ghosts of Berkeley Square*, with Robert Morley, Felix Aylmer, and Yvonne Arnaud. He was also in *Mine Own Executioner*, another well-crafted film based on the popular novel by Nigel Balchin, in which he appeared as a psychiatrist — the first of many film psychiatrists he was to play. The film was entered at the Cannes Film Festival in 1947 and, although failing to win a prize, was highly commended and enjoyed wide distribution in the British cinema.

The following year was a particularly busy one for Miller, matching the expansion in British film production. His credits include such titles as *Counterblast*, in which he played a Dutch seaman, and *Bonnie Prince Charlie*, an ambitious costume drama produced by Alexander Korda. Shot in technicolour, the film portrays the 1745 Jacobite rebellion, which was intended to restore the house of Stuart, in the person of Charles Edward, the 'Bonnie Prince Charlie' of the title, to the English throne. Miller had a substantial role as King George II, but, unfortunately, the film was a critical and financial disaster.[84] It was Korda's pet project, for which he hired David Niven (then in Hollywood under contract to Samuel Goldwyn) who, according to Niven himself, was paid the then very substantial sum of $150,000, to secure Niven's services on loan. However, the film was poorly received in London, driving Korda to run paid advertisements defending the film against its critics, but these had a limited effect and the film's box-office returns failed to recoup the original investment. If contemporary criticism was scathing, subsequent critics have ridiculed the film, one asserting that 'Time has made it the film industry's biggest joke'.[85] Miller ended 1948 with a fleeting appearance as a barman in Carol Reed's classic *The Third Man*, made initially on location in Vienna, although Miller's brief role was shot at Shepperton Studios in London.

In a film career spanning some twenty-five years, Miller appeared in fifty-four feature films.[86] While few could be considered works of art, many were interesting mainstream productions, made by accomplished directors such as Anthony Asquith, Michael Powell, Blake Edwards, Robert Siodmak, Nicholas Ray, and Otto Preminger — and featured well-known stars like Cary Grant, Dirk Bogarde, Paul Newman, and many others. In Anthony Asquith's *Libel* (1959), an old-fashioned courtroom drama, he played the role of Dr Schrott, appearing alongside Olivia de Havilland and Dirk Bogarde. While this was a successful role for Miller, he reached the peak of his film career — somewhat late in life — with his outstanding role as the psychiatrist Dr Rosen in the controversial *Peeping Tom* (1960).

Peeping Tom is a horror film, scripted by wartime cryptographer Leo Marks, and produced and directed by Michael Powell. A study in voyeurism, it tells the story of Mark Lewis, a serial killer who murders women, using a portable camera to film their dying expression of terror. The technical execution of the film was highly

---

84   See <https://en.wikipedia.org/wiki/Bonnie_Prince_Charlie_(1948_film)> [accessed September 2016].

85   Cited in *Halliwell*, p. 100.

86   Cf. Bedrich Rohan, *Wo Marx die Revolution erfand* (Freiburg im Breisgau: Herder, 1989), p. 123.

accomplished, using the camera, for example, to make the audience share the point of view of the murderer. However, when the film was released, its subject-matter provoked a critical backlash so loud and so negative that it almost wrecked the distinguished career of director Michael Powell. More recently, the film has been rehabilitated; it is now regarded as a minor masterpiece, and Miller's performance as Dr Rosen is widely admired. His appearance is a five-minute cameo, during which he chats to Mark, telling the young man that he is familiar with his father's work as a psychiatrist, later relating details of the conversation to the police: a crucial turning-point in the story. By the time *Peeping Tom* was released on 16 May, Miller was already involved in shooting a film which was undoubtedly closer to his heart: the epic Hollywood movie *Exodus*.

Exodus, a screen version of the best-selling novel, became as popular as it was controversial. The film was produced and directed by Otto Preminger, once, like Miller, an Austrian, but by 1960 a major American film director working in Hollywood. Leon Uris's best-selling novel had been widely criticised for historical inaccuracy and for being little more than Zionist propaganda, a charge that could be made equally against the film. Starring Paul Newman, it portrays events on the ship *Exodus* when the vessel was briefly blockaded by the British in Famagusta Harbour and its subsequent voyage to Palestine, touching superficially on the Arab-Israeli conflict and culminating in the declaration of the state of Israel in May 1948. Miller's role was that of Dr Odenheim, a ship's doctor on board the *Exodus* bound for Palestine, another small cameo role, but incisively acted. What he thought of the Zionist slant of the film and whether he discussed the former glories of Viennese theatre with Otto Preminger can only be matters of speculation.

The year 1963 was a busy one for Miller, in which he appeared in *The VIPs*, a film scripted by Terence Rattigan and starring Richard Burton and Elizabeth Taylor, Maggie Smith and Orson Welles. Miller played the part of Mr Schwatzbacher, a comic character who links the scenes by moving between groups in an airport VIP lounge. In the same year Miller appeared in *55 Days at Peking*, an action spectacular based on the events of the Boxer Rebellion in 1900. Set in China but shot in Spain, the film was directed by Nicholas Ray and starred Charlton Heston, Ava Gardner, and David Niven. Miller played a minor role as Hugo Bergmann. Also in 1963 he acted in *The Pink Panther*, a highly successful film featuring Peter Sellers as Inspector Clouseau, perhaps Seller's best-loved role, with Miller in a minor role as the photographer Pierre Luigi.

As television began to replace cinema as the main form of popular entertainment, Miller also embraced the new medium, enjoying a notable career, starting in 1951 and continuing throughout the 1950s and 1960s.[87] On television too, he was regularly cast in 'foreigner' roles, for example as Rabbi Menasseh Ben Israel in *Portrait by Rembrandt* in 1952, or Dr Waldersee in Robert E. Sherwood's *Idiot's Delight* in 1955. In 1957, he played Papa Kolinsky in an episode of the popular series *Dixon of Dock Green*. In the field of popular television, Miller performed on several

---

87 This, and much of what follows, is taken from BBC Written Archives Caversham (WAC), Martin Miller, TV Art 1, 1951–1962, and TV Art 2, 1963–1969.

occasions with Eric Sykes and Hattie Jacques, appeared in two episodes of *Doctor Who* (1964), and one of *Maigret* (1968), while in 1967 he played a minor character in the legendary television epic *The Forsyte Saga*. He also made guest appearances in several other popular series, including *The Saint* (1965), *The Avengers* (1965), and *The Prisoner* (1967).

However, it was in the comic television role of Hyman Kaplan, the irrepressible Jewish immigrant and student of basic English, that Miller appears to have enjoyed an unqualified success, with Antony Jay of the *Tonight Programme* informing him not only that 'I enormously enjoyed your performance' but that the author, Leo Rosten himself, had been 'delighted and enchanted with your interpretation of the character'. The role had been played before by other actors, but in Rosten's opinion, there had been 'nothing to touch your rendering'.[88]

While Miller continued to make film and television appearances during the 1960s, he was seen less frequently in the West End, partly because he could now afford to be selective about his stage roles, often choosing to appear outside London. He acted twice, for example, with the Glasgow Citizens Theatre, then consolidating its reputation as one of Britain's leading repertory theatres, firstly in a production of Harold Pinter's *The Birthday Party*, directed by the actor Albert Finney, in which Miller's performance was acclaimed as 'superfine comedy'.[89]

Five years later he returned to Glasgow to act in a remarkable but little-known play, *The Strange Case of Martin Richter* by Stanley Eveling (which the *Scotsman* called 'an intriguing parable of modern Germany'). Miller played the title role, a character described as 'a Jew who has escaped the gas chambers'.[90] First produced by the Citizens Theatre at the Close Theatre club in November 1967, the play was directed by Michael Blakemore, who was shortly to join the National Theatre.

The play is a study in megalomania which partly subverts the norms of recent history. It takes place in an unnamed country which is Germany in all but name, in which the racial minority are called 'Swebians', a name Eveling intended presumably as a distancing device. However, when the curtain opens, the Horst Wessel song is playing in the background and a stage direction instructs the actors to speak 'in those accents which people affect as versions of a German accent'.[91]

There are only half a dozen characters in the play, most of whom are servants in a rich man's house. All of them have a past in recent history that they prefer to conceal, either as active members of the 'National Health Party' or, in Richter's case, as a victim: he is a 'Swebian'. In the absence of the owner, Richter, while concealing his own origins, incites the other servants to take over the house, recapture their past, and act it out. As the *Glasgow Herald* noted:

> Mr Miller's Richter, small, elderly (and of course unmistakably ['Swebian']), haranguing his wretched worn-out followers and leading them by the nose

88   Antony Jay to Martin Miller, 23 August 1961, BAC, Martin Miller, TV Art 1.
89   *Daily Express*, 8 April 1962.
90   *Scotsman*, 9 November 1967.
91   'The Strange Case of Martin Richter', in Stanley Eveling, *The Balachites and The Strange Case of Martin Richter* (London: Calder and Boyars, 1970), p. 83.

('You are to believe what you are ordered to believe; truth cannot be more important than the end it serves') is a terrifying figure.[92]

In the play's long central scene, Richter's followers carouse and celebrate after taking over the house. Richter plies them with drink and encourages them to relive the heady brutality of earlier days, reproducing the dreadful bestialities of Nazism and its essential nihilism. The final toast 'To Nothing!' (p. 126) is the proper climax to this recognisable nightmare.

The *Glasgow Herald* recognised the dramatic power and originality of 'this very remarkable play — the best new work that the Close has introduced to us so far', also noting that it gave Miller 'the chance for a tremendous virtuoso performance'.[93] The play was produced the following year in London at the Hampstead Theatre Club, though without Miller, the part of Richter being taken by Leonard Rossiter, but, perhaps unsurprisingly in view of its challenging subject-matter, it never transferred to the West End.

Miller evidently enjoyed acting in Scotland. In addition to his appearances in Glasgow, he performed several times at the Edinburgh Festival, appearing in 1957 in *Nekrassov*, the first production by the English Stage Company to go to Edinburgh, in 1960 in *The Dream of Peter Mann* by Bernard Kops, taking the role of Jason, an undertaker, and in a revival of *Daphne Laureola* in 1968. In fact, his last stage role was also in Edinburgh, in the key role of Kulygin in Chekhov's *Three Sisters* in November 1968.

While Miller appeared in the West End largely in comic roles, he always maintained that he could never decide whether he preferred to play comedy or tragedy. In his entry in *Who's Who in Theatre*, he named his two favourite theatrical roles as Shylock in *The Merchant of Venice* and Caliban in *The Tempest*. But in Britain he was never offered such parts: 'My one big regret', he remarked in a newspaper interview, 'is that I have never been able to play Shakespeare in English'.[94]

This aspect of Miller's career typifies the fate of the actor in exile. Actors depend crucially on language, the very tool of their trade: on a foreign stage, their opportunities are limited by accent and delivery, but they can make a virtue out of a necessity, creating a particular stage or film niche. Thus Miller made his name in the West End with a series of cameo roles as an eccentric or mysterious Central European. For a time, he threatened to become the victim of his own success: no sooner had he performed one role than he was asked to play something similar. His good fortune, however, was that his performances transcended the limitations of language, enabling him to overcome such stereotyping.

One outstanding attribute was his gift for mime, as marvellously demonstrated in his performance in *Mountain Air*, a little-known play at a little-known theatre in 1947. One critic declared that his 'sketch of a plump, middle-aged man getting out of bed in the morning is one of the most natural and funniest things seen for a very long time', an indication of Miller's talent for physical comedy.[95]

---

92 'Hair-raising Study of Nazism', *Glasgow Herald,* 9 November 1967.
93 Ibid.
94 In an interview, as cited in an unidentified press cutting in MN-MA.
95 *Playgoer,* March/April 1948.

While Miller had a strong stage presence, his success on the English stage ultimately rested on a protean ability for disguise: all of his outstanding performances were essays in impersonation. When he appeared as Mátyás Rákosi in *Shadow of Heroes*, critics commented on his startling likeness to the Hungarian dictator. In fact he was a very physical actor, his stage likeness to Rakosi being an example of his ability to inhabit the character he was playing. He was the consummate character actor, a man of many faces who ultimately disappeared behind his various disguises.

Miller's reputation in Vienna had rested not least on his gift for parody, an aspect of performance which notably eludes translation. His impersonations of well-known German and Austrian actors were embedded so deeply in their own cultural context that they could not readily be transferred to another: humorous exaggeration, the basis of parody, has to be recognisable and can only really be produced in the language of the original. Nonetheless, it was Miller's gift for parody that launched his career in London, but only because, in the case of Adolf Hitler, his impersonation was instantly recognisable and could be readily appropriated for propaganda purposes.

A measure of the reputation Miller acquired was the company he kept on stage, whose names represent a who's who of the English theatre at that time: Michael and Vanessa Redgrave, Edith Evans, Peggy Ashcroft, Richard Attenborough, Dirk Bogarde, Robert Donat, and Valerie Hobson, among others. In 1966, he was the only member of the original cast to appear in a London revival of *Arsenic and Old Lace* at the Vaudeville Theatre, in which the company included Athene Seyler and the famous theatrical couple Lewis Casson and Sybil Thorndike. Although Miller frequently played alongside such famous actors, he was rarely overshadowed — indeed it was often he who stole the limelight.

Despite their refusal to return to the German-speaking world, Martin and Hannah Miller never abandoned their roots in the German language and in the German and Austrian exile communities in London. In the post-war years, Hannah pursued her career with the BBC World Service, while also appearing in various radio and television plays as well as films, such as *Sunday, Bloody Sunday*. Even while consolidating his career on the English stage, Martin Miller continued to be involved in German-language broadcasting, assuming the role of cultural intermediary between his native and host countries.[96]

Beginning in 1949, for example, he was responsible for producing the programme 'Österreicher in England' [Austrians in England] which presented Austrian authors living and working in Britain to an Austrian audience. Miller undoubtedly considered it his cultural duty to return these authors to their 'natural readership' in Austria. Among those featured in the series were Theodor Kramer, the novelist Joe Lederer, and the young poet Erich Fried, whose work Miller introduced to an audience who had probably never heard his name before.

Fried himself confirmed that Miller had gone out of his way to help him during his early career. In 1941, for example, he had invited Fried, then aged twenty, to give his first public reading of his poems under the auspices of the Free German

---

96 See Brinson, 'The Go-between'.

League of Culture. In an even more direct intervention, he personally financed the publication of Fried's second volume of poetry, *Österreich* [Austria] — a contribution which Fried was at pains to acknowledge many years later.[97]

Miller also wrote scripts for regular series in the Austrian Service including 'Austrian Entertainment Notes', as well as 'Englishmen I Know', presenting some of the famous figures with whom he had worked on the English stage, including Laurence Olivier, Edith Evans, whom he had served with one brandy after another in *Daphne Laureola*, and Richard Attenborough, whose stage career he had accompanied from *Awake and Sing* to *The Mousetrap*. BBC records also include a script, written by Miller and transmitted in 1960, on the stage director Peter Hall.

During the 1950s and 1960s, Miller became an established figure, both as writer and actor, in German-language programmes for British schools and colleges which were broadcast on the BBC Home Service and Third Programme. Throughout his life he continued to act as an intermediary between German and English culture.

Miller always remained conscious of his grounding in the German-speaking theatre. In October 1949 he produced and directed a one-off performance of *Iphigenie auf Tauris* [Iphigenia in Tauris] at Wyndham's Theatre. The performance took place under the auspices of the British Goethe Festival Society — 1949 was the Goethe Bicentenary Year — and with Sir Laurence Olivier and Vivien Leigh as his patrons, offering a rare opportunity to see German classical theatre on the English stage in the original language. The production of *Iphigenie* was evidently a success, judging by a review put out in the BBC German Service in its 'Arts and Entertainments' series, in which Leonie Hiller lamented the general lack of British interest in German classical drama before expressing her satisfaction that it had been possible, 'largely thanks to Martin Miller, to perform Goethe's play 'in a large West End theatre, played in German and before a festive audience that filled every seat in the house'.[98] So great indeed was the demand for tickets that a repeat performance had to be arranged at the Embassy Theatre.

If there is one constant thread running through Miller's career, it is his dramatic readings from the Austrian writer Karl Kraus, satirist, parodist, and polemicist of *fin de siècle* Vienna.[99] Miller shared Kraus's love of the German language, giving his readings — not so much readings as dramatic renderings — a flavour and authenticity that helped to explain their enormous popularity. Kraus had died in 1936, meaning that his own public readings remained in the memory of many in the Austrian exile community in London.

Miller's readings from Kraus span the entire thirty years he spent in Britain. He gave his first only two months after arriving, as part of a concert organised by the Austrian Circle for Arts and Sciences, 'Ewiges Österreich' [Eternal Austria]; in the following year he took part in what must have been a noteworthy 'Karl Kraus Evening' at the Austrian Centre, in which his fellow performers were

97 See Erich Fried, 'Vorwort', in *Frühe Gedichte* (Düsseldorf: Claassen, 1986), p. 7. *Österreich: Gedichte* was originally published by Atrium in Zurich [London] in 1946.

98 A copy of the script for 'Arts and Entertainments' is held in MN-MA.

99 For Kraus, see Edward Timms, *Karl Kraus: Apocalyptic Satirist* (New Haven, CT, & London: Yale University Press, 1989).

Heinrich Fischer, Kraus's literary executor, and Georg Knepler, Kraus's former accompanist.[100]

After the war, Miller gave frequent Kraus readings, many of which he undertook at the invitation of the Anglo-Austrian Society. Thus, on 8 December 1957, at the society's request, Miller gave a one-man show at the Royal Court Theatre consisting entirely of scenes from Kraus's apocalyptic masterpiece *Die letzten Tage der Menschheit* [The Last Days of Mankind].[101]

In 1964, twenty-five years after his arrival in London, Miller finally returned to the German stage to play Sam in Peter Ustinov's *Endspurt* [The Photo Finish], the occasion being the re-opening of Cologne's Theater am Dom in a new auditorium.[102] Though the production was well received, it was in an accompanying show in Cologne that Miller seems to have surpassed himself, when he gave an evening of readings from Karl Kraus.[103] Miller's performance, wrote former fellow-exile Wilhelm Unger in the *Kölner Stadt-Anzeiger*, had been nothing short of 'a special experience [...] the brilliance of Kraus's language is inimitable, equally inimitable the rendering by Martin Miller'. In every line, Unger maintained, 'one can feel Miller's respect for the Austrian genius and his enthusiasm to serve his compatriot and to introduce him particularly to a younger generation'.[104]

For all his success on the English stage Miller always remained a member of the exile community in London, partly because of his awareness of his Jewish heritage and possibly also because he recognised his own good fortune.[105] Although he made many friends in the English theatre, he kept up old friendships with fellow-exiles. His son Daniel remembers many occasions (usually Sunday evenings) when Austrian and German guests came to the house in Decoy Road. Such guests included old friends such as Fritz Schrecker, with whom he had acted at the Laterndl, and Lilly Kann, whom he had first met in Nazi Berlin.

Indeed one of the most striking aspects of Miller's long stage career was the tremendous regard and affection in which he was held by his professional colleagues. His correspondence documents his long friendship with Richard Attenborough. In the course of his work for the BBC German Service, Miller broadcast several appreciations of his friend and fellow-actor: in one, he claimed the right to speak highly of Attenborough since there was no-one who knew him better: 'After all, I was his grandfather, his father — and his psychiatrist!'[106] Attenborough responded

---

100 Programmes for both these events (held on 24 May 1939 and 12 May 1940, respectively) can be found in MN-MA.

101 MN-MA contains correspondence regarding this production, as well as programmes for this and other Anglo-Austrian events.

102 Founded in 1957, the Theater am Dom had moved to a new location, re-opening with Ustinov's *Endspurt* on 29 October 1964.

103 See, for example, 'Guter Start mit Endspurt', *Kölner Stadt-Anzeiger*, 31 October/1 November 1964,

104 W[ilhelm] U[nger], 'Künstler und Mensch: Martin Miller verabschiedete sich mit Karl Kraus', *Kölner Stadt-Anzeiger*, 8 December 1964.

105 On this, see for example Rohan, p. 125.

106 Martin Miller, *Englishmen I Know: Richard Attenborough*, from which this quotation is taken, was broadcast by the German Service on 10 September 1954 and repeated by the Austrian Service a week

warmly to Miller's tribute: 'I was most touched by the enchanting things you said about me in the broadcast: greatly exaggerated [...] but nonetheless most warming to read. You are a very sweet person, mon cher grandpère', signing the letter, 'yours ever, Dickie'.[107]

The actor Robert Hardy, anticipating their appearance together in *The Dream of Peter Mann*, wrote, 'I'm so thrilled that we're going to be together again [...] Sally sends her love to you both, as I do. Hurrah, hurrah, hurrah. And you shall certainly have the curtain every night'.[108] Others, who knew Miller less well, were unstinting in their praise of his acting. Michael Blakemore, for example, wrote regarding *The Strange Case of Martin Richter*:

> Incidentally, may I say how pleased I am that you want to play in it for us. I've long been an admirer of yours and remember most vividly your performance in *The Birthday Party* up here which I saw in fact, before I was associated with the theatre.[109]

The most poignant tribute came from Richard Eyre, then associate director of the Lyceum Theatre, Edinburgh, and later director of the National Theatre. In a handwritten note he thanked Miller for his performance in Chekhov's *Three Sisters*, stating: 'I have learned more about Chekhov from you in three weeks than reading him for five years'.[110] Miller's performance as Kulygin, the most affecting role in the play, was his last stage part. After Miller's death Eyre produced Tolstoy's sketch *Traveller and Peasant,* which Miller had first sent him in his own translation, in the Lyceum's studio theatre in 1971, 'as a mark of affection for Martin'.[111]

Although Miller acted again in Germany, he never returned to the Austrian theatre and refused even to re-visit Vienna, which had once been the scene of his earliest stage performances, but which now held too many bitter memories. Yet, it was ironically in Austria that he died after suffering a heart attack while on location in Innsbruck for the film *The Last Valley* in 1969.

later. The script, surviving only in an English-language version, is in MN-MA; Miller had played Attenborough's grandfather in *Awake and Sing* and his psychiatrist in *Sweet Madness.* An interview he conducted with Attenborough, *Ein Mann von Rang* [A Man of Standing], was broadcast on 3 August 1960.

107   Richard Attenborough to Martin Miller, 3 November 1954, in MN-MA.
108   Robert Hardy to Martin Miller, 13 July 1960, in MN-MA.
109   Michael Blakemore to Martin Miller, dated 'Friday' [October? 1967], in MN-MA.
110   Richard Eyre to Martin Miller, 6 December 1968, in MN-MA.
111   Richard Eyre to Hannah Norbert-Miller, 5 October 1971, in MN-MA. Further correspondence confirms that Hannah Norbert-Miller later attended a performance of the play in Edinburgh.

CHAPTER 19

Lilly Kann:
'Lilly Is Superb'

Tomorrow the World gave Lilly Kann her first experience of a box-office success in the West End: the play continued to run for some three months after the end of the war, finally reaching a total of 398 performances. Moreover, success in the West End was followed by a provincial tour, in which the first stop was Portsmouth. Although she had a contract for the tour, she was prevented from taking part in it, after she fell and broke her ankle while walking home from an evening rehearsal. The accident may have been a blessing in disguise. She had mixed feelings about this long run, which obliged the actors to give the same performance over and over again, 'like a gramophone record, repeating the same lines eight times a week, like a parrot'.[112] In fact, she deplored the English (commercial) theatre practice of allowing a play to run as long as it could attract audiences, that is, as long as it remained profitable.

As *Tomorrow the World* approached the end of its West End run, Kann was offered the role of Princess Caroline, scorned wife of the later George IV, in the play *The First Gentleman*. She turned the part down in the belief that a costume drama of this kind would not have a long run.[113] In fact, as she admitted in retrospect, she misread the mood of post-war audiences; the play ran for two years in the West End, the part of Princess Caroline being taken by Kann's fellow-refugee Amy Frank.

Kann returned to the stage at the beginning of 1946, when she was invited to join the Arts Theatre Group, a touring company directed by Alec Clunes and sponsored by CEMA (shortly to become the Arts Council) which performed in various towns in the north west, including small towns in the Lake District. She particularly remembered *Dutch Family*, a play set in wartime Holland during the Nazi occupation in which she played the mother of the eponymous family, the kind of matriarchal role in which she excelled.

A reviewer who saw a performance in Kendal thought it was superbly acted:

> There are two tremendous performances — those of Lilly Kann as the Aryan mother and Arnold Marlé as the Jewish father. Miss Kann's emotional intensity is such that it simply dominated the play. She laughs, quarrels, loves, spurs

---

112 Kann, p. 104.
113 Ibid., p. 84.

the faint-hearted and weeps with an equal and unrestrained power, and the defiant grief with which, as the play ends, she turns up the hidden radio and lets the national anthem surge out in honour of her dead son has a splendour unforgettable.[114]

Two weeks after the end of the tour, the play opened for a short season at the Arts Theatre in London, running for twenty-five performances and receiving good reviews.

It was almost two years before Kann acted again on the London stage. Writing in retrospect on this long absence, she confirmed she was all too aware of the personal shortcomings which made it so hard to find suitable parts. 'It was difficult; I was far from beautiful, I had a foreign accent, I was a tragedienne, whose main ability was to move people — and how many leading roles are there like that?' The inevitable consequence was that there were 'long periods when I earned almost nothing'.[115]

To earn a living during these early post-war years, she had to turn to film work, which was easier to find. Although highly selective in her stage roles, she was much less discriminating in her attitude to film work. As the British film industry increased its output, she appeared in various films, often in minor roles. Following her modest entrée into British cinema during the war, she returned to the screen in 1945 in *Latin Quarter* — an ambitious thriller set in 1890s Paris, in which a mad sculptor murders his wife and hides her body in his latest exhibit. Kann played 'Maria', a brief but effective role, while the film also included a short cameo by Martin Miller as a lugubrious morgue keeper. Over the coming years, Kann and Miller came into contact less frequently, but they both appeared (fleetingly) in Carol Reed's *The Third Man* in 1948, though neither of them was credited. Significantly, Kann makes virtually no mention in her memoirs of the numerous films in which she played, except for those, such as *Background*, which derived from stage success.

One of Kann's better roles was in the 1947 film *Mrs Fitzherbert*, a historical drama in which she played Queen Charlotte to Frederick Valk's King George III. A contemporary review described the film as 'another costume drama from British National with convincingly lavish settings and costumes [...] Both the leads are far too meek and mild [...] but the supporting cast are on the whole excellent [...] Lilly Kann is very good as the Teutonic Queen Charlotte'.[116] The film included at least one striking anomaly. Valk was apparently cast as George III on account of his German accent, whereas George had in fact been born in England and was the first Hannoverian king to speak English without an accent. Valk may have been aware of this anomaly, but he considered film work 'excellent business':[117] Lilly Kann may well have shared his opinion.

Kann's next stage appearance was in *I Remember Mama*, in which she once more played alongside Frederick Valk. Despite the play's relative failure in London, the critics enjoyed many of the individual performances, not least Kann's Aunt Jenny. W. A. Darlington in the *Daily Telegraph*, for example, praised Valk's 'wonderful,

114 'A Window into Occupied Holland', *Manchester Evening News*, 5 March 1946.
115 Kann, pp. 87–88.
116 'Mrs Fitzherbert', *Film Industry*, December 1947.
117 Valk, p. 17.

intimidating, outsize great-uncle' while adding that 'the aunts of Adrienne Gessner, Lilly Kann and Amy Frank are in beautiful contrast'.[118]

Given such excellent reviews of the acting, the failure of *I Remember Mama* seems rather surprising. For Kann, in particular, it was an untimely reminder of the uncertainties of life in the British theatre. Shortly before the production opened, she had been granted British naturalisation. Faced with the prospect of remaining in Britain or returning 'home', she had applied for British naturalisation at the first opportunity, not only out of gratitude to the country which had given her refuge, but also as a matter of expediency. Her German passport had long since expired, leaving her technically stateless, and the prospect of British nationality thus gave a measure of security to herself and her daughter. Her British naturalisation came through in February 1948.[119]

In November 1948 Kann appeared in Strindberg's *The Father*, a play that had not been seen on the English stage for over twenty years, reflecting the unwillingness of British theatre audiences to engage with Strindberg's work, which was considered dark and misogynistic. The production opened at the Embassy Theatre, outside the West End, where, coincidentally, the play had last been produced in 1927, with the distinguished actor Robert Loraine in the title role.

Strindberg's naturalistic drama is a study of marital conflict: the marriage of Adolf, a cavalry captain, and his wife Laura is declining into violent argument between the couple over the education of their daughter. In the course of the play, the captain is driven slowly mad by his wife's calculated insinuation that he is not the father of their child, and his mental breakdown finally leads to his death. The role of the captain was played by Michael Redgrave, his wife Laura by Freda Jackson. Lilly Kann played Margaret, the old nurse, a role which is a crucial accompaniment to the captain's mental disintegration.

There was general admiration for the players, if not the play. The *Sunday Dispatch*, for example, called the play 'this gloomy misogynistic drama', but praised Redgrave for his 'really powerful performance'; Freda Jackson was 'cold and wicked as a Strindberg woman should be', while 'Lilly Kann played the old nurse with good effect'.[120] Kann's performance was indeed widely praised: 'Miss Lilly Kann draws a warm, breathing picture of the nurse', the only character with any compassion.[121] She was particularly effective in handling the crucial scene which brings on the play's denouement. As the captain's mental state disintegrates, 'His only sympathy is from his old nurse, beautifully played by Lilly Kann [...] The most moving moment is when the nurse lulls the frantic man with memories of his childhood and tricks him into putting on a straitjacket'.[122]

The play had a six-week run at the Embassy, before transferring to the West End in early 1949 for a four-week season at the Duchess Theatre, where its performance

118 W. A. Darlington, 'Charming Play with no Plot', *Daily Telegraph*, 2 March 1948.
119 Her certificate of naturalisation from the Home Office was dated 24 February 1948, see Lilly Kann Papers.
120 *Sunday Dispatch*, 2 December 1948.
121 *The Times*, 25 January 1949.
122 *Queen*, 2 February 1949.

formed part of the celebrations of the centenary of Strindberg's birth.[123] The production was only one of a series of events in 1949 to celebrate the Strindberg centenary, including talks, performances, broadcasts, and luncheons. There was, for example, a two-week Strindberg Festival on the BBC, beginning with a broadcast of *The Father* in the 'World Theatre' slot on the Home Service on 21 January.

The highlight of the centenary events was the fixing of a plaque to commemorate Strindberg's arrival at Gravesend Pier on the occasion of his only visit to Britain in 1893. Michael Redgrave, Freda Jackson, and Lilly Kann were invited to attend the ceremony when the plaque was unveiled on 22 January — the dramatist's birthday. In fact, Redgrave was responsible for bringing the plaque, arriving with his fellow-actors by river to disembark at the pier where Strindberg had landed. The plaque itself was a gift to Gravesend from Anthony Hawtrey, the director of the Embassy Theatre. It was put in place by the Swedish chargé d'affaires and officially unveiled by Redgrave. The plaque is no longer in place; it had to be removed and is currently in storage. At the time, the event transcended local interest and received national news coverage, even earning an editorial in *The Times*.

Possibly Lilly Kann's greatest triumph on the English stage was as Becky Feldermann, the leading role in *The Golden Door* by Sylvia Regan. *The Golden Door* was a chronicle play covering twenty-one years in the life of a Jewish immigrant family in New York. Seven years after her success in *Awake and Sing*, Kann was once again cast as a New York Jewish matriarch.[124] The play had been successful in the USA under the title *The Morning Star*, but since a play by Emlyn Williams with the same title had been produced in London only shortly before, it was decided to change the play's title for the British stage to *The Golden Door*, a phrase aptly taken from the poem inscribed on the Statue of Liberty.

The play was produced at the Embassy, a local theatre which usually changed its programme every fortnight to cater for a largely local audience. However, *The Golden Door* proved to be an unprecedented success. The Embassy suddenly had a hit on its hands, enjoying a long succession of full houses. The production attracted the interest of West End critics, who did not always venture into North London to review productions at the Embassy. The *Daily Mail* called the play 'a sprawling patchwork', adding 'but as a collection of warm-blooded character studies it offers rich rewards. The richest come from Lilly Kann as the lovable head of a family in constant turmoil'.[125] The *Daily Telegraph* was more measured: 'An excellent company acts the piece. Lilly Kann brings her usual integrity to the part of the mother of the family'.[126]

The production also marked the English stage debut of Meier Tzelniker, a veteran of Yiddish Theatre.[127] Tzelniker played the role of Aaron Greenspan, an immigrant from Russia — where Tzelniker himself had acted in Yiddish theatre earlier in

---

123   Duchess Theatre, 24 January–19 February 1949, 32 performances.
124   Sylvia Regan was, coincidentally, a childhood friend of Clifford Odets, the author of *Awake and Sing*.
125   Cecil Wilson, 'A Patchwork but It Warms the Heart', *Daily Mail,* 22 September 1949.
126   W. A. Darlington, 'Play About US Immigrants', *Daily Telegraph,* 22 September 1949.
127   Anna Tzelniker, *Three for the Price of One* (London: Spiro Institute, 1991), pp. 189–90.

his career. Among others in the cast were Alfie Bass and Leonard Sachs, both of whom gave noteworthy performances. But it was Kann who carried the whole production. Playing the Jewish matriarch across two generations, she was on stage almost throughout the play. The evolution of her character's life over twenty years required some hurried changes of costume back stage, a problem heightened when there were matinee performances. Following the matinee, she had to transform herself back into a younger woman, changing make up and transforming her hair style while preparing for the same rapid costume changes back stage. Matters were made worse by the dilapidated state of the theatre building, which had been badly damaged during the Blitz and had never been properly renovated. Since the roof was leaking badly, a large canvas awning was put up back stage to keep the rain off.

Becky Feldermann was none the less Kann's favourite part. She recalled that 'the role was a huge success, some people called it a triumph. The reviews were so good that my agent's partner said she had never before read reviews like them. "Lilly is superb" was the headline of one review'.[128] After filling the Embassy for several successive weeks, the production went on tour, visiting provincial theatres before returning to the Alexandra Theatre, Stoke Newington, and from there to other London suburban theatres, some of which, Kann remembered, were just as dilapidated as the Embassy.

Kann's long periods of absence from the stage were probably made longer by her selective attitude to which parts she played. In the theatre she was determined to preserve her artistic integrity, as she stressed in an interview given while she was still appearing in *The Golden Door*:

> I want to work in plays of literary worth and value [...] I don't want to work in two hours of escapism. I'd prefer to play in something which gives a chance to develop human and artistic personality rather than drown it in unworthy material.[129]

In autumn 1950, she also reprised her role as Bessie Berger in a revival of *Awake and Sing*, staged in the West End at the Saville Theatre as the last in an experimental 'season of Jewish plays', presented under the auspices of Bernard Delfont. The experiment was not successful and Delfont did not venture to repeat it.

A few months after her success in *The Golden Door*, Lilly Kann appeared in a radio adaptation of G. B. Stern's novel *The Matriarch*, broadcast on the BBC Home Service in the series 'Saturday Night Theatre'. She played the role of Anastasia Rakonitz, the matriarch of the title, whose word is law within her widespread family and who is described simply as 'indomitable'. The preview in the *Radio Times* stated that:

> Her language is as unique as her character. She speaks an English all her own — which is fitting. The woman who moulded and controlled a family as widespread as the Rakonitz will not be disturbed by such a minor problem. 'If one speaks from the heart, one has not much need of the tongue,' she says. Hers, fortunately for our entertainment, is still pretty constantly in use.[130]

---

128 Kann, p. 88.
129 'Hard Work Made Lilly Kann a Fine Actress', *Weekly Sporting Review*, 22 December 1949.
130 *Radio Times*, 17 November 1950.

It was evidently a part in which Lilly Kann could turn her foreign accent to decided advantage.

It was the first of several radio plays in which she acted. In 1951 she took part in *Jolson Sings On*, based on the career of the 'jazz singer', Al Jolson, who had died only a few months earlier. Kann played Jolson's wife in a series of domestic scenes, Meier Tzelniker played the actor/singer Eddie Cantor, while Jolson's songs were sung by Max Bygraves.[131] In fact, Kann was in some danger of becoming typecast. A year after acting in *The Matriarch*, she reverted to playing Becky Feldermann in a radio production of *The Golden Door*, broadcast as the BBC's 'Monday Matinée' on 3 December 1951.[132] The role of Becky Feldermann is a leitmotif running through her later career. In 1960 she played it yet again in a revival of *The Golden Door* in Edinburgh.

One of Kann's outstanding performances on the West End stage was as 'Nanny Braun' in *Background* by Warren Chetham-Strode, who had made his name a couple of years earlier with *The Guinea Pig*. Chetham-Strode was a dramatist with a gift for turning social problems to dramatic effect. In *Background* the plot concerned the emotional impact of divorce, particularly on the children. Opening at Westminster Theatre on 17 May 1950 and directed by Norman Marshall, the production played to good reviews, running for some three months and eighty-four performances.

Though there was some criticism of the mechanics of the plot and quibbles about the characterisation of the parents, there was universal praise for the cast, who often transcended the inherent limitations of the drama. The cast included three child actors, one of whom, John Charlesworth, was already a well-known performer. Defying the stage adage never to appear together with children or animals, Lilly Kann gave a moving performance as the devoted nanny, perhaps the play's only sympathetic adult character. 'Miss Lilly Kann gives a lovely performance, offering delicate implications of tragedy as a German nanny'.[133]

Other reviewers were even more emphatic:

> John Charlesworth [...] with his stubborn, dazed resentment, pet rabbit and unruly hair, is superb, eclipsed only by Lilly Kann as a stout nanny from Mittel-Europa. Miss Kann, in homely humours, casual undertones of private tragedy and outbursts of fierce candour, acts everybody else off the stage most of the time she is on it.[134]

The success of the play quickly led to a film version, starring Valerie Hobson, then a major British star, though when the film was released in 1953, it was Kann who stole several scenes: 'The old Swiss nurse is a brilliant little portrait, as brilliantly played by Lilly Kann'.[135] The play was also adapted for other media, including a television version and a radio production for the BBC Home Service, Lilly Kann appearing in both of them. According to her own recollections, she also translated

131 Tzelniker, p. 199.
132 *Radio Times*, 30 November 1951.
133 *Punch*, 31 May 1950.
134 *Tatler and Bystander*, 26 May 1950.
135 'Divorce, Death and Disaster', *Daily Telegraph*, 3 October 1953.

the play into German, a version that was broadcast by a radio station in Stuttgart, though she did not appear in it, or any other German version.

In 1951 Kann was briefly reunited with Martin Miller in two plays, though neither production was particularly successful. In April, they appeared as Yousuff and Fatima Birka in the American comedy *Collector's Item* which was tried out at Golders Green Hippodrome, but failed to transfer to the West End. Her last stage appearance with Miller came later that year in *Magnolia Street Story*, a stage adaptation by Emanuel Litvinoff of Louis Golding's best-selling novel of the relations between Jews and Gentiles in the northern industrial city of Doomington (generally acknowledged to be Manchester, Golding's birthplace). Martin Miller played the central role of Mr Emmanuel, while Lilly Kann played his domineering sister, Milly. Also in a distinguished cast were Alfie Bass as a Jewish marriage broker and Irene Handl, as the gossiping neighbour.

The play was produced at the Embassy Theatre and Anthony Hawtrey must have hoped that the production would repeat the success of *The Golden Door*, but such hopes were dashed by a clumsy adaptation. Acknowledging the problem of transferring a long and sprawling novel to the stage, Litvinoff had chosen to simplify it, narrowing the time-span of the novel to the two years 1914–1915, reducing the many characters and concentrating the action into two settings — Mr Emmanuel's house and the street outside — alternated by the device of the revolving stage. Critics nonetheless found fault with the confusing number of characters, the episodic nature of the plot, and the slow pace of the production: 'It is a long play made longer by the tempo'.[136] They were much kinder to the actors than to the adaptation, praising a number of sharply-defined character studies. The *Sunday Times* called the play 'a well-meaning but ill-arranged homily on the stupidity of war, in which Miss Lilly Kann, Mr Martin Miller and Mr Alfie Bass give good performances'.[137] *The Times* commented that Mr Emmanuel was 'beautifully played by Martin Miller',[138] and Lilly Kann's performance was widely praised, among others by Kenneth Tynan, already a distinctive critical voice:

> In the first half [...] there is some beautifully fluent and expressive playing. Miss Lilly Kann, who resembles a harvest moon, deploys her bulk with mother-of-pearl delicacy, distributing out of her largesse such gentle pleasures as that of hearing her say: 'Don't shush me. I'm not a pussycat'.[139]

Despite such performances, the play's structural faults and the poor reviews it received condemned it to failure. A recent *Guardian* obituary of Emanuel Litvinoff called the production 'a spectacular flop'.[140]

Magnolia Street Story was the last play in which Martin Miller and Lilly Kann appeared together. Thereafter, their careers diverged, though their personal friendship continued. She also had links to other theatre exiles, including 'my friend

---

136   *The Stage,* November 1951.
137   *Sunday Times,* 11 November 1951.
138   *The Times,* 9 November 1951.
139   *The Spectator,* 16 November 1951.
140   *Guardian,* 26 September 2011.

and colleague Gerhard Hinze/Gerard Heinz'. She and Heinz appeared together in the film *The Clouded Yellow* as the refugee couple Karl and Minna Cesare, giving them the opportunity for a brief but effective cameo. A notable film, *The Clouded Yellow* also enjoys a minor place in British cinema history as the first of thirty-two films to result from the team of producer Betty Box and director Ralph Thomas.

In the 1950s Lilly Kann made a steady career in Britain. Though she appeared rarely on stage, she was to be seen frequently in film, and later, television. Many of the films she appeared in were made as undemanding entertainment, a typical example being the comedy *A Day to Remember*, another film by the Betty Box-Ralph Thomas partnership. Made and released in 1953, it followed the adventures of a London pub darts team on a day trip to France. Kann appeared in one episode of the film as a French *grandmère*, earning the approval of one critic who, after conceding that the film had its moments of comedy, added 'and there is also some *real* acting by Lilly Kann as a French granny and Odile Versois, as her granddaughter'.[141] Praise indeed!

Background, filmed on the basis of a stage success, was almost the only one of the numerous films in which she appeared to be mentioned in her memoirs. She was, by instinct and experience, a stage actress for whom film acting was a financial necessity but not a career enhancement. She clearly did not always relish the ambience of the film set or the style of acting required. Her comments even include the reproach that some film directors seemed to have forgotten the very concept of rehearsal. She recalled that on some occasions she was given the script, or perhaps only a small portion of it, on the same day that the scene was to be shot, so that there was scarcely a chance to learn the lines, let alone to think herself into the role. Despite these reservations, Kann continued to play film roles. In all, she acted in a total of twenty-seven films, some of which were undistinguished, made in the production gold rush of the early post-war years. Her last film role was in *The Long Shadow,* an independent film made in 1961 in black and white at Pinewood Studios, in which she played, perhaps inevitably, the part of an old lady.

She found herself more at home in television drama, featuring in several notable television series including 'London Playhouse' (1955), the long-running 'Sunday Night Theatre', and 'Douglas Fairbanks Jr. Presents'. The BBC's 'Sunday Night Theatre', a popular series of television plays, ran from 1950 to 1959, being transmitted live during its first five years, for both economic and technical reasons, emphasising the theatrical basis of much early television drama. She enjoyed one of her most successful roles in the BBC mini-series *Jo's Boys*, based on Louisa May Alcott's novels (*Little Men* and *Jo's Boys*). Shot in black and white, the series ran for seven thirty-minute episodes in 1959; Kann, playing the role of Nursie Hummel, appeared in all seven episodes. The advent of independent television in 1954–1955 also provided new opportunities, including various appearances in the series 'Douglas Fairbanks Jr. Presents', an anthology series hosted by Fairbanks himself. Kann appeared in four television films in this popular series between 1954 and 1956. She had very warm memories of Fairbanks himself, writing: 'Douglas is the most

---

141 'Grace Conway on Films', *Catholic Herald*, 6 November 1953.

handsome boss I ever had and stern only in one demand: that everybody who works for him should be happy'.[142] Not all her memories of acting for television were so positive, but in these early days — which many remembered as the golden age of television drama — she found television theatre preferable to film, since it more closely resembled theatre performance than film production did, or could.

Lilly Kann never acted again on the German stage, though this was less a matter of reluctance than of missed opportunity. In 1950, while she was still acting in *The Golden Door*, the actor Fritz Kortner had telegraphed her with the offer of a guest appearance in Munich as Alexandra, Mariamne's mother, in a production of Hebbel's *Herodes und Mariamne* [Herod and Mariamne]. The offer was immediately attractive and in other circumstances she might well have gone, but having just signed a contract to go on tour with *The Golden Door*, she was unable to accept the opportunity, leaving her to wonder whether such a performance might have led her to return permanently to the German stage. One can only speculate how far this might have altered the trajectory of her career. Being able to act again in her native language might well have given her greater access to the kind of classical roles (ranging from Medea to Lady Macbeth to Mrs Warren) which had once been her stock-in-trade and from which her foreign accent had sadly excluded her in Britain, but she was by then already in her mid-fifties, an age at which many roles become no longer available. She would also have had to contend with the sometimes grudging reception given to returning émigrés in Germany. Not even Fritz Kortner was able to re-establish himself fully in the German theatre.

Lilly Kann's final appearances on stage were in Edinburgh in 1960, where she appeared at the Lyceum Theatre with Donald Wolfit in a rather routine thriller, *A Stranger in the Tea*. One reviewer reported that Wolfit 'received prolonged applause', adding that 'Lilly Kann, as Lotte Grossbek, the German housekeeper, is a most engaging personality. Her German accent is impeccable'.[143] At the same theatre, she also reprised her role as Becky Feldermann in a revival of *The Golden Door*, her last major appearance on the British stage.

By then, Kann was suffering increasingly from the chronic arthritis which eventually forced her to retire from acting. For a time, at the beginning of the 1960s, she played occasional minor roles in television films which are now long forgotten, before her career finally petered out. In February 1973 she took her last bow, appearing with the soprano and lieder singer Ilse Wolff at a Heine memorial meeting in London, sponsored by the Goethe Institute. The evening had a nostalgic ring, not least for those few in the audience who could still recall Kann's recitations of Heine at the matinee performances which had made her name in Düsseldorf forty-five years earlier.[144] It was a fitting finale to a theatrical career of over sixty years, in which she had sometimes reached the heights of dramatic performance.

---

142 Lilly Kann, autobiographical outline, dated 13 January 1957, Lilly Kann Papers.
143 'Wolfit Triumphs in Thriller', *Edinburgh Evening News*, 17 May 1960.
144 *Rheinische Post,* 10 February 1973; *AJR Information*, January 1979.

CHAPTER 20

Lucie Mannheim:
The Long Homecoming

Of the five actors discussed in this study, only Lucie Mannheim returned to Germany, but even for her there was no immediate homecoming. Berlin, the city she had once loved — and which had loved her — lay in ruins, divided by the conquerors of the Third Reich. The tensions of the Cold War would make this division permanent for forty years. However, even in the early post-war years, she and Marius Goring attempted to restore contacts between Germany and Britain. In 1947 they returned to Germany together under the auspices of the British military authorities to make an extensive tour of the British zone of occupation, presenting Ibsen's *Rosmersholm*, Shaw's comedy *Too True to be Good*, and Chekhov's *The Cherry Orchard*.[145] Performing for both British troops and German audiences, they played alternately in English and German, a feat which Mannheim remembered as completely exhausting.[146] Still pursuing their efforts at cultural reconciliation, they returned the following year to Berlin in a production of the London stage success *Daphne Laureola*, in which Mannheim took the role of Lady Pitts, acted in London by Edith Evans, and Goring, adopting a Berlin accent, played the role of the waiter, performed in London by Martin Miller. The time and effort they spent in touring Germany confirms their passionate determination to help repair Anglo-German relations, at least in the theatre.

Later in 1948, Mannheim finally returned to the English stage in a season of classic, mainly continental plays, produced at the Arts Theatre, where Alec Clunes continued to provide a welcome for serious modern drama. The Arts had just been refurbished, with new seating, and had now become, as one critic put it, 'one of the pleasantest playhouses in London'.[147] Following the continental pattern, the producer Peter Powell had assembled his own company, based around Mannheim and Marius Goring, but also featuring Joyce Heron, Stafford Byrne, and Charles Lloyd Pack. The season of plays was styled as 'A Festival of International Comedy and Drama', and gave Mannheim every chance to demonstrate her remarkable gift for both.

145 See obituaries for Marius Goring in the *Independent*, 1 October 1998, and *Daily Telegraph*, 10 October 1998.
146 Lehnhardt, *Die Lucie-Mannheim-Story*.
147 Philip Hope-Wallace, *Manchester Guardian*, 10 July 1948.

FIG. 10. Lucie Mannheim as Rebecca West with Marius Goring as Rosmer
in *Rosmersholm*, London 1948 (Bristol University Theatre Collection,
John Vickers Archive)

The six-month season opened with productions of *Rosmersholm* and *Too True to be Good*, performed in repertory; both plays had been among those Mannheim and Goring had only recently performed in Germany. *Rosmersholm* is sometimes considered Ibsen's greatest play — and it is certainly the play in which he expounded most clearly his ideas for social advance. Mannheim played the leading role of Rebecca West, with Goring as John Rosmer. *Rosmersholm* was not new to the London stage, having been first produced in London in 1891, but had rarely been seen since then. It had received only one notable production in London during the 1920s — by Barry Jackson at the Kingsway Theatre in 1926 — when it attracted considerable attention but was not a commercial success. Another notable production, by Tyrone Guthrie, had featured Flora Robson as Rebecca West at the Festival Theatre, Cambridge, in 1929–1930, a significant landmark in Robson's career.

Mannheim was an ideal interpreter for one of Ibsen's key roles, having already played such parts as Nora, Hedda Gabler, and Regina in *Ghosts*. While the critics were divided about the merits of the production, they were in no doubt as to her superlative performance: 'Lucie Mannheim's Rebecca West is acting of a high order. Her surface is beautifully restrained and increasingly we glimpse how great is the cost of keeping it so, the strength of the passionate currents racing beneath it'. The disappointment, according to this reviewer, was Marius Goring's performance as Rosmer: 'his figure is a figure of straw, got up to look the part, but not breathing or living'.[148]

There was also admiration for Mannheim's remarkable acting technique:

> Lucie Mannheim is an actress so accomplished as to be almost handicapped by her own ability. One tends to watch the faultless mechanism of the player and to forget Miss West herself. It is a fine performance which might be speeded up at the close.[149]

The production was given seventeen performances during July and August 1948, played in repertory with Shaw's comedy *Too True to be Good*, a play which had not been performed for well over a decade. Shaw subtitled the play 'A Collection of Stage Sermons', which aptly summarises the second act, in which the characters conduct philosophical discussions about science, politics, and religion. The play was first performed in 1932 at the Malvern Festival, but had not been seen since, and the revival was greeted with enthusiasm by *The Times*:

> The play's satire upon purposeless vitality has increased in force since its first production. Partly this recovery is made possible by the author's superb mastery of the rhythm of English prose and partly by the brilliant production and acting of a cast in which the honours go to Miss Joyce Heron, Miss Lucie Mannheim and especially Mr Marius Goring, who has all the mockery under easy control.[150]

The central character is a young woman who lives a life of idle luxury. Mannheim

148   *New Statesman*, 17 July 1948.
149   An uncaptioned and unsigned review of the first night performance, V & A TPA.
150   *The Times* 14 July 1948.

played 'Sweetie', her nurse, who is planning to rob her patient, assisted by her boyfriend Aubrey, a role played by Goring. For Mannheim, it was above all a long-awaited opportunity to display her talent for comedy. The *Observer* critic commented: 'Marius Goring acts suavely as the cleric-cum-crook and Joyce Heron prettily as his dupe, but Lucie Mannheim is formidably funny as the bogus nurse'.[151]

Later that year the theatre produced Chekhov's one-act comedy *The Bear*, played in a double bill with Gogol's 'farcical comedy' *Marriage*. The choice of these plays was doubtless initiated by Mannheim, who directed both plays, as well as acting in them. *The Bear*, described as 'a joke in one act', has a simple plot in which a widow, still mourning her dead husband, is wooed by a boorish and misogynist suitor. Mannheim played the widow, Madame Popov, with Goring as her suitor. One critic observed that 'Mr Goring here drops into burlesque. As the widow, Miss Mannheim gives every indication of knowing how the part ought to be played'.[152] Indeed she did, for she had first played Madame Popov some twenty years earlier in Berlin, under the direction of Jürgen Fehling, while she had also appeared, at the very start of her career, in Gogol's *Marriage*.[153]

In the Arts Theatre production of *Marriage*, Goring played the leading role of Podkolyossin, a bashful middle-aged man in search of a wife, while Mannheim played Fyolka, the match-maker to whom he turns. Other parts were played by Stafford Byrne as Starikov and the German exile Paul Demel as Yaichnitsa (Omelette). There was unanimous praise for Mannheim's performance, *The Times* commenting that 'Miss Mannheim makes an admirable character study of the match-maker' and the *Daily Telegraph* adding that Mannheim 'was at the top of her form'.[154] There was also royal endorsement, when Princess Margaret attended the first night. Thereafter, the double bill played to full houses for thirty performances during October and November.

The final play in this season at the Arts Theatre, opening on 10 November, was Louis Verneuil's *Monsieur Lamberthier*, played under the title of *The Third Man*. It was the first production of the play in London, doubtless initiated by Mannheim, who had appeared in the play with Albert Bassermann in Berlin twenty years earlier. In London she directed the production as well as acting in it. Set in 'a small top floor flat in Montmartre', the play has only two roles — a painter and his mistress, played by Goring and Mannheim. The third man of the English title, though pivotal to the plot, is kept off stage: a voice on the telephone.

This dramatic device evidently appealed to the critics. The *Daily Telegraph*, for example, called the play 'a model of ingenious stagecraft', while the *Manchester Guardian* went further, declaring that 'the play remains unsurpassed as a tour de force of ingenious construction and was extremely well-acted by Mannheim

151 'Shaw Revival', *Observer*, 18 July 1948.
152 Peter Forster, *Observer*, 17 October 1948.
153 Mannheim appeared in *Marriage* at the Volksbühne, Berlin, in 1919 in the much younger role of Agafya.
154 *The Times*, 15 October 1948; *Daily Telegraph*, 15 October 1948.

and Goring'.[155] Their perfect rapport was widely acknowledged. The *Observer* commended 'their 'delicate interplaying'; another (anonymous) critic called their performance 'a great achievement: Lucie Mannheim and Marius Goring are blessed with so much natural variety and act with such complete conviction that the attention of the audience is absorbed from curtain-rise to curtain-fall'.[156]

Reviewers particularly acknowledged the range and subtlety of Mannheim's performance. Philip Hope-Wallace, who had criticised aspects of her performance as Rebecca West, was completely won over:

> Miss Mannheim and Mr Goring (husband and wife in real life) sustain the jealous tension with great skill, but are not quite fairly matched, for hers is the wider range by far. [...] Miss Mannheim, though still handicapped by a strong German accent, plays so expressively that that she succeeds in a remarkable way in externalising the thoughts which are passing through the woman's mind and we watch her face closely throughout, knowing that there we shall first see the clue.[157]

In paying fulsome tribute to her acting technique, he also suggested, perhaps inadvertently, her debt to Stanislavski, whose early performances in Germany had been such a revelation to her.

Despite this personal triumph, Mannheim had already decided to shift the focus of her career back towards Germany. This was in fact her last stage performance in Britain, though not her last performance in *Monsieur Lamberthier*, a play with which she and Goring remained strongly associated. Eight months after their performance at the Arts Theatre, they returned to it, this time in a radio adaptation by Goring himself, once more under the title *The Third Man*, broadcast by the BBC Home Service in July 1949; the broadcast was repeated in January 1951, this time under the play's original title.

Mannheim's experiment at the Arts Theatre had been a considerable success, but it only strengthened her desire to recapture her former career in Germany. From 1949, she returned to (West) Germany for a series of 'guest performances'. Her own comments make clear that her return to the German stage was above all a return to her native language.[158] She had never become completely accustomed to performing in what remained a foreign language. And she had never managed to lose her German accent, which inevitably restricted her stage opportunities: many of the roles she played on her return would simply not have been available to her in London. Her role as Frau John in Gerhart Hauptmann's *Die Ratten* [The Rats] is a case in point. Hauptmann's play is a German counterpart to Gorki's *The Lower Depths*, in which she had first acted — with Veit Harlan, later the Nazis' favourite film director — as early as 1922. *Die Ratten* had remained very much part of the German theatre repertoire, but there was, and still is, no serviceable English translation of the play, which has never been performed professionally in Britain or the USA. Among other roles she played were Shakespeare's Lady Macbeth and

155 *Daily Telegraph*, 11 November 1948; *Manchester Guardian*, 12 November 1948.
156 Typescript, signed 'HGM', in the production file held in the V & A Performance Archive.
157 Philip Hope-Wallace, *Manchester Guardian*, 12 November 1948.
158 Cf. Lehnhardt, p. 63.

Rosa in Tennessee Williams's *The Rose Tattoo*. Like Lilly Kann, Mannheim had played Lady Macbeth more than once in Weimar Germany, but, like Kann, had no prospect of playing the role on the English stage. Her role in *The Rose Tattoo*, which she played in Berlin in 1952, would have been equally unlikely in London.

Despite her renewed success, Mannheim continued to divide her time between England and Germany, retaining her house at Hampton Court, near London, with Marius Goring. She never rejoined a theatre company in Germany: all her appearances during the 1950s were 'guest engagements'. Much had indeed changed during her absence. Before 1933 many of her greatest triumphs had been achieved with Jürgen Fehling and she would gladly have renewed their professional relationship, but by the time of her return Fehling's career was already faltering and she was never able to act again under his direction.

While Mannheim, like Goring, considered herself primarily a stage actor, who enjoyed her compact with the audience, she also managed to appear in some fifteen film roles in post-war Germany; while mostly unremarkable, they at least emphasise the length and strength of her screen comeback. The first of these was the highly successful *Nachts auf den Straßen* [Nights on the Road], starring the enormously popular Hans Albers, as Heinrich Schlüter, a long-distance lorry-driver who picks up an attractive hitchhiker, played by Hildegarde Knef (who had starred in Germany's first post-war film in 1946) who becomes his lover. Mannheim played Schlüter's wife, to whom he eventually returns, while Marius Goring was also featured as a small-time crook. The film was named the best German feature film of its year in 1953.

Despite this successful return to the German screen, Mannheim's next two appearances in 1952 were both in British films, though still together with her husband. In the same year, they both appeared in *So Little Time*, a wartime drama set in occupied Belgium. The film was unusual for its time in showing the German characters in a sympathetic light. Post-war British audiences were unused to this kind of story-line and the film met with several protests. Fifty years later the film was reissued in Germany with a dubbed soundtrack, prompting a revival of the original version that briefly saw Mannheim and Goring restored to the British screen.[159]

Later in 1952 Goring and Mannheim acted together again in *The Man Who Watched Trains Go By*, a British film based on a Simenon novel, starring Claude Rains as a small-town accountant and Mannheim as his wife. Goring played a Parisian police inspector, pursuing his inquiries. Despite its splendid source and an accomplished international cast, the film remains of interest mainly as the last film in which Goring and Mannheim appeared together. Thereafter, they went their separate ways, he continuing a busy career in the British cinema, while she refocused her career towards Germany.

After 1948 Mannheim did not appear again on the London stage, but she made several television film appearances in Britain. She was quick to adapt her formidable

159 The film was reissued in Germany in 2005 under the title *Wenn das Herz spricht* [When the Heart Speaks].

stage technique to the new medium, appearing in both the ITV 'Play of the Week' series and the BBC's 'Sunday-Night Theatre'. Her most notable appearance was in the ITV production of *The Adventures of the Scarlet Pimpernel,* a costume drama based on the novel by Baroness Orczy. The series proved popular, running for eighteen episodes, starring Goring as the title character, with Mannheim, as Countess La Valliere, appearing in seven episodes.

Mannheim's last British film role in 1965 was a small part in *Bunny Lake is Missing,* a psychological thriller, filmed in black and white, directed and produced by Otto Preminger. The leading role was played by the American actress Carol Lynley, but the backbone of the film was Laurence Olivier's performance as a police superintendent. Mannheim played a cameo role as the cook, in a cast which also included Noel Coward. *Bunny Lake is Missing* is now remembered not so much in its own right as for the stipulation — repeated in all the publicity for the film — that nobody would be admitted after the film had started. The film itself failed to live up to this promise of tension and excitement, being dismissed by the critics, and by Otto Preminger himself, as insignificant.

Apart from her role in *Bunny Lake is Missing,* Mannheim pursued her career entirely in Germany during the 1960s, appearing in a succession of television films, culminating in Anouilh's *Cher Antoine* in 1970. After 1974 she settled in Germany, where she died in 1976.

ACT V

Final Curtain

CHAPTER 21

Final Curtain

The five actors discussed in this book came to Britain at different times — and with very different prospects. Lucie Mannheim, who came in 1934, expected to continue her career in London and was able to do so. The others, who came in 1938–1939, had little hope of continuing their careers in Britain. Most of them initially spoke little English — or if they did, with a marked accent. Yet by mid-1942 they had all made the transition to the English stage.

Banned from acting in Germany, they were forced abroad in 1933 and — with the exception of Mannheim — experienced a second exile in 1938–1939, as Nazism advanced inexorably across Central Europe. Like other refugees, they came to Britain on the tide of historical events, indeed for most refugees Britain was at this time not a destination of choice, but of necessity: Britain was almost alone in offering visas to refugees from Czechoslovakia. Once in Britain, they were obliged to adapt to a new language and a new theatre system, but before they had been able to adjust, war broke out.

The war turned German refugees overnight into 'enemy aliens', a fate which befell Mannheim, Kann, Miller, and Hinze. Valk, as the holder of a Czech passport, was designated a 'friendly alien'. It is worth remembering, if only because it has not really been acknowledged before, that Martin Miller's brilliant satirical impersonation of Hitler, which the BBC considered a propaganda coup, was made while he was still officially an 'enemy alien', a designation which faded in significance as the war progressed.

In the tense atmosphere of 1940, as Britain feared a German invasion, the government ordered the mass internment of 'enemy aliens', but the measure was not uniformly applied. Gerhard Hinze, for example, was interned and then deported to Canada, whereas Martin Miller was left at liberty, apparently because the BBC considered him vital to its war propaganda. Valk avoided internment by reason of holding a Czech passport.

All these five actors were in mid-career when they were summarily excluded from the German stage. None of them, except Lucy Mannheim, had been a star name in Germany and none became one in Britain, but they all pursued successful careers. Success is not merely a matter of celebrity, being defined much more by critical approval, audience appreciation, and respect within the profession.

Of these five, only Mannheim and Valk were able to make a rapid transition to the English stage. The others turned first to the refugee theatres, where they could practice their craft but could not expect to earn a living. In some cases, their material existence was ensured by work with the BBC, but it was the refugee theatres which aided their transition to the English stage. Their performances were intended for refugee audiences, but were also attended by British actors or directors who sometimes acted as talent-spotters.

Despite Valk's early appearance in the West End, his real breakthrough came only later, when he was cast as Dr Kurtz in *Thunder Rock*; his performance in what quickly became his signature role can still be seen in the film version of the play. Tyrone Guthrie, who saw him in this role, recruited him to the Old Vic company, casting him as both Shylock and Othello. In playing Shylock, Valk turned his foreign accent to advantage, emphasising the Jew's standing as an outsider.

Thunder Rock heralded a change in the London theatre repertoire, as some theatres turned to new plays that explored topical themes, not least the war itself. Such plays, which came largely from America, also contained parts in which a foreign accent was acceptable, or even desirable, thrusting a few refugee actors into the spotlight of the West End stage.

Valk's achievement in playing leading Shakespearean roles with Britain's principal theatre company was unparalleled, but as the war went on, the absence of many British actors on military service created unexpected opportunities for the refugees. Remarkably, three other actors were able to make the transition to the English stage by mid-1942. Even more remarkably, they had the good fortune to act in long-running plays, some of which ran on well into peacetime: Gerhard Hinze, despite spending eighteen months in internment, made his British stage debut in August 1942 in *Flare Path*, appearing in 680 performances during an eighteen-month run. Martin Miller gave a total of 1337 performances in *Arsenic and Old Lace*, which opened in December 1942 and finally closed in 1946, while Lilly Kann appeared in almost 400 performances of *Tomorrow the World* which ran for practically a year in 1944–1945. By the end of the war, they had all clearly been assimilated into the British theatre.

Their considerable success is a tribute to their own confidence and commitment, but also to the support of sympathetic British colleagues. Valk's rapid success owed much to Herbert Marshall who cast him in *Thunder Rock*, and even more to Tyrone Guthrie, who brought him to the Old Vic. Lilly Kann, whose London debut was mediated by Alec Clunes, paid tribute to the generous support of the 'prince of the English stage', John Gielgud. There were other examples.

The achievements of refugee actors like Valk and Kann, however outstanding, were always episodic. In 1942–1943 Valk, appearing with the Old Vic, won the rapt attention of theatre audiences and the unreserved admiration of critics like Agate and Tynan, but his triumphs were isolated events. When the Old Vic returned to London in 1944 under the auspices of Olivier and Richardson, there was no place for Valk because a repertoire which favoured the history plays offered no parts for which he was considered suitable. He was, at best, able to repeat his success as Othello in the West End alongside Donald Wolfit.

Refugees were of course more likely to be typecast than other actors, though this could sometimes work to their advantage. Alec Clunes, for example, chose Miller and Kann to play the leading roles in *Awake and Sing* precisely because, as refugees, they knew at first hand the problems of migration. They also appeared, separately or together, in several plays that depicted aspects of their own Jewish background. Kann particularly relished her role as the Jewish matriarch in *The Golden Door,* but she was also able to escape type-casting, excelling as the Mother Superior in Gielgud's production of *Cradle Song*. Gerard Heinz was especially commended for his portrayal of a refugee who cannot quite trust the evidence of his own freedom, but was also praised for his performance in the comedy *Dear Charles*.

All of them found their careers in Britain framed by questions of language and nationality. Frederick Valk had received a Czech passport in 1936, which enabled him to enter Britain freely in 1939. He was frequently referred to as 'the Czech actor Frederick Valk', indeed more than one reviewer commented on his 'strong Czech accent'; Valk, perhaps wisely, did not demur. Miller made his name through his pitch-perfect impersonation of Adolf Hitler, first performed at an Austrian refugee theatre, but despite these impeccable Austrian credentials, he too was sometimes described as 'the Czech-born actor', a description which was only geographically correct. Prior to her British stage debut in 1942, Lilly Kann doubted whether the audience would understand her accent, well aware that it was also 'the accent of the enemy'. She was, however, perfectly understood and loudly applauded.

The strength of feeling against Germany and Germans, reinforced during the war by government propaganda, continued in the decade after 1945 with the full revelation of Nazi war crimes at the Nuremberg trials. It did not seem to affect adversely the careers of German-speaking actors in Britain. British audiences had the good sense to accept them as actors — and judge their stage performance on its own merits.

Most refugees who chose to remain in Britain took British nationality at the first opportunity after the war: Valk and Miller in 1947, Kann and Hinze in 1948. Despite this, they did not become British actors: with few exceptions, émigré actors were not allowed to tackle the leading roles of English classical theatre. Even Valk, though recognised as an outstanding Shakespearian actor, was permitted to play only Shakespeare's two outsiders, Othello and Shylock, while Kann waited in vain for the tragic roles, such as Lady Macbeth, that she had once played on the German stage.

Perhaps more notably, Valk and Kann were often overlooked when it came to casting supporting roles, sometimes for fear that their powerful acting style would eclipse the leading actors. One critic noted of Valk's award-winning performance as Old Karamazov that he 'commits the fault of acting his neighbours off the stage'. A similar comment was made about Lilly Kann, who recalled in her memoirs that she was once passed over by Sam Wanamaker after giving a strong audition for a supporting role. Both actors were forced to fall back on film work, often in parts which were quite unrepresentative of their achievements on stage.

A film performance is intrinsically more durable than its stage counterpart. Stage performance is always fleeting, making it impossible to document and retrieve (unless in another medium) whereas film performances are usually preserved, and available for future reference. In fact, one of the ironies inherent in this study is that the only remaining examples of these actors at work are in their film performances, even though these were only rarely representative of their work in the theatre. Frederick Valk is a case in point. His performances as Shylock and Othello have been all but forgotten; he is now remembered, if at all, as the psychoanalyst Dr von Straaten in *Dead of Night*.

In keeping with media developments in post-war Britain, émigré actors, like their British counterparts, relied increasingly after 1945 on work in film, and later television. Kann's memoirs make clear that she did not always feel at home on the film set. She adapted more easily to television drama where, like Martin Miller, she was able to make a mark.

Miller became possibly the best-known of these five actors. During an English stage and film career lasting almost thirty years, he was never out of work. Yet today his name is largely unknown, confirming the ephemeral nature of fame — and of acting itself. Miller was in fact one of the few actors who could have lived comfortably from his work in the theatre. He appeared in several long-running plays, including *The Mousetrap*, in which he gave over a thousand performances as the mysterious foreigner, but even in much less successful productions, his performance was always well noticed. He was a character actor, who could perform cameo parts as though they had been written for him, and although he was usually cast in supporting roles, his performance often stole the show.

Miller was quickly typecast as a comedy actor on the British stage, but he was also a tragedian manqué. Assessing his own career in Britain, he wrote that his greatest regret was that he had never been able to play the leading Shakespearean roles he had performed earlier in his career, naming as his two favourite parts Shylock and Caliban. Significantly, the best dramatic parts he was offered were usually outside London: in *The Strange Case of Martin Richter*, or as Kulygin in *Three Sisters*. Despite these limitations on his career, Miller's considerable impact on the British stage can be measured by the tributes which followed his untimely death, including a memorial production by Richard Eyre. Whatever his reputation, Miller, like Valk, had no influence on performance styles; he remained a brilliant exponent, not a trend-setter.

This raises the question of 'culture transfer'. In the 1920s the German theatre had been more modern and more innovative than the British theatre, prompting the question: what impact did actors who came from this environment have on theatre in Britain? The answer is, probably very little. British theatre paid scant regard to what was happening on the Continent. In general, actors have no influence on the theatre system or the production values it represents. In the case of émigré actors, they were best able to pursue their careers by fitting in, adapting to the system, not changing it.

Valk, for example, had a powerful performance style, which made a profound impression on audiences and theatre contemporaries in Britain: he received the Best Actor award in 1947 for his performance in Peter Brook's production of *The Brothers Karamazov*. While his acting style was admired by critics and audiences alike, it did little to influence other actors or change acting styles on the British stage. He died in July 1956, a month before Bertolt Brecht. Later that year, the visit to London of Brecht's Berliner Ensemble made a more lasting impression, not least on one of Valk's greatest admirers, Kenneth Tynan. Brecht's 'epic' theatre required, however, a completely different style of performance from that of Valk.

Like Valk, Lilly Kann had an intense and distinctive performance style which won the appreciation of both critics and audiences. Like him, she had long periods of absence from the stage in the 1950s, suffering from the same lack of parts for which they were deemed suitable. And like him, she was rarely able to play the classical roles she aspired to, and had in many cases already played in Germany.

German-speaking actors were, however, prominent in attempts to establish modern European classics in the British stage repertoire. While heading her own company at the Duke of York's in 1939, Lucie Mannheim attempted to re-introduce Ibsen to the London stage, playing Nora in *A Doll's House* — one of the greatest female roles in the modern theatre. Despite critical acclaim, theatregoers showed little interest, such was the insularity of British audiences in the 1930s. In the first post-war decade, both Frederick Valk and Lilly Kann contributed to a modest revival of serious European drama in London. Valk played Solness in *The Master Builder* to great critical excitement while Kann enjoyed excellent reviews for her performance in Strindberg's *The Father*, yet neither production was a box-office success.

None of the actors in this study ever transferred their full potential to the British stage, despite the acclaim which often greeted their individual performances, prompting the question whether they would have achieved even more if they had returned to Germany after the war. Their opportunities in Britain were always limited by a foreign accent which restricted their choice of roles, and none of them had the same breadth of career in the theatre as they might have enjoyed in Germany. On the other hand, media developments in both countries followed a similar path, so that in Germany too they would have faced greater reliance on film and television parts.

If Valk had returned to Germany, as he originally intended, he would have been able to act again in the German classics. The English stage during the 1940s and 1950s offered little or no opportunity to play Schiller or Lessing, let alone Büchner or Brecht. He did make some brief working visits to Germany, mainly for film work on location, but he felt detached from the country and its people: Germany had become a familiar yet distant land. Hinze too acted again in Germany, but not in the theatre. He returned only for short working visits and, according to his son, never felt comfortable there, feeling that nothing had really changed.

Lilly Kann might also have enjoyed a greater range of stage roles in Germany, although by the end of the war she was already over fifty, an age at which many actresses find their opportunities are restricted. Martin Miller did return once to the stage in Germany, but not until 1964, twenty-five years after he had left Berlin for London. Despite his admiration for Karl Kraus, he never acted again in Austria and shunned Vienna, which he never forgave for the intense anti-Semitism he had experienced there in the 1930s.

Only one of these actors, Lucie Mannheim, pursued her stage career in Germany, going back to a divided country. Her return to the German stage at the age of fifty was above all a return to her native language. Despite her relative success in London, she had always felt that the English language came between her and her audience. Her return was also a sign of her dissatisfaction with the limitations of the London theatre. She was impatient with the West End practice of assembling a company for a single production, which would run for as long as it continued to make money. Acting again in Germany gave her greater scope to find rewarding roles. Even though she retained her home near London, she did not return, even briefly, to the London stage.

The transition of German-speaking actors to the English stage during the Second World War, when some of them were still designated 'enemy aliens', is a unique episode, but it also stands for a wider development. At a time of heightened nationalism, fostered by government intervention, and semi-isolation imposed by the conditions of war, it is striking that British theatre became more, not less international. Many successful plays arrived from the USA (well before the arrival of American troops in 1944) and many actors were foreign nationals who usually spoke English with a foreign accent, giving British theatre a more international character than in the previous decade. It is hoped that the present account will stimulate further interest in British theatre during and immediately after the war, a crucial but still under-researched period of theatre history and above all will encourage a more searching investigation of the connections and interactions between British and German theatre.

BIBLIOGRAPHY

AKADEMIE DER KÜNSTE, BERLIN (ed.), *Geschlossene Vorstellung: Der Jüdische Kulturbund in Deutschland 1933–1941* (Berlin: Hentrich, 1992)

ALDGATE, ANTHONY, and JEFFREY RICHARDS, *Britain Can Take It: The British Cinema in the Second World War*, 2nd edn (London: I. B. Tauris, 2008)

ALLEN, JERRY C., *Conrad Veidt: From Caligari to Casablanca* (Pacific Grove, CA: Boxwood Press, 1987)

BABLET, DENIS, *Edward Gordon Craig* (London: Heinemann, 1966)

BEARMAN, MARIETTA, and OTHERS, *Out of Austria: The Austrian Centre in London in World War II* (London & New York: Tauris, 2008)

BERGFELDER, TIM, and CHRISTIAN CARGNELLI (eds), *Destination London: German-speaking Emigrés and British cinema 1925–1950* (New York & Oxford: Berghahn, 2008)

BERGHAUS, GÜNTER (ed.), *Theatre and Film in Exile: German Artists in Britain 1933–1945* (Oxford, New York, & Munich: Berg, 1989)

BERGHAUS, GÜNTER, 'The Emigrés from Nazi Germany and their Contribution to the British Theatrical Scene', in *Second Chance: Two Centuries of German-speaking Jews in the United Kingdom*, ed. by Werner Mosse and Julius Carlebach (Tübingen: Mohr, 1991), pp. 297–314

BERGNER, ELISABETH, *Bewundert viel und viel gescholten: Unordentliche Erinnerungen* (Munich: Bertelsmann, 1978)

BERSTL, JULIUS, *Odyssee eines Theatermannes* (Berlin: Sarani, 1963)

BILLINGTON, MICHAEL, *State of the Nation: British Theatre since 1945* (London: Faber, 2009)

BONNELL, ANDREW G., 'Shylock and Othello Under the Nazis', *German Life and Letters*, 63/2 (April 2010), 166–78

BRINITZER, CARL, *Hier spricht London: Von einem der dabei war* (Hamburg: Hoffmann & Campe, 1969)

BRINSON, CHARMIAN, 'The Go-Between: Martin Miller's Career in Broadcasting', in *German-speaking Exiles in the Performing Arts in Britain after 1933*, ed. by Brinson & Dove, pp. 3–16

BRINSON, CHARMIAN, and RICHARD DOVE, *A Matter of Intelligence: MI5 and the Surveillance of Anti-Nazi Refugees 1933–50* (Manchester: Manchester University Press, 2014)

—— *Politics by Other Means: The Free German League of Culture in London 1939–1945* (London & Portland, OR: Vallentine Mitchell, 2010)

BRINSON, CHARMIAN, and RICHARD DOVE (eds), *Stimme der Wahrheit: German-Language Broadcasting by the BBC*, Yearbook of the Research Centre for German and Austrian Exile Studies, vol. 5 (Amsterdam & New York: Rodopi, 2003)

—— *German-speaking Exiles in the Performing Arts in Britain after 1933*, Yearbook of the Research Centre for German and Austrian Exile Studies, vol. 14 (Amsterdam & New York: Rodopi, 2013)

CALDER, ANGUS, *The People's War* (London: Pimlico, 1992)

CLARKE, ALAN, 'They Came to a Country: German Theatre Practitioners in Exile in Great Britain 1938–45', in *Theatre and Film in Exile*, ed. by Berghaus, pp. 99–120

DIETZEL, PETER, *Exiltheater in der Sowjetunion 1932–1937* (Berlin: Henschelverlag, 1978)

——'Theater im sowjetischem Exil', in *Handbuch des deutschsprachigen Exiltheaters*, ed. by Trapp & others, I, 289–318

D'MONTE, REBECCA, *British Theatre and Performance 1900–1950* (London: Bloomsbury, 2015)

ELSOM, JOHN, *Post-war British Theatre* (London: Routledge, 1979)

EVELING, STANLEY, *The Balachites and The Strange Case of Martin Richter* (London: Calder & Boyars, 1970)

FLADUNG, HANS, *Erfahrungen: Vom Kaiserreich zur Bundesrepublik* (Frankfurt am Main: Roderberg 1986)

FLESCH-BRUNNINGEN, HANS, *Die verführte Zeit: Lebenserinnerungen* (Vienna: Brandstätter, 1988)

FRIED, ERICH, *Frühe Gedichte* (Düsseldorf: Claassen, 1986)

GADBERRY, GLEN W. (ed.), *Theatre in the Third Reich, the Pre-war Years: Essays on Theatre in Nazi Germany* (Westport, CT: Greenwood Press, 1995)

GAY, PETER, *Weimar Culture: The Outsider as Insider* (London: Secker & Warburg, 1968)

GILLMAN, PETER and LENI, *Collar the Lot!* (London: Quartet, 1980)

GREENE, GRAHAM, *The Pleasure Dome: Collected Film Criticism 1935–1940*, ed. by John Russell Taylor (Oxford: Oxford University Press, 1972)

GROSS, JOHN, *Shylock: A Legend and its Legacy* (New York: Simon & Schuster), 1993

HAIDER-PREGLER, HILDE, 'Exilland Österreich', in *Handbuch des deutschsprachigen Exiltheaters*, ed. by Trapp & others, I, 97–155

HEINRICH, ANSELM, 'It is Germany Where He Truly Lives: Nazi Claims on Shakespearean Drama', *New Theatre Quarterly*, 28/3 (2012), 230–42

——'Theatre in Britain during the Second World War', *New Theatre Quarterly*, 26/1 (2010), 61–70

HÜPPING, STEFAN, *Rainer Schlösser (1899–1945): Der 'Reichsdramaturg'* (Bielefeld: Aisthesis, 2012)

JORDAN, JAMES, 'Audience Disruption in the Theatre of the Weimar Republic', *New Theatre Quarterly*, 1/3 (1985), 283–91

KANN, LILLY, *Der Ritt über'n Bodensee: Erinnerungen einer Schauspielerin*, ed. by Charmian Brinson and Richard Dove (Bern: Peter Lang, 2017)

KERSHAW, BAZ (ed.), *The Cambridge History of British Theatre*, 3 vols (Cambridge: Cambridge University Press, 2004)

KOCH, ERIC, *Deemed Suspect: A Wartime Blunder* (Toronto: Methuen, 1980)

KORTNER, FRITZ, *Aller Tage Abend* (Munich: Kindler, 1959)

LAW, JONATHAN (ed.), *The Methuen Drama Dictionary of the Theatre* (New York: Methuen, 1999)

LEHNHARDT, ROLF, *Die Lucie-Mannheim-Story* (Rommerskirchen: Remagen-Rolandseck, 1973)

LESKE, BIRGIT, and MARION REINISCH, 'Exil in England', in *Exil in der Tschechoslowakei, Großbritannien, Skandinavien und Palästina*, ed. by Ludwig Hoffmann and others, *Kunst und Kultur im antifaschistischen Exil 1933–45*, vol. 5 (Leipzig: Reclam, 1980), pp. 197–276

LONDON, LOUISE, *Whitehall and the Jews 1933–1948: British Immigration Policy, Jewish Refugees and the Holocaust* (Cambridge: Cambridge University Press, 2001)

MCFARLANE, BRIAN (ed.), *The Encyclopedia of British Film*, forward by Philip French (London: Methuen, 2008)

MAGEE, BRYAN, *Growing Up in a War* (London: Pimlico, 2007)

——*Wagner and Philosophy* (London: Penguin, 2000)

MARTINEZ-SIERRA, GREGORIO and MARIA, *The Cradle Song* (London: Samuel French, 1945)

MEYER, MICHAEL, *Not Prince Hamlet: Literary and Theatrical Memoirs* (London: Secker & Warburg, 1989)

NEUMANN, ROBERT, *Ein leichtes Leben* (Munich: Desch, 1963)

PALMIER, JEAN-MICHEL, *Weimar in Exile: The Anti-Fascist Emigration in Europe and America* (London: Verso, 2006)

RATTIGAN, TERENCE, *Flare Path*, intro. by Dan Rebellato (London: Nick Hern Books, 2011)

REDGRAVE, MICHAEL, *In My Mind's Eye* (London: Weidenfeld & Nicholson, 1983)

REISNER, INGEBORG, *Kabarett als Werkstatt des Theaters* (Vienna: Theodor Kramer, 2004)

RICHTER, FRIEDRICH, 'Auf Theatertour in England', in *...gelebt für alle Zeiten: Schauspieler über sich und andere*, ed. by Renate Seidl (Berlin: Henschel 1980), pp. 293–307

RITCHIE, J. M., 'Exiltheater in Großbritannien', in *Handbuch des deutschsprachigen Exiltheaters*, ed. by Trapp & others, I, 341–65

ROHAN, BEDRICH, *Wo Marx die Revolution erfand* (Freiburg im Breisgau: Herder, 1989)

ROVIT, REBECCA, *The Jewish Kulturbund Theatre Company in Nazi Berlin* (Iowa City: University of Iowa Press, 2012)

ROWELL, GEORGE, *The Old Vic Theatre: A History* (Cambridge: Cambridge University Press, 1993)

SCHNEIDER, HANSJÖRG, 'Exiltheater in der Tschechoslowakei', in *Handbuch des deutschsprachigen Exiltheaters*, ed. by Trapp & others, I, 157–92

——'Das Neue Deutsche Theater Prag in den dreißiger Jahren', in *Exiltheater und Exildramatik 1933–1945*, ed. by Edita Koch and Fritjhof Trapp (Maintal: Exil, 1991), pp. 104–17.

TANITCH, ROBERT, *London Stage in the 20th Century* (London: Haus Publishing, 2007)

TIMMS, EDWARD, *Karl Kraus: Apocalyptic Satirist* (New Haven, CT, & London: Yale University Press, 1989)

TRAPP, FRITHJOF, and OTHERS (eds), *Handbuch des deutschsprachigen Exiltheaters 1933–1945*, 2 vols (Munich: K. G. Saur, 1999)

TRUSSLER, SIMON, *The Cambridge Illustrated History of British Theatre* (Cambridge: Cambridge University Press, 2000)

TYNAN, KENNETH, *He That Plays the King* (London: Longman, 1950)

TZELNICKER, ANNA, *Three for the Price of One* (London: Spiro Institute, 1991)

VALK, DIANA, *Shylock for a Summer* (London: Cassell, 1958)

VÖLKER, KLAUS, *Elisabeth Bergner: Das Leben einer Schauspielerin* (Berlin: Hentrich, 1990)

WALKER, JOHN (ed.), *Halliwell's Film and Video Guide* (London: HarperCollins, 1999)

WEARING, J. P., *The London Stage 1930–1939: A Calendar of Plays and Players* (Metuchen, NJ, & London: Scarecrow Press, 1990)

—— *The London Stage 1940–1949* (Metuchen, NJ, & London: Scarecrow Press, 1991)

—— *The London Stage 1950–1959* (Metuchen, NJ, & London: Scarecrow Press, 1993)

WILLETT, JOHN, *The Theatre of Erwin Piscator: Half a Century of Politics in the Theatre* (London: Eyre Methuen, 1978)

—— *The Weimar Years: A Culture Cut Short* (London: Thames & Hudson, 1984)

WILLIAMSON, AUDREY, *Old Vic Drama: A Twelve Years' Study of Plays and Players* (London: Rockliff, 1948)

INDEX OF NAMES

❖

INDEX OF PLAYS

❖

Lightning Source UK Ltd.
Milton Keynes UK
UKOW07n0637111117

312476UK00004B/58/P

9 781781 884737